SIGILLVM · VNIVERSITATIS · SCOLARIVM · STVDII · PRAGENSIS

A BOOK OF FANS

ŌGI NO SŌSHI

A BOOK OF FANS

ŌGI NO SŌSHI

扇の草子

Facsimile of an illustrated collection
of old Japanese poems

With essays by
Helena Honcoopová
Joshua S. Mostow
Makoto Yasuhara

Charles University in Prague
Karolinum Press 2016

JAPAN FOUNDATION

The Japan Foundation contributed a six-week fellowship for the research concerning the subject of this book.

サントリー文化財団 SUNTORY FOUNDATION

The Suntory Foundation kindly supported the printing costs of the Prague version of A Book of Fans.

Reviewed by
Prof. Anthony V. Líman (University of Toronto)
Prof. Zdenka Švarcová (Charles University in Prague)

ISBN 978-80-246-2518-8

CONTENTS

PREFACE AND ACKNOWLEDGEMENTS

This facsimile of a unique collection of illustrated Japanese *waka* poems dating from the late 16th to the early 17th century is the result of a new type of transcontinental cooperation among Japanese art and literature specialists from Japan, North America and Europe. This cooperation has been enabled by the recent advancement of electronic technologies resulting in the development of a new academic discipline labelled "digital humanities." Japan has always been at the vanguard of technical developments and it started digitizing its cultural assets two decades ago so that many of its research institutes, universities, libraries, museums and other public and private institutions have created databases of a wide range of resource materials, and have made them available to interested people around the globe. The international network of digitized data enables free research of cultural resources hidden in the depths of archives, libraries and depositories in Japan that had been hitherto accessible only after much strain and long distance traveling on the part of Japanese studies scholars. The only problem regarding these useful databases lies in the fact that they are mostly in Japanese and only a few of them also provide basic orientation and search instructions in the international language of today, English. Therefore the role of Japanese studies specialists in accessing these data is still imperative.

The National Gallery, Prague's collection of Japanese manuscripts and illustrated books from the former estate of the important Czech collector, fiction and travel-book writer Joe Hloucha (1881–1957) contains a rare illustrated manuscript entitled *Ehon Wakashū* which Hloucha purchased in Japan in 1906. It is a bound book of the *Nara-ehon* type consisting of forty pages, 311 x 236 mm in size, and recently dismantled into twenty numbered sheets of thick *gampi* paper. Each of the forty pages displays three fan-shaped colour illustrations and three adjoining *waka* poems written quite irregularly in fluent *hentaigana* calligraphy. It is not only a unique piece of mediaeval Japanese poetry, dating from the late Muromachi to early Edo period, but also a beautiful work of art with *Yamato-e* style illustrations, exemplifying the work of an anonymous town painter (*machi-eshi*), probably from Kyōto or Ōsaka. The four hundred year-old Prague manuscript of the genre called Book of Fans (*ōgi no sōshi*) deserves publication in the form of a facsimile as a rare, well-preserved and complete Japanese codex. Besides the fan illustrations, we have included six other still unpublished old pictures of the seated poets type (*kasen-e*) from Prague. Both sets belong among the oldest secular Japanese paintings in Czech collections.

Research into *A Book of Fans* started in 1972 when I first transliterated the rare manuscript into Hepburn script, being able to identify and translate about 30 poems from the total without having the capacity to go much further from behind the Iron Curtain. After its fall, and after my life-long work in the position of a curator of Japanese art in the National Gallery, Prague, I was able to go a step further and translate the complete Book of Fans, as well as the poems in the captions (if not stated otherwise). In 2002, we exhibited the manuscript at the Kyōto National Museum and its exceptional quality was underlined by the authority of Prof. Hiroyuki Kanō, unquestionably one of the finest Japanese connoisseurs of art. Soon after that, a Japanese researcher from Rikkyō University, Dr. Makoto Yasuhara, arrived in Prague to examine the book, and a year later she published her comparative study of various extant versions of *Ōgi no sōshi* (*Ōgi no sōshi no kenkyū – asobi no geibun*, Pelikan-sha, Tōkyō, 2003). She proved that the Prague version with 120 illustrated poems is the most complete surviving manuscript of the Book of Fans genre out of the approximately fifty manuscripts remaining in the world.

In cooperation with Dr. Yasuhara, who was the first one to venture into the *ōgi no sōshi* field, and Prof. Joshua Mostow from The University of British Columbia, a well-known expert on old Japanese poetry, we decided to translate this unique manuscript into English and into Czech and publish it together with commentaries and transcriptions in modern Japanese. Professor Mostow made the English translation the theme of his advanced course for Japanese studies students at The University of British Columbia in Vancouver in the spring semester of 2011. In the meantime I translated the volume into the Czech language and my further research in Japan was supported by a six-week fellowship from the Japan Foundation, and carried out in affiliation with the Japanese literature experts from the Art Research Centre (ARC) at Ritsumeikan University in Kyōto in 2012. The five essays included in this publication provide the general public with a wider literary and artistic context for this volume, and were originally written in Japanese and English by the three cooperating authors.

Our thanks go to all the institutions that kindly allowed for publishing their art reproductions, as credited in the captions of the roughly seventy illustrative figures included throughout the volume and especially to the National Gallery, Prague, which has provided for copyright of the facsimile and most of the illustrations. We would like to express our special appreciation to the British Museum in London, the Freer Art Gallery in Washington, and the National Institute of Japanese Literature in Tōkyō, for their enlightened copyright policies, which permit small-size images to be reproduced free of charge in research publications. Vlasta Winkelhöferová helped us with selecting brocade samples from her collection for the cover binding and inner book design. We are greatly grateful for the research support of the Japan Foundation and the printing costs support of the Suntory Foundation. Thanks to the cooperation of various research institutions in Japan (such as the Art Research Centre of the Ritsumeikan University in Kyōto, Nichibunken, Tōbunken, Hōsei University, Waseda University, Keiō University, Kyōto and Tōkyō National Museum) the Japanese art collections in the Czech Republic are gradually being integrated into an international context. We are obliged to Professors Ryō Akama, Hiroyuki Kanō, Eiko Tsuji, Tōru Ishikawa, Takaaki Kaneko, Tōru Takahashi, Haruki Ii, Keiko Suzuki et al. for individual consultations and advice. The publishing house of Charles University in Prague generously acted as the producer of the publication, which was kindly read by Prof. Anthony Líman and Prof. Zdenka Švarcová. All these individuals and institutions deserve our sincere gratitude.

Helena Honcoopová, April 2016

序と謝辞

このたび刊行した、16 世紀末に日本で制作された極めてユニークな作品の影印本は、日本、北アメリカ、ヨーロッパの日本文学研究者が協力して翻刻にあたるという新たな試みによって制作されました。この協力関係は、〈デジタルヒューマニティーズ〉と呼ばれる最新の学術的な方法論として発達しつつある、近年の科学技術の進展により可能となりました。日本は常に科学技術の発達の先頭に立ってきた国であり、その文化資源も 20 年前からデジタル化されてきました。そのため、多数の研究機関や大学、図書館、美術館、その他の公共及び私立の機関が、広範にわたる文化資料のデータベースを構築し、それらに関心を持つ世界中の人々が利用可能な状態にあります。

以前は、一部の日本文学研究者が日本まで出かけて行かなければならないなどのかなりの努力を要しましたが、国際的なデジタルネットワークの構築により、日本の公文書館、図書館、所蔵施設に保管され、容易に見ることのできなかった文化資源の、自由な調査、研究が可能になったのです。このように便利なデータベースではありますが、一つの問題があります。それは、ほとんどが日本語で書かれており、今日の国際的言語である英語による基本的な解説や調査の方法もごく僅かしか提供されていないということです。それゆえ、今なおこれらのデータを活用するにあたり、日本文学研究者が果たす役割は少なくないといえます。

プラハ国立美術館に所蔵される日本の古典籍資料や絵入り本のコレクションは、チェコの重要な美術コレクターで、小説や旅行作家として知られるヨエ・ホロウハ（1881 ― 1957）が収集したものです。その中に、江戸時代のはじめごろに作られた 1 冊の個性豊かな絵入り本が含まれています。それは、1906 年にホロウハが日本で購入したもので、表紙には「絵本和歌集」と墨書されています。この作品は、奈良絵本と呼ばれる冊子本形態の作品であり、40 頁から成っています。各頁の大きさは 311mm×236mm ですが、近年綴じ糸が外され分解されたため、20 枚の厚用の雁皮紙というかたちで現存しています。1 頁ごとに 3 つの扇絵と、その周囲に 3 首の和歌が描かれています。また、和歌は流麗な変体仮名で、非常に不規則な配列で記されています。本作品は、室町時代後期から江戸時代初期における近世日本の珍しい和歌集であるのみならず、町絵師と呼ばれる、京都や大阪で活躍していたと推測される作者不詳の絵師の好例をなす、大和絵系の挿絵が描かれた美しい芸術作品でもあります。プラハ国立美術館に所蔵される 400 年前に作られた、この「扇の草子」と総称される作品は、それだけで影印本として刊行する価値のあるものですが、私たちはそれに加えて、プラハ個人蔵の、いまだかつて出版されたこのとのない 6 枚の桃山時代の「歌仙絵」も掲載することにしました。両者は、プラハに現存する日本の世俗的な絵画の作品の中で、最も古い日本美術に属します。

私は、「扇の草子」の調査を 1972 年から始めました。はじめ、この稀少で貴重な資料に書かれているすべての和歌のうち 30 首の内容を確認し翻訳するために、ローマ字表記に改めました。しかしながらその頃は、いわゆる「鉄のカーテン」から逃れられない状況下にあったので、その崩壊後、また私が永年勤続していたプラハ国立美術館の日本美術の学芸員を定年退職した後、さらに踏み込んだ調査を再開することができました。

2002 年には、プラハ国立美術館所蔵の「扇の草子」が、京都国立博物館で展示され、それが並はずれて優れた作品であることが、日本美術研究における疑いのない最も優れた専門家である狩野博幸氏によって明確に示されました。その後まもなく立教大学の若手研究者だった安原眞琴氏が、この作品を調査するために、日本からプラハ国立美術館にやってきました。彼女は一年後、『『扇の草子』の研究―遊びの芸文』（ぺりかん社、2003 年）という、現存する諸本を比較検討した研究書を出版し、およそ 50 点の伝本が世界中に伝存していることを明らかにしました。その中にあるプラハの「扇の草子」の伝本は和歌が一番多く入っています。

「扇の草子」研究の第一人者である安原氏と、日本の和歌の著名な研究者であるブリティッシュコロンビア大学教授のジョシュア・モストウ氏の協力のもと、私たちはこの非常にユニークな作品を英語とチェコ語に翻訳し、加えて注釈と影印をほどこして出版することを決めました。モストウ氏は、バンクーバーにある本務校の 2011 年春学期の授業において、彼のもとで日本研究を専攻する大学院生たちに本作品の英訳を課し、その間に私はチェコ語への翻訳を行いました。また私は、2012 年に国際交流基金の 6 週間の研究奨学制度によって日本を訪れ、京都にある立命館大学アートリサーチセンターの日本文学の専門家である赤間亮氏や金子貴昭氏などの協力を得て、さらに詳細な調査を行うことができました。読者の方々には、この本書のエッセイを通して、3 名の共著者により 広範囲にわたる文学的、芸術的コンテクストに触れていただけるでしょう。

私たちは、本書の随所に掲載されている 66 枚の絵画の出版を許可してくださったプラハ国立美術館をはじめとするすべての機関に感謝申し上げます。特に、見識ある著作権ポリシーを持って、非営利目的の学術図書の出版のために無料で図版を提供してくださいました、ロンドンの大英博物館、ワシントン D.C. の国立スミソニアン協会フリーア美術館、東京の国文学研究資料館に深謝申し上げます。また、国際交流基金の研究支援とサントリー文化財団の海外出版助成金に大変助けられました。さらに、京都立命館大学アートリサーチセンター、国際日本文化研究センター、東京文化財研究所、法政大学、早稲田大学、慶應義塾大学、京都国立博物館、東京国立博物館、辻英子、狩野博幸、赤間亮、石川透、高橋亨、井伊春樹、鈴木桂子（以上、敬称略）などの日本の研究機関と研究者、及び、徐々に国際的コンテクストに組み込まれつつある、チェコ共和国内にある日本美術の複数のコレクションのご協力に感謝申し上げます。そして、本書の出版に尽力してくださった プラハのカレル大学出版局と、校閲に携わっていただいたアンソニー・リーマン氏、ズデンカ・シュヴァルツォヴァー氏に感謝申し上げます。上記のすべての個人及び研究機関に、私たちの心からの感謝を捧げます。

2016 年 4 月　ヘレナ・ホンコポヴァー

安原眞琴訳

A BOOK OF FANS

ŌGI NO SŌSHI

FACSIMILE

English translation Joshua S. Mostow et al.

The following English translation of the Prague *Ōgi no sōshi* was undertaken in seminar at The University of British Columbia in the spring of 2011. The students were Julien Butterlin, Vincent Chan, Alexey Lushchenko, Otilia Milutin, Anthea Murphy, Samuel Shooklyn, and Ethan Windschitl. The results have been edited by Joshua Mostow, who would also like to thank Prof. Ii Haruki and Dr. Yasuhara Makoto for their assistance. Any errors remain my responsibility.

J. S. Mostow

Notes

The international Hepburn script is used for the transcription of Japanese in the explanatory texts of this volume. In the transcription of the Japanese text in the facsimile part, however, the *hentaigana* characters of the original are maintained in the Latin letters, thus the particle *wa* is transcribed as *ha*, *dzu* stands for pallatelized *tsu*, while *zu* is used for pallatelised *su*, *jhi* is used for pallatelized *chi*, while *ji* for pallatelized *shi*, *afu* is used for long *ō*, *he* or *we* is used for *e*, *wi* for *i*, *wo* for *o* etc. - which is a service for students of old Japanese culture, who may use this volume as a textbook for reading practice of traditional Japanese texts (*bungo*).

Poems in the Prague version of *Ōgi no sōshi* come from many possible sources. Those included in the translation footnotes are selective and for a more thorough listing readers should refer to Dr. Makoto Yasuhara's study (*Ōgi no sōshi no kenkyū – asobi no geibun*, Pelikan-sha, Tōkyō, 2003).

The Prague version of A Book of Fans consists of 20 numbered sheets, each containing two pages that were originally bound in the Japanese manner from the back to the front. The obverse pages are labelled as A (omote), the reverse as B (ura). Each B-A pair represents the original double-pages and enables to follow mutual links among pairs of three fans and poems on each double-page.

ALPHABETICAL LIST OF ABBREVIATIONS
used in the Notes to the translation

BZS. *Butsukoku zenshi shū*, collection of Zen poems, Kōhō Kennichi (1241–1316).
FWS. *Fuboku wakashō*, ca. 1310. Japanese *waka* organized by themes and containing over 17,000 poems.
GM. *Genji monogatari*, ca. 1008. Lyrical novel in 54 chapters describing the court life of Prince Genji in Kyōto, by Murasaki Shikibu (ca.978–ca.1014).
GSIS. *GoShūi (waka) shū*, 1075–1086. Fourth imperially-commissioned anthology of Japanese poetry.
GYS. *Gyokuyō (waka) shū*, 1311–1312. Fourteenth imperially-commissioned anthology of Japanese poetry.
HI. *Hyakunin isshu*, 1236. Joshua S. Mostow. *Pictures of the Heart: The Hyakunin isshu in Word and Image*. Honolulu: University of Hawai'i Press, 1996.
HM. *Heike monogatari*, 1330. Chronicle of the battles between the Taira (Heike) and Minamoto (Genji) clans.
IM. *Ise monogatari*, ca. 950. *The Ise Stories*, translated by Mostow and Tyler; see Bibliography.
ISN. *Izumi Shikibu Nikki*, 1008. A diary with poems by the court lady Izumi Shikibu (978?–1036?).
KKS. *Kokin (waka) shū*, 905. *Kokin Wakashū*: *The First Anthology of Japanese Poetry*, translated by Helen Craig McCullough. Stanford: Stanford University Press, 1985.
KGS. *Kanke goshū*, a private collection of the god of poetry Tenjin, alias Sugawara Michizane (845–903).
KYS. *Kin'yō (waka) shū*, 1112–1127. Fifth imperially-commissioned anthology of Japanese poetry.
Kokon chomonjū, 1254. Collection of 726 *setsuwa* tales by Tachibana Narisue.
MS. *Makura no Sōshi*, 1002. The Pillow Book, collection of essays *zuihitsu* by Sei Shōnagon (ca.966–ca.1025).
Murasaki Shikibu nikki, 1008–1010. Literary diary of the famous poet and writer court lady.
Shinsen Tsukubashū, 1470. Collection of *renga* compiled by Sōgi Hōshi (1421–1502).
Shinsen Inu Tsukubashū, 1524–1532. Collection of humorous *haikai no renga* compiled by Yamazaki Sōkan (1465–1553).
SKS. *Sankashū*, a private collection of ca. 1500 poems by Saigyō Hōshi (1118–1190).
Shōkaku Kokushi shū, a private collection of Musō Soseki, also known as Shōkaku Kokushi (1275–1351).
ShKKS. *ShokuKokin (waka) shū*, 1259–1266. Eleventh imperially-commissioned anthology of Japanese poetry.
SIS. *Shūi (waka) shū*, 1005–1007. Third imperially-commissioned anthology of Japanese poetry.
SKKS. *ShinKokin (waka) shū*, 1201–1205. Eighth imperially-commissioned anthology of Japanese poetry.
SKS. *Shika (waka) shū*, 1144–1151. Sixth imperially-commissioned anthology of Japanese poetry.
SSZS. *ShinSenzai (waka) shū,* 1359. Eighteenth imperially-commissioned anthology of Japanese poetry.
SZS. *Senzai (waka) shū*, 1181–1188. Seventh imperially-commissioned anthology of Japanese poetry.
TBS. *Tsukubashū*, 1356. The first official collection of *renga* compiled by Nijō Yoshimoto.
Tsurezuregusa, 1324. Buddhist discourses in *zuihitsu* form by the monk Kenkō Hōshi.
WKRS. *Wakan rōei shū*, 1013. J. Thomas Rimer & Jonathan Chaves, (trans.): *Japanese and Chinese Poems to Sing: The Wakan rōei shū*. New York: Columbia University Press, 1997.

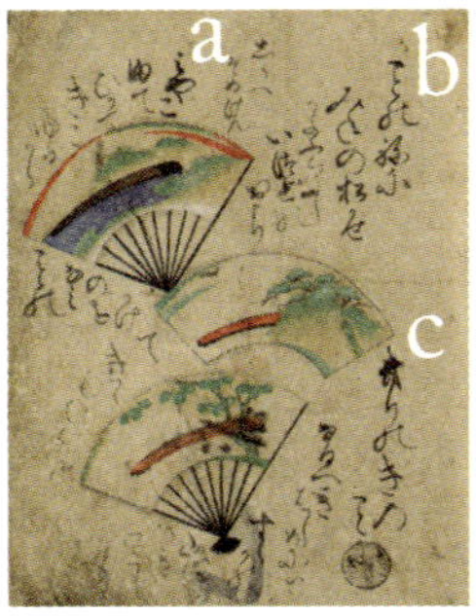

a/01

ミやこまて
ひかてきこゆる
からことの
なミのをかけて
ききもひかせん

miyako made
hikade kikoyuru
kara-koto no
nami no wo kakete
kiki mo hikasen

The Chinese zither
of Karakoto, heard as far as the capital
though unplucked–
stroking its strings of waves,
how I wish to make it hum.

b/02

ことのねに
みねの松かせ
かよふらし
いつれのおより
しらへそめけん

koto no ne ni
mine no matsu-kaze
kayofurashi
idzure no o yori
shirabe-someken

The wind through the pines
on the peak closely resembles
the sound of the zither–
from which slope or string
does it begin to play?

c/03

きりのきの
ことになるへき
はしめにハ
すゝかの山
ひきわたしけり

kiri no ki no
koto ni narubeki
hajime ni ha
suzuka no yama
hiki-watashikeri

At the start
the wood of the palownia
–destined to become a zither–
was pulled down from
the mountain of Suzuka.

NOTES SHEET 1A

01. *Kokinshū* XVII (Misc. 1): 921. Monk Shinsei, "Composed at a place called Karakoto ('Chinese zither')": *miyako* made / *HIBIKI KAYOHERU* / *karakoto ha* // *nami no wo SUgete* / *KAZE ZO HIKIKERU*. "This Karakoto, / the 'Chinese zither' noted / in the capital: // its strings are made of billows / and the player is the wind" (McCullough). The *koto* is a vertical harp-like instrument, here translated as "zither". Karakoto is "Chinese zither", but also a place-name on the Inland Sea–thus it is "heard of" as far as the capital. The poet compares the waves of Karakoto Bay to the strings of a zither.

02. *Shūishū* 451. The Ise Priestess (Princess Kishi, 949–986), "Composed on the topic 'Pine-wind enters the zither of night', when performing a *kōshin* vigil at Nonomiya"; Noh play *Senju*. O can mean both "mountain slope" and "string (of a musical instrument)".

03. *Mottomo no sōshi* (1632). "Various plucked instruments": *kiri no ki no* / *koto ni narubeki* / *TAMESHI ni ha* // *susuKI no yama wo* / *hiki-WATARU KANA*. "As an example / of the palownia tree / fated to become a zither, // it is pulled down from / the mountain of Suzuka." Mt. Suzuka is in Ise province, and famous as a barrier on the Ōmi road. "Suzuka" includes the word "suzu", or "bell", suggesting that it is because of this name that the zither has a beautiful, bell-like sound.

a/04

したもみち
かつちるやまの
ゆふしくれ
ぬれてやしかの
ひとりなくらん

shita-momijhi
katsu chiru yama no
yufu-shigure
nurete ya shika no
hitori nakuran

The evening showers
of the mountains where the lower leaves
of the autumn foliage are gradually falling–
dampened, the stag
is no doubt alone, crying.

b/05

なかむれは
たけのはしろく
月さへて
つもらぬゆきそ
はらふあきかせ

nagamureba
take no ha shiroku
tsuki sahete
tsumoranu yuki zo
harafu aki-kaze

As I look out,
the leaves of the bamboo are white,
the moon shining clearly,
and it is the autumn wind that scatters
the ungathered snow!

c/06

のゝミやの
あきのちくさの
はなくるま
われもむかしに
めくりきにけり

nonomiya no
aki no chigusa no
hana-kuruma
ware mo mukashi ni
megurikinikeri

A carriage of flowers
adorned with the autumn grass-flowers
of Nonomiya–
like it, I too have come
to return to the past.

NOTES SHEET 1B

04. *ShinKokinshū* 437. Fujiwara no Ietaka, "At the Waka Bureau, when the courtiers had composed poems on the topic 'deer at evening." (last lines: *nureta ya hitori / shika no nakuran*).

05. *ShinSenzaishū* (Autumn I): 416. GoToba Kunaikyō, "On wind in the bamboos before the moon": *IRO KA-HENU / take no ha shiroku / tsuki saEte // tsumoranu yuki zo / harafu aki-kaze*. "The leaves of the bamboo / – unchanging of color– / are white, and the moon bright; // the autumn wind brushes off / the unaccumulating snow".

06. (Noh) *Nonomiya*. Based on the "Sakaki" chapter of *The Tale of Genji*, when Genji goes to visit his former lover, the Lady Rokujō, at Nonomiya, where she is staying with her daughter, the Ise Priestess.

おもしきはなはのたゝしく月さして
はかなくぬれまき
そてらふおきなを

志くすみちは
ちるやぬれゆふ
志くれ
ぬき
ゝてや
志くれ
いろすら
ん

ゆきやの
めきれ
ちらくき
ひかるみ
くるまはも
むら小

めくりきみ
らん

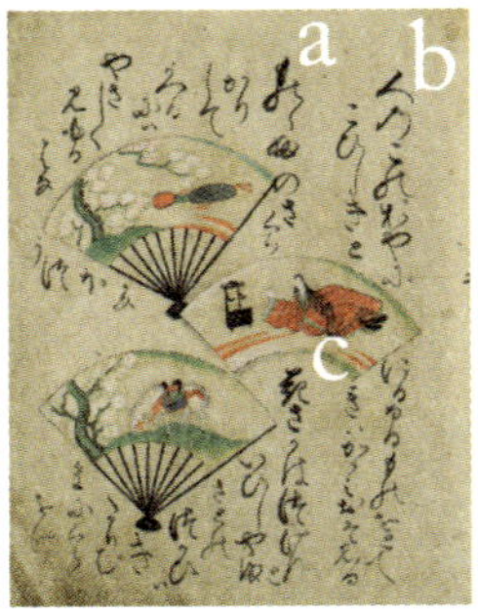

a/07

ものゝふの	mononofu no	A warrior
さくらかりして	sakura-gari shite	hunting for cherry-blossoms
かへるにハ	kaheru ni ha	and in his returning baggage
やさしくみゆる	yasashiku miyuru	a quiver of blossoms
はなうつほかな	hana-utsuho kana	appearing so refined!

b/08

人のこの	hito no ko no	Thinking that they say
おやににるなる	oya ni niru naru	that a person's child
ものをとて	mono wo tote	resembles her mother,
こひしきときハ	kohishiki toki ha	whenever I long for her
かゝミおそみる	kagami o zo miru	it is in a mirror that I look.

c/09

花さかは	hana sakaba	They said that
つけんといひし	tsuken to ihishi	if the cherries bloom, they would send word.
やまさとの	yama-zato no	From the mountain village
つかひハきたり	tsukahi ha kitari	a messenger has come–
むまにからをけ	muma ni kura oke	saddle the horses!

NOTES SHEET 2A

07. *Tsukubashū* (1356–57), with minor differences.
Shasekishū (1279-83), 5-22 [trans. Morrell, p. 174]:
This happened while Gotō Ikinokami Motomasa (1214-1267) of Kamakura was living in the capital. Once when returning from the mountains west of the city where he had been flower viewing, he placed a sprig of blossoms in his quiver. As he was proceeding on his way, a lady-in-waiting, seated on a high viewing platform, called out:

Yasashiku miyuru — Ah! The quiver of blossoms
Hanatsubo kana — So pleasant to look at!

Motomasa got down from his horse and replied:

Mononofu no — The warriors,
Sakuragari shite — Gone hunting for cherry blossoms:
Kaeru niwa — Their return baggage.

08. The Noh play *Matsuyama-kagami: ko ha oya ni niru naru mono to omoharete kohishiki toki ha kagami wo zo miru* ("A girl's features resemble her mother's, it seems; Yearning after the dead, she looks in the mirror" [Ueda]).

09. A similar poem appears in the *Minamoto Sanmi Yorimasa shū* and the Noh play *Kurama Tengū*.

くのこみわやみ
こひしきと
あらぬのさくら
かりそ
ろなぬい
やきしく
えゆる
とまる

うけれわ
ゑ

はるかるまれとて
きいかくとおそえる
あきらはけけれんと
いひしやぬ
さきみ

けらひい
き
くらひ
まぬろう
よけ

a/10

あらかねの
つちよりいてゝ
いかなれは
そらいろにさく
つゆくさのはな

arakane no
tsuchi yori idete
ika nareba
sora-iro ni saku
tsuyu-kusa no hana

Coming forth from earth
of hard iron
how is it, then,
that they bloom sky-blue,
the blossoms of the dayflower?

b/11

うしの子に
ふまるなにハの
かたつふり
つのありとても
ミをなたのミそ

ushi no ko ni
fumaru na niha no
katatsuburi
tsuno ari tote mo
mi wo na tanomi so

Don't get stepped on
by the calf of the bull,
o garden snail!
Although you too have horns,
do not rely on your strength!

c/12

みちのへの
たよりのさくら
おりそへて
たきゝやおもき
はるのやま人

michinobe no
tayori no sakura
ori-sohete
takigi ya omoki
haru no yama-bito

Ah, the Spring mountain-man
with his bundle of brushwood
made heavy by the addition
of the messenger-cherry blossoms
of the wayside!

NOTES SHEET 2B

10. No source identified.
11. Jakuren Hōshi, *Fuboku waka shō* 266 (*Ushi no ko ni / fumaru na niha no / katatsuburi // tsuno AREBA tote / mi woBA tanomi so*); the kyōgen *Gyūba*.
12. Junsō, *Ungyoku waka shū* (1514), attrib. Kuronushi; also the Noh play *Shiga*.

うれしさにふるさとをいでしかはゆり
はのはりそても
こよひたのそて
めぐりあひみつら
みちのくの
ちりいそて
はなれ
いるまて
さくらあり
そて
そらいろぬ
はるや
さく
あさき
は

とま
れ
ゆき

とる
れ
やぬん

a/13

むさしのハ
けふハなやきそ
わかくさの
つまもこもれり
われもこもれる

musashi no ha
kefu ha na yaki so
waka-kusa no
tsuma mo komoreri
ware mo komoreru

Oh no, please, today
do not burn Musashi Plain!
Tender as young grass,
my darling is hiding here,
and I too am hiding here.

b/14

さほひめの
ふてかとそ見る
つく〱し
ゆきかきわくる
はなのけしきハ

saho-hime no
fude ka to zo miru
tsukudzukushi
yuki kaki-wakuru
hana no keshiki ha

Ah, the Spring landscape
where the horsetails
that look as if they were the brushes
of the spring Princess Sao
push up through the snow!

c/15

をとにきく
つゝミのたきを
うち見れハ
たゝやまかハの
なるにそありけり

woto ni kiku
tsudzumi no taki wo
uchi-mireba
tada yama-kaha no
naru ni zo arikeri

Striking out to gaze
at Drum Falls
of high repute
I see it is made by no more than a mountain
stream
which is what makes its noise.

NOTES SHEET 3A

13. KKS 17, anon.; *The Ise Stories* (*Ise monogatari*), episode 12 (trans. Mostow & Tyler).
14. *Fuboku waka shō* (ca. 1310), bk. X, a hundred-poem sequence from 1224, grasses: 20 poems, "horsetails", Mibu no Kyō Tame'ie (1198–1275).
15. SIS 556, "When Kiyowara no Motosuke was governor of Higo, he went once to see a place in that province called Drum Falls, and a strange-looking priest composed [the following]"; *Eiga no ittei* (trans. Brower); the Noh *Tsutsumi no Taki*.

さほひめの
かつそめる
はくしほれ
そにこるなは
のゝし
きい

むまし
ぬい
ふいなや
きそわくらきみ

流ま
ともうて
まり
まれ
まる

とこよまくは
えんめきと
うらえ
まい
はやぬ
うゑ
なる
あゆ
ゑり

a/16

わかこひハ	waga kohi ha	My longing
たゝまるおけに	tada maru-oke ni	is just like a square lid
よはうふた	yohau futa	on a round container–
なにとまハせと	nani to mahasedo	however I turn it, they never meet,
あハぬつまかな	ahanu tsuma kana	like my love and I.

b/17

ミつのおもに	midzu mo omo ni	When I count
てる月なミを	teru tsuki-nami wo	the shining moon-waves
かそふれは	kazofureba	on the surface of the water
こよひそあきの	koyohi zo aki no	I realize that tonight indeed
もなかなりけり	monaka narikeri	is the middle of autumn!

c/18

かさゝきの	kasasagi no	When I see the whiteness
わたせるはしに	wataseru hashi ni	of the frost that lies
おくしもの	oku shimo no	on the bridge the magpies spread,
しろきを見れは	shiroki wo mireba	then do I know, indeed,
よそふけにける	yo zo fukenikeru	that the night has deepened.

NOTES SHEET 3B

16. Souce unidentified. "*Tada maru-oke*" may also be read as "*waga kohi ha tatamaru*"–"my longing piles up".
17. SIS 171: "On a screen, the fifteenth night of the Eighth Month, where someone was amusing themselves at a house with a lake, Minamoto no Shitagō"; WKRS.
18. SKKS 620, Yakamochi; HI 6 (trans. Mostow).

わこ君たち
御ゆるしけふよ
ちうかこ

なみて
ゆせ
さ
あかぬ
れまる

よそ
御けふ
けり

こよひかいてる月のかし
とりそへまいらせんこらし
そめきぬもの
すいゐり
めてきれ
にこせる
ちりぬめく
さもれ
さるゝ
とりまいらせん

a/19	たつねきて	tadzune-kite	Lost in contemplation
	はなにくらせる	hana ni kuraseru	of the blooms all day,
	このまより	ko no ma yori	then from the flower-shrouded
	まつとしもなき	matsu to shi mo naki	darkness between the trees, unexpected,
	山のはの月	yama no ha no tsuki	the moon on the mountain ridge!

b/20	かりくらし	kari-kurashi	Having spent the day hunting
	かたのゝましは	katano no mashiba	at Katano, we break off brushwood
	おりしきて	ori-shikite	and spread it out
	よとのかハせの	yodo no kahase no	and now we see the moon
	月をこそ見れ	tsuki wo koso mire	on the river-shallows of the Yodo.

c/21	あふミなる	afumi naru	Let them now begin
	つくまのまつり	tsukuma no matsuri	the Tsukuma Festival
	とくせなん	toku senan	Ōmi Province loves,
	つれなき人の	tsurenaki hito no	for I want to see how many pots
	なへのかす見ん	nabe no kazu min	crown your girlish innocence.

NOTES SHEET 4A

19. SKKS (Spring 1): 94, "When he submitted a set of fifty poems", Fujiwara no Masatsune
20. SKKS (Winter): 688, "Composed on the topic of hawking," Middle Captain of the Left Inner Guard, [Fujiwara no] Kinhira [1158-1193], with the last line reading "*tsuki wo miru kana*".
21. The *Ise Stories* (*Ise monogatari*), 120: "Back then this man learned that a woman he thought was still an ingénue was actually involved with a ranking gentleman. Sometime after that he sent her [the following poem]" (trans. Mostow & Tyler). The Tsukuma Festival required the local women to make a procession to the shrine with a pot on her head for every lover she had had.

かりくらしたなはた
つめにやとからん
あまのかはらに
われはきにけり

せわこれ
ゆりゆりに
うしも
すれふ
わその月

みす
見ん

ゆふたちのすゝて
月とそ見えき
あつさのかけくる
わまつらとく
せあん
つき
すれく
わあへ

a/22

花もうし
あらしもつらし
もろともに
はれはそさそふ
さそへハそちる

hana mo ushi
arashi mo tsurashi
moro-tomo ni
hareba zo sasofu
sasoheba zo chiru

The cherry blossoms are frail,
and the gales are cruel:
together,
when the blossoms scatter, indeed, they entice;
when the wind entices, indeed, they fall.

b/23

よりてこそ
それかとも見れ
たそかれに
ほの〱見ゆる
ゆふかほのはな

yorite koso
sore ka to mo mire
tasogare ni
hono-bono miyuru
yufu-gaho no hana

I will come closer
and see who she is–
the evening face
faintly visible
in the dim light at dusk.

c/24

あきのよの
かたハれ月の
かた〱ハ
ありけるものを
いけのみきハに

aki no yo no
katahare-tsuki no
kata-gata ha
arikeru mono wo
ike no migiha ni

The light, here and there,
of the crescent moon
of the autumn night–
although it is there, it is also
on the lake's waterside too.

NOTES SHEET 4B

22. *Ungyoku waka shū*, 92. Within the original collection, the commentary describes this poem as one speaking of a man and a woman, who, after spending night together, blame each other. The man blames the woman, saying that is because her "blossoms scatters" that they "enticed" him. The woman, on the other hand, claims that it is because of the "wind" that her "blossoms scattered". The poem also appears in the Noh play, *Sakuragawa* (Huey 1983).
23. *The Tale of Genji*, "Yūgao".
24. The closest verse found is from the *Kanke Kingyoku shū*, bk. 4, with the second hemistch "*ochite midzu no / soko ni arikeri*" (even after it sets, it remains / on the bottom of the water).

花もうし
おもひきて
はらしめる
ちそふみ
それそ
さそふ
さそへ
てらる

らて
こそ

あれのまま
ひさ遣月
むくらい
ゆりはしまれ
とひのみきふ

それ
かとも
見遣ぬそ

一
みち
なふ白
見るる
かれ
なふ

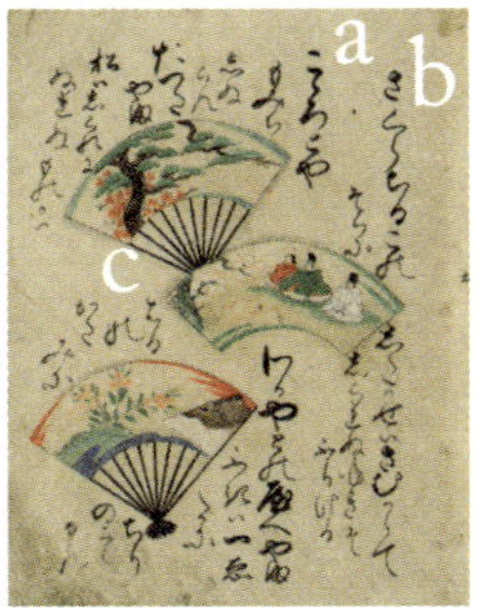

a/25

こゝろとや
もみちしぬらん
たつたやま
松ハしくれに
ぬれぬものかハ

kokoro to ya
momijhi shinuran
tatsuta-yama
matsu ha shigure ni
nurenu mono ka ha

Do the leaves themselves
decide to change color?
Mount Tatsuta!
Or are its pines something, then,
never dampened by showers?

b/26

さくらちる
このしたかせハ
さむからて
そらにしられぬ
ゆきそふりける

sakura chiru
ko no shita kaze ha
samukarade
sora ni shirarenu
yuki zo furikeru

The wind that blows beneath the trees
with their falling cherry blossoms
is not cold
but in the sky falls
an unknown snow.

c/27

わかやとの
やへやまふきハ
一ゑたに
ちりのこるらん
はるのかたみに

waga yado no
yahe-yamabuki ha
hitowe dani
chiri-nokoruran
haru no katami ni

Double-petalled *yamabuki*
blooming near my lodging,
how I wish at least one layer
would remain
as a reminder of spring!

NOTES SHEET 5A

25. SKKS 527, "On 'autumn leaves', when he composed a hundred-verse sequence at the house of the Lay Monk and Former Regent-Chancellor [Fujiwara no Kanezane, 1149-1207], Fujiwara no Shunzei [1114-1204]. Second line: "*momijhi ha suran*", adopted here. It was believed that it was the Autumn showers that were responsible for the changing color of the leaves.

26. SIS 64, "At a poetry-contest at the Teishi-in," Tsurayuki.

27. SIS 72, topic unknown, author unknown. *Yamabuki* is the Japanese rose (kerria japonica).

さくらちるこれ
そらふ
志てこのせいさむゝて
志らまぬゆきそ
ふりけり

このころや
みちしぬらん
たつたやま
松い志くれに
ぬきぬ
ぬれみつ

いつやまとれ戀へやゐ
うれい一念
ふみ

ちる
れ
吹く
みふ

ちり
のうて
ちん

a/28

しゝならは	shishi naraba	With boars,
十六つれて	jifuroku tsurete	four times four,
ゆくへきに	yukubeki ni	should make sixteen.
くゝきもるゝか	kuku ni moruru ka	says multiplication, but have they escaped?
ひとりはしるハ	hitori hashiru ha	–there is only one running.

b/29

とらと見て	tora to mite	Although
いしにたつやも	ishi ni tatsu ya mo	the arrow pierces the stone
あるものを	aru mono wo	mistaken for a tiger,
なとわかこひの	nado waga kohi no	why can't I pass
とをらさらめや	toworazarame ya	through to my love?

c/30

しつのめか	shidzu no me ga	The humble woman
松のおちはを	matsu no ochi-ba wo	grows used to raking up
かきなれて	kaki-narete	the fallen pine needles–
あすのたきゝに	asu no takigi ni	for tomorrow's firewood
あらしをそまつ	arashi wo zo matsu	she waits for the storm.

NOTES SHEET 5B

28. Source unidentified. *Kuku* is a word for "multiplication"; *shishi* means *inoshishi*, or boars, but can also be taken to mean "four times four".

29. *Shiji* (Records of the Historian, by Sima Qian, ca. 145-85 BCE). In the legend of General Li. Li Guang of Han went to hunt and having mistaken a stone in the grass for a tiger, he shot an arrow, piercing the stone. The same episode is also found in Book 7 (A matter of General Li) of The Tales of the Soga Brothers (*Soga monogatari*, mid-fourteenth century: *tora to mite / iru ya no ishi ni / tatsu mono wo // nado wa ga kohi no / toorazarubeki*). The story of an arrow sticking in a stone came to be used as a proverb. In general, it means that nothing is impossible if one is sufficiently determined.

30. *Seisuishō*, a collection of humorous tales, that were widely popular among *shōmin*, or commoners. A massive collection put together by Anrakuan Sakuden (1554-1642), a tea-master from Kyōto (1623).

こゝに見えていつはり鹿やもあるよし

おとなしこゝろみ

とさらさうめや

志かのうちえ

十六

つまて

ゆく色

きみ小

くみ小

めくりつ

ひとりちゝ御い

ねふ

小

あつ

よそ

まつ

志ぬれめる

松のみち

くされ

あれて

あされ

a/31	ゆくミつに	yuku midzu ni	The greater folly
	かすかくよりも	kazu kaku yori mo	lies not in writing figures
	はかなきハ	hakanaki ha	on a flowing stream,
	おもハぬ人を	omohanu hito wo	but in loving loyally
	おもふなりけり	omofu narikeri	one who has no love for you.
b/32	うつをとの	utsu woto no	The sound of its beating
	しはしとたゑて	shibashi todawete	has stopped for a while
	きこへぬハ	kikohenu ha	and what cannot be heard
	いまやきぬたを	ima ya kinuta wo	right now, is when the fulling blocks
	まきかへしけり	maki-kaheshikeri	are being rolled.
c/33	ふしのねハ	fuji no ne ha	The height of
	としにたかさや	toshi ni takasa ya	Mt. Fuji's peak
	まさるらん	masaruran	seems to increase with every year.
	きへぬるうへに	kihenuru uhe ni	On top of the unmelted snow,
	つもるしらゆき	tsumoru shira-yuki	white snow piles up ceaselessly.

NOTES SHEET 6A

31. KKS 522, *Ise monogatari* 50 (trans. Mostow & Tyler).
32. *Waka teikinshō* (ca. 1326), 2, [Nijō Tamezane], with the last lines: *ima ya koromo wo / maki-kahesu hodo* ("now, when the robe is being rolled up"). See as well the Noh play *Kinuta*.
33. Noh play *Fuji-yama*, (atrrib. to both Zeami and Zenchiku): *fuji no take ha / toshi ni takasa ya / masaruran / kienu ga uhe ni / tsumoru yuki no.*

うれしともしらしとこゝろてきこえぬ
いかやこきぬこ　とかれつゝけり

ゆくとにふぬ
みなもく
ちりも
ちるまれい
ねてつぬ
人をと
ねあふありけり

うつよ
流もる
しつゆれ

ゆみねは
やまにも
なれつ
さや
ゆきる
らん
きえぬらん

a/34

もゝとせに	momotose ni	Only one year shy,
ひととせたらぬ	hitotose taranu	she is, of a full hundred,
つくもかミ	tsukumo-gami	with her seaweed hair,
われをこふらし	ware wo kofurashi	and I believe she loves me.
おもかけにたつ	omokage ni tatsu	There she is: that haunting face.

b/35

月かけの	tsuki-kage no	As the moonlight strikes,
さすにまかせて	sasu ni makasete	so do the oars of
ゆくふねハ	yuku fune ha	the departing boats.
あかしのうらや	akashi no ura ya	Will they stop per chance
とまりなるらん	tomari naruran	at the bright bay of Akashi?

c/36

やまてらの	yama-dera no	When I come
はるのゆふへを	haru no yufube wo	to see the spring twilight
きて見れは	kite mireba	of the mountain temple
いりあひのかねに	iri-ahi no kane ni	the blossoms scatter
はなそちりける	hana zo chirikeru	with the evening bell.

NOTES SHEET 6B

34. *Ise monogatari*, 63 (trans. Mostow & Tyler), with the last verb "*miyu*" rather than "*tatsu*".
35. KYS, 221, "Composed on 'the moon over the water", Fujiwara no Sanemitsu. "*Sasu*", "to strike", refers to both the moonlight and oars.
36. SIS 115, "Composed when he was in a mountain village", Nōin; with "*yufugure*" rather than "*yufube*". Also in *Teika Jittei* (45), and the Noh play *Mii-dera*.

風のけはきすゝ海のそてしくしらへ
わかのうらや潮りなるらん

ことせに
ひとよ
みるみ
なかくて
かつき
見えを
ふら
かさはか
こひ

かねに
はなそ
ちりける

やまさとの
はるのゆふ
くれきて
見れは
いりあひの

a/37

ゆきふれは
身にひきそふる
はしたかの
たゝさきのはや
しらふなるらん

yuki fureba
mi ni hiki-sofuru
hashi-taka no
tada-saki no ha ya
shirafu naruran

When the snow falls,
accompanied by
my sparrow-hawk
on my left wrist – its wings
will no doubt turn white.

b/38

いそかすは
なか〱ぬれし
たひころも
あとよりはるゝ
のちのむらさめ

isogazuba
naka-naka nureji
tabi-koromo
ato yori haruru
nojhi no murasame

If he hadn't hurried–
they would not have got so wet,
the travel-robes!
the passing shower over the country road
where it later cleared!

c/39

ものゝふの
よろひにまさる
かミのきぬ
かせのいりやも
とをらさりけり

mononofu no
yorohi ni masaru
kami no kinu
kaze no iru ya mo
toworazarikeri

Even though the paper robe
has replaced the armor
from the past,
the arrow that the wind shoots
does not pierce it.

NOTES SHEET 7A

37. *Shōji shodo hyakushu*, 1570, Fujiwara no Norimitsu; *Fuboku waka shū*, 1277.

38. *Bokeishū*, personal poetry collection of Ōta Dōkan (1432-1486), with 2nd and 3rd lines as: *nurezaramashi wo / tabi-bito no* ("he would not have been soaked / the traveller").

39. *Kokon ikyoku shū* (1666), Rensei Hōshi (Kumagai Naozane), with the first two lines as: *inishihe no / yorohi ni kawaru*, yeilding: "Even though a paper robe / has replaced my armor / of the past, / the arrow that the wind shoots / does not pierce it".

ゆ乃宝ん
男ふひ
きそふる
とかけれ
負されの
とや志ふ
するらん

あまの
そでひに
ゆきさる
めつられ
きぬ

むら
さめ

をれいろや
ときは
まつ
らり

いそなつむ
なく
ぬまの
こころ
あこもり
もろく
のち

a/40

やま人の	yama-bito no	The mountain man:
かさもたきゝも	kasa mo takigi mo	both his umbrella and brushwood
うつもれて	udzu-morete	are leaking and
ゆきこそくゝれ	yuki koso kugure	the snow indeed blows under them
たにほそみち	tani [no] hoso-michi	on the narrow road of the valley.

b/41

わかやとの	waga yado no	The white dew of the mums
きくのしらつゆ	kiku no shira-tsuyu	at my house,
けふことに	kefu goto ni	today and year after year,
いくよつもりて	ikuyo tsumorite	how many ages will accumulate
ふちとなるらん	fuchi to naruran	and it turn into deep pools?

c/42

とひきゆる	tobi-kiyuru	The heron
くも井のさきの	kumowi no sagi no	flying off into the clouds
をのつから	wonodzukara	all alone,
わかいろこほす	waga iro kobosu	shedding its own color
ゆきのあけほの	yuki no akebono	upon the snowy dawn.

NOTES SHEET 7B

40. Noh play *Katsuragi*, with the last lines: *yuki koso kudare / tani no michi wo* ("the snow falls indeed / on the road of the valley").
41. WKRS 265; Noh play *Kantan*; SIS 184: "For a screen at the coming-of-age ceremony of the Empress of the Third Ward, on [a scene depicting] the ninth day of the Ninth Month, [Kiyowara no] Motosuke".
42. *Shūgai Kasen* (1665), "Snowy dawn", Shōtetsu (1381–1459): *shira-sagi no / kumowi haruka ni / tobi-kihete / ono ga ha kobosu / yuki no akebono* ("The white heron / flies off / into the clouds afar, / shedding the color of its wings / upon the snowy dawn").

やまくれは
つなかも
なそし
うれ
めまて
ゆきえて
くれは
かそ
みち

ゆやとは
きくのたつ
はなふ
とふいくよ
はかり
て
うちと
あるらん

さひきゆら
くもゐは
きたの
とはは
のうら
いろはそ
ゆれは
あけ
はの

a/43

おのつから
あふときなれや
やとれとハ
ミつもおもハす
月もたつねす

onodzukara
afu toki nare ya
yadore to ha
midzu mo omohazu
tsuki mo tadzunezu

When, by chance,
they meet, do they say:
"Let's lodge together"?
The water does not think it;
the moon does not ask for it.

b/44

こくらくの
うちにもこしを
かけはこそ
そとハなにかハ
くるしかるへき

gokuraku no
uchi ni mo koshi wo
kakeba koso
soto ha nani ka ha
kurushikarubeki

Inside Paradise, as well,
since I take a seat, indeed,
what can be bad
about doing it outside?

c/45

くさのなも
ところによりて
かハりけり
なにハのあしハ
いせのはまをき

kusa no na mo
tokoro ni yorite
kaharikeri
naniha no ashi ha
ise no hama-wogi

Even the names of grasses,
depending on where you are,
change!
The "reeds" of Naniwa
are the "rushes" of Ise.

NOTES SHEET 8A

43. *Sōkinshū* 1050, Shōtetsu (1381–1459).

44. Noh play *Sotoba Komachi*: *gokuraku no / uchi naraba koso / ashikarame / soto ha nani ka ha / kurushikarubeki* ("My crime in Paradise most grave post it without quite free of every blame" (trans. Tyler 1978).

45. *Tsukuba shū* (1356), with third line: kaharu nari; similar thoughts are also expressed in the Noh play *Ashikari*.

こゝら見うらみを
そことはあふらくる

萩流つゝめふれとも
きれや
やさしと
とい
言も
枕の字
月も色

秋すゞ

こゝとかけにて
志ろうしき

なきれ身ことろ
ふまりてつら
かり京ふ見
あい
なお
よれ

a/46		
やまたもる	yamada moru	Near a small hut
いほちかくなく	iho chikaku naku	that guards the mountain paddies,
しかのねに	shika no ne ni	the voice of a deer
おとろかすれて	odorokasurete	surprises me,
おとろかすかな	odorokasu kana	and so surprising him!

b/47		
ものゝふの	mononofu no	The warrior
ゆミはり月の	yumi hari-dzuki no	draws his bow by the light
かけ見へて	kage mihete	of the crescent moon and,
あけぬにもなく	akenu ni mo naku	ah, the rooster at the barrier
せきのにハとり	seki no niha-tori	who cries though it is not dawn!

c/48		
ゆきならは	yuki naraba	If it were snow
いくたひそてを	iku tabi sode wo	how many times then would I
はらハまし	harahamashi	brush my sleeves–
はなのふゝきの	hana no fubuki no	the mountain-pass of Shiga
しかのやまこへ	shiga no yama-kohe	in a flowery blizzard!

NOTES SHEET 8B

46. SKKS 448, Saigyō, with the first line *woyamada no* ("the small mountain paddies") and the fourth line *odorokasarete* (the Prague version is ungrammatical, suggesting a scribal error).

47. Source unknown. The poem contains a *kake-kotoba*, or "pivot-word": *mononofu yumi hari* ("the warrior strings his bow") and *yumi-hari-tsuki*, ("a moon in the shape of a strung bow", i.e., a crescent moon). The poem seems to refer to an episode in *Shiji* (Book of History) about Lord Mengchang of Qi being able to flee through Hangu Pass by having one of his soldiers imitate a rooster's cry, thus making the guards at the barrier think it was dawn and so open the gate.

48. *Rokka waka shū* (Muromachi period), 271, Lady Nakatsukasa; the poem is quoted in the Noh plays *Shiga* and *Miidera*.

まちの夜のゆふされ月のかけつて
あけぬるかとおもふく
せきのかいより

ゆくへもいく
鳥ひそてと
ちらい御
ちるも
ぬくきみ
志らのやま
こへ

やまた
もる
いなら
かく
すく
志ゐ
ねに
ねと

わすれまてをとろかす
なる

a/49

ふてもよし	fude mo yoshi	The brush is good;
すミよしいかて	sumi-yoshi ika de	the ink good – Sumiyoshi –
かゝさらん	kakazaran	how then should I not paint it –
なにハあたりの	naniha atari no	the landscape of Spring
はるのけしきを	haru no keshiki wo	in the vicinity of Naniwa?

b/50

いかたしよ	ikadashi yo	Hey, Raftsman!
まてこととハん	mate koto tohan	Wait! There's something I would ask you:
みなかミハ	minakami ha	at the headwaters,
いかはかりふく	ikabakari fuku	how hard did it blow,
やまのあらしそ	yama no arashi zo	the storm in the mountains?

c/51

花ならは	hana naraba	If they were flowers,
いくたひそてに	iku tabi sode ni	how many times on my sleeves
うけてまし	uketemashi	I'd receive them–
ゆきのふゝきの	yuki no fubuki no	the mountain pass of Shiga
しかのやまこへ	shiga no yamagoe	in a snowy blizzard!

NOTES SHEET 9A

49. Source unknown, though the last two lines appear in a poem by Nōin (b. 988). In a *kake-kotoba* (pivot-word) "Sumiyoshi" is both the name of a place in Naniwa and the phrase "the ink is good".

50. SKKS (Spring) 76, "During the time of Retired Emperor GoReizei; Lord Fujiwara no Sukemune." The man onshore asks how hard the wind upstream blew because of the flooded waters.

51. Source unknown; an apparent variation on poem 48, above.

ぬれてゝし
すゝし
いそ
のゝ
きゝん
なふい
あそりし
ちるの
ゆき
きと

やま
れ
おち
て

花のちかくおもそてに
うけつゝ
ゆきの
ぬく

きゝ
しみ
やま
え

いかにしても
かとゝなかめ
とりかへ
いつとかり
う

a/52

こまとめて	koma tomete	There is no shelter
そてうちはらふ	sode uchi-harafu	for me to stop my horse
かけもなし	kage mo nashi	and brush off my sleeves –
さのゝわたりの	sano no watari no	a snowy twilight
ゆきのゆふくれ	yuki no yufugure	crossing the Sano Ford.

b/53

このうちも	ko no uchi mo	He envies
うらやましきハ	urayamashiki ha	even the one in the cage
やまからの	yamagara no	– the mountain-tit –
ミのほとかくす	mi no hodo kakusu	hiding himself in the shelter
ゆふかほのやと	yufu-gaho no yado	of the evening-face gourd-blossoms.

c/54

かきりあれは	kagiri areba	Since there is a limit,
かやかのきはの	kaya ga noki-ba no	I have come to see the moon
月もミつ	tsuki mo mitsu	over eaves of thatch.
しらぬハ人の	shiranu ha hito no	What I don't know is the sky
ゆくすゑのそら	yukusuwe no sora	over the destinations of others.

NOTES SHEET 9B

52. SKKS (Winter), 671, "When a hundred-poem sequence was offered to the emperor; Lord Fujiwara no Teika". Note that the bridge at Sano Ford was a *funabashi*, that is, a bridge made by lashing boats together, and not a plank bridge, as depicted.

52. GYS 1312; *Fuboku waka shū* 12884, Master of the Law Jakuren; also included in Book 8 of *Heike monogatari*, with the second line: *naho urayamashi*.

53. This poem appears to be a variation of a poem composed by Retired Emperor GoToba in exile on Oki Island, included in the *GoToba Oki entō hyakushu*, the *Masu Kagami* (attributed to Emperor GoDaigo), and Zeami's *Kintōsho* (there attributed to Retired Emperor Juntoku): *inochi areba / koya no nokiba no / tsuki mo mitsu // shiranu ha hito no / yukusuwe no sora* ("Because I still live, / I have seen the moon / over eaves of thatch. // What I do not know is the sky / over the destination of others").

このうらとうつやまきハやまのみ
みねほとかくせて
ゆふつねやと

駒とめて
そて
うち
はらふ
かけ
もなし
さのゝ
わたりの
ゆきの
ゆふくれ

もゝの
そち

かりあまた
やりぬき
えの月
ことに
あきぬ
くれ
ゆく

a/55

くまのなる
おとなしかハに
わたさはや
ひんこのともの
さゝやきのはし

kumano naru
oto-nashi kaha ni
watasabaya
bingo no tomo no
sasayaki no hashi

If only I could pass
the silent Otonashi River
of Kumano
by the Sasayaki Bridge of whispers,
companion of Bingo Province!

b/56

見わたせは
やなきさくらを
こきませて
みやこハはなの
けしきなりけり

mi-wataseba
yanagi sakura wo
koki-mazete
miyako ha haru no
nishiki narikeri

When I gaze afar,
the hue of the cherry mixes
with that of the willow–
forming the Spring brocade
of the capital.

c/57

さきそめし
わかききのさくら
かせふけは
ちりもならハて
はないかにせん

saki-someshi
wakakiki no sakura
kaze fukeba
chiri mo narahade
hana ika ni sen

When the wind blows
on the cherry-blossoms of the young trees
that have just begun to bloom,
not yet learning how to scatter,
what will the flowers do?

NOTES SHEET 10A

55. *Fuboku waka shō*, 9492, with the last line: *shinobi ni shinobi ni* ("secretly, secretly"). *Oto-nashi* means "soundless" and *sasayaki* "whisper". Otonashi River is the headwater of the Kumano River, in the former province of Kii, present-day Wakayama; Sasayaki Bridge is in the modern prefecture of Hiroshima. The poem is also included in the *otogi-zōshi Saru Genji* (before 1597).

56. KKS (Spring) 56: "Composed on gazing at the capital from afar when the cherry-blossoms were in full bloom," Master of the Dharma Sosei. The poem is also quoted in the Noh play *Saigyō and the Cherry Tree*.

57. Various partial sources, including *Kanke goshū* and the *Tenri-bon Tenji emaki*.

見にこそたやすれ
みやこいへ

さくらとこれ御せれ
ゆれのふきまかり
さこそそう
にこれきれの
さくらせ
ぬはた
ちりも
あらつそ
たみ
いふ

せん

くゆれ
なるもと
あつゐふ
ゆきらや
こんこれのうて
のさて
やき
のれ
ら

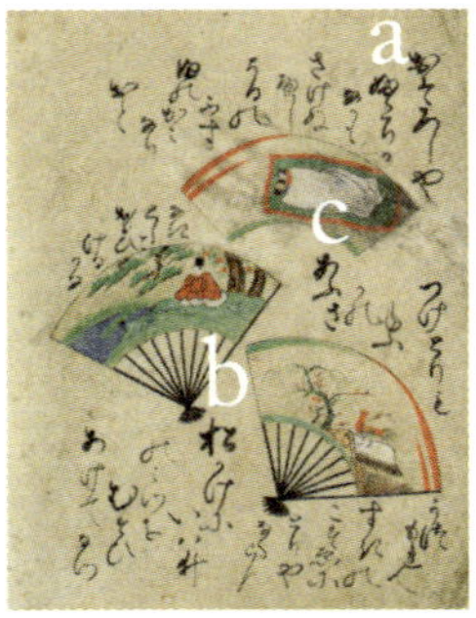

a/58

おそろしや
ふたりかなかも
さけぬへし
よるのふすまの
かミなりのおと

osoroshi ya
futari ga naka mo
sakenubeshi
yoru no fusuma no
kaminari no oto

Oh, how terrible!
It will certainly lead
to our separation:
the thundering sound
of my paper robe at night!

b/59

松かけに
いハ井のミつを
むすひあけて
なつなきとしと
おもひけるかな

matsu-kage ni
ihawi no midzu wo
musubi-agete
natsu naki toshi to
omohikeru kana

In the shade of the pines,
scooping up pure water
from the stone pool,
I find myself thinking
that it is a year without summer!

c/60

あふさかの
ゆふつけとりも
うつもれて
すきのこすゑに
とりやなくらん

afusaka no
yufu tsuke tori mo
udzu-morete
sugi no kozuwe ni
tori ya nakuran

Even the beribboned cock
of Ōsaka Barrier
they drown out
the birds that must be singing
in the branches of the cedar.

NOTES SHEET 10B

58. *Seisuishō* (c. 1615), VI, "Composed by a child when he was wearing new paper bed-clothes"; *Shinkyū kyōka haikai kikigaki*, Love; both with the third line: *omofu naka wo mo saketsubeshi* ("even true lovers must surely be parted") and the fifth line: *narukami no oto* ("the sound of the thunder god"). Cf. KKS 701.

59. *SIS* (Summer), "When he was cooling himself at the source of a spring at the Kawara-In", Egyō Hōshi; WKRS (Summer, Keeping cool), with the third line: *musubitsutsu*.

60. Source unknown; the poem resembles one attributed to Fujiwara no Toshiyuki (d. 901) in the *Nishi Hongan-ji-bon Sanjūroku-nin shū: afusaka no / yufu tsuke ni naku / tori no ne ha // kiki-togamete zo / yuki-suginikeru* ("As for the sound of the bird, / that sings, beribboned / on Afusaka Barrier– // hearing it, I find fault / that it has gone too far").

おそろしや
ゆくり
おこし
さけぬ
のし
うるに
うす
ゆにかこ
おり
おと

あれ
こと
思ひ
ける
る

みそりも
しほに
はれ
あふさ

うれて
あきて
すれに
こそ京に
そりや
あらん

松のけふ
いいけ
にかいと
もそい
あけてきの

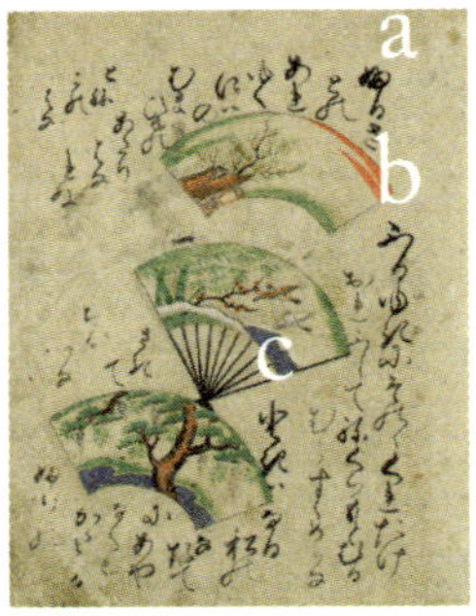

a/61	ふるさとの	furu-sato no	Ah, the flowers of the attending ash
	あれゆくにハの	are-yuku niha no	do not go far from
	むまひゆの	muma-biyu no	the purslane
	あたりはなれぬ	atari hanarenu	in the declining garden
	とねこのはな	tone[ri]ko no hana	of the old village.
b/62	ふるゆきに	furu yuki ni	In the falling snow,
	そのゝくれたけ	sono no kure-take	the bamboo of the garden
	おれふして	ore-fushite	bends and topples and
	ねくらもとむる	negura motomuru	oh! the flock of sparrows
	むらすゝめかな	mura-suzume kana	searching for another roost!
c/63	ときハなる	tokiha naru	The evergreen
	松のなたてに	matsu no na-date ni	pine is famous but
	あやなくも	aya naku mo	uselessly
	かゝれるふちの	kakareru fujhi no	the wisteria clinging to it
	さきてちるかな	sakite chiru kana	blooms, and then scatters.

NOTES SHEET 11A

61. *Rokka waka shū* (Winter) 1188, Fujiwara no Tame'ie (1198-1275). *Toneriko* is the ash tree, while *toneri* means "attendant."

62. GYS (Winter), "Bamboo covered by snow", Saigyō, with the first line: *yuki udzumu* ("covered by snow").

63. WKRS 136; ShKKS 172, Ki no Tsurayuki.

a/64

かハつなく	kahadzu naku	Do their reflections
かミなひかハに	kaminabi-gaha ni	appear in the Kaminabi River,
かけ見へて	kage mihete	where the frogs cry,
いまやさくらん	ima ya sakuran	and is it now that they are blooming,
やまふきのはな	yamabuki no hana	the flowers of the yellow kerria?

b/65

よもあけは	yo mo akeba	Come dawn's early light
きつにはめなて	kitsu ni hamenade	oh yes, in the tank you go,
くたかけの	kutakake no	you obnoxious bird,
またきになきて	madaki ni nakite	to learn to cock-a-doodle
せなをやりつゝ	sena wo yaritsutsu	my darling away so soon.

c/66

からころも	kara-koromo	Robe from far Cathay
きつゝなれにし	kitsutsu narenishi	long and comfortably worn,
つましあれは	tsuma shi areba	bound by love to stay
はる〱きぬる	haru-baru kinuru	I cover these distances
たひをしそおもふ	tabi wo shi zo omofu	shrouded in melancholy.

NOTES SHEET 11B

64. SKKS, topic unknown, Prince Atsumi (892–966).
65. *Ise monogatari*, episode 14, with last word *yaritsuru* (trans. Mostow and Tyler). *Kitsu* was by many commentators taken to mean "fox", but none is depicted here.
66. KKS IX (Travel): 410, Ariwara no Narihira; *Ise monogatari*, episode 9 (trans. Mostow and Tyler). The poem is an acrostic (*oriku*), with the first syllable of each line spelling out the word "*kakitsubata*", or iris. The painting depicts *Yatsubashi* ("Eight Bridges") where the poem was composed.

かはつなく
かみなひかはに
かけみえて
いまやさくらん
やまふきのはな

よもあけはきつにはめなて
くたかけのまたきになきて
せなをやりつる

からころも
きつつなれにし
つましあれは
はるはるきぬる
たひをしそおもふ

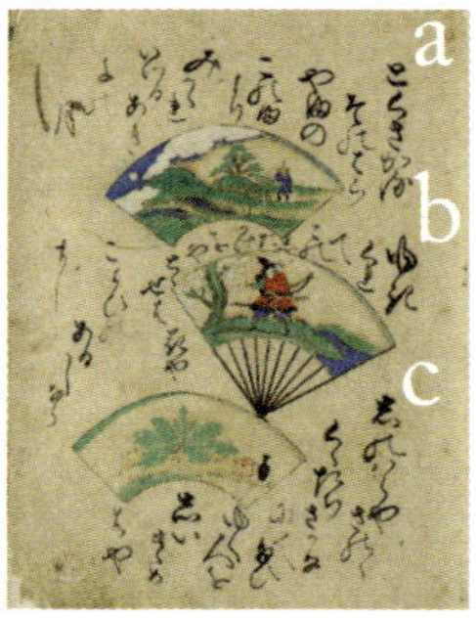

a/67

とくさかる	tokusa karu	Reaping weeds,
そのはらやまの	sonohara-yama no	from the space between the trees
このまより	ko no ma yori	of Mount Sonohara
みかゝれいつる	migakare-idzuru	it emerges, all polished–
あきよの月	aki [no] yo no tsuki	the moon of the autumn night!

b/68

ゆきくれて	yuki-kurete	Journeying on,
このしたかけを	ko no shita-kage wo	were I to make the shade beneath the trees
やとゝせは	yado to seba	my shelter for the night,
花やこよひの	hana ya koyohi no	then the cherry blossoms would be
あるしならまし	aruji naramashi	my hosts for the evening.

c/69

しのハらや	shinohara ya	The low bamboo field,
さのゝくゝたち	sano no kukutachi	with greens from Sano
さかなにて	sakana nite	as tidbits–
たひゆく人を	tabi-yuku hito wo	if only we could hold back
しいとゝめはや	shii todomebaya	the traveler, even against his will!

NOTES SHEET 12A

67. Noh play *Tokusa*; *Fuboku waka shō* 8443: "Mount Sonohara, Shino. In the first year of the Hōen era [1134], from the poetry contest held at the house of Middle Captain Ienari, Minamoto no Nakamasa". The last line should read: *aki no yo no tsuki*.

68. *Heike monogatari*, Bk IX, Taira no Tadanori. Written on the topic "On Blossoms at a Travel Lodging"; according to the tale, this poem was hidden within the quiver of the slain warrior and served as the only means for the victors of this particular battle to identity the fallen soldier.

69. *Fuboku waka shō* 9957, "Drinking sake in a field", Minamoto no Nakamasa (b. ca. 1066).

とくきかは
そなたら
やまの
こなたちり
みつまき
いつるあき
よみほ
し

ゆれ
まて
こなて
やとけたえ
ちせん花や
こらひの
ある
ちしあう

志れつゝや
さそく
くたらさる
ゐて見
ゆくと
志い
さか
そや

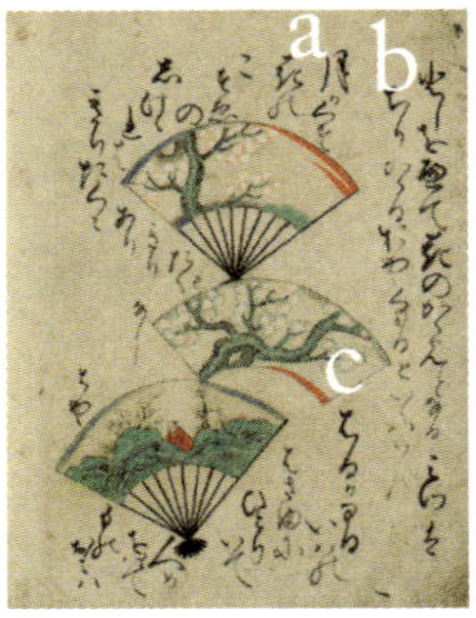

a/70	月かくす	tsuki kakusu	When the branches
	花のこすゑの	hana no kozuwe no	of the cherry blossoms grow thick
	しけゝれは	shigekereba	and hide the moon
	きりたくもあり	kiritaku mo ari	I both want to cut them
	きりたくもなし	kiritaku mo nashi	and do not want to cut them.
b/71	としをへて	toshi wo hete	The years pass and
	花のかゝみと	hana no kagami to	as for the waters that become
	なるミつは	naru midzu ha	a mirror to the blossoms–
	ちりかゝるおや	chiri-kakaru o ya	when they scattered should we say
	くもるといふらん	kumoru to ifuran	that they are clouding the mirror?
c/72	はるかなる	harukanaru	Ah, to be alone
	いハのはさまに	iha no hasama ni	among the rocks
	ひとりいて	hitori ite	far away,
	人めをもハて	hito-me womohade	heedless of people's stares,
	ものおもハはや	mono-omohabaya	thinking of my love!

NOTES SHEET 12B

70. *Shinsen Inu Tsukuba shū* (ca. 1532), 207. The lower hemistich is given first, and then three capping verses, one of which is: *sayaka naru / tsuki wo kakuseru / hana no eda* ("the branch of cherry blossoms that hide the shining moon").
71. KKS (Spring) 44, Lady Ise.
72. SKKS XII (Love 2), 1099, topic unknown, Master of the Law Saigyō.

山を越て花のかゝみとする こゝを
ちりかゝるわかやまとさそふらん

月かくて
花の
こそ思
の
志けき
ん
まさりたる
あり
こゝろ
たくも
あ
ちや

ちるを見る
いつれ
えさぬめり
ひとつそ
くや
とても
まし
なけ

a/73

くものいへに
あれなるこまハ
つなくとも
ふたみちかくる
人ハたのまし

kumo no ihe ni
arenaru koma ha
tsunagu to mo
futa-michi kakuru
hito ha tanomaji

Even if one can snag
a wild horse
in a spider web,
one cannot rely on a man
drawn down two roads.

b/74

よそに見て
かへらん人に
ふちのはな
はひまつハれよ
ゑたハおるとも

yoso ni mite
kaheran hito ni
fujhi no hana
hahimatsuhareyo
weda ha oru to mo

They look elsewhere
and make to go home–
twine around them!
o wisteria blossoms,
even if your limbs are broken!

c/75

よこはしる
あしまのかにの
いかなれや
あきさむしとて
ミつにいるらん

yoko-hashiru
ashi-ma no kani no
ika nare ya
aki samushi tote
midzu ni iruran

The crabs that run
sideways between the reeds–
is it because
they think autumn cold
that they run into the water?

NOTES SHEET 13A

73. Apparently an old folk verse, cited by Kenkō in his *Essays in Idleness* (*Tsurezure-gusa*); also quoted in the Noh play *Kanawa*.

74. KKS (Spring): 119: "Composed and sent to some women who, returning from Shiga, entered Kazan, stood under some wisteria, and then left"; Sōjō Henjō.

75. *Tametade-ke godo hyakushū* (1135), 514, Minamoto no Nakamasa (1066–ca.1137); *Fuboku waka shō*: Animals, Crabs, Snow Between Reeds: *yoko-hashiru / ashi-ma no kani no / yuki fureba / ana samuge ni ya / isogi-kakuru-ru* ("Running sideways / the crabs between the reeds / when snow falls- / ah! is it because of the cold / that they hurry to hide?").

よそにみてかへらん人にふちのはな
はひまつはれよ
えたはおるとも

くもの
うへに
あまかける
こまは
なかれく
るて
ゝき
みち
くる
くるま
の

よこさは
かはなみの
おりうめ
いつ
されや
あれさ
もとも
とふ
いらん

a/76

あふときハ	afu toki ha	Although I think
かたりつくすと	katari-tsukusu to	I have exhausted all I had to say
おもへとも	omohedomo	every time we meet,
わかれとなれは	wakare to nareba	when it is time to part
のこることのは	nokoru koto no ha	there are words still left unspoken.

b/77

むさしのは	musashino ha	There are no mountains
月のいつへき	tsuki no idzubeki	from which the moon can rise
山もなし	yama mo nashi	on Musashi Plain–
くさよりいてゝ	kusa yori idete	it rises from the grasses and
くさにこそいれ	kusa ni koso ire	into the grasses, indeed, it sets.

c/78

山てらの	yama-dera no	What kind of thing
こひのこゝろハ	kohi no kokoro ha	are the feelings of love
いかなれは	ika nareba	in a mountain temple?
あふとはすれと	afu to ha suredo	Although they do "meet",
うちうしろむく	uchi-ushiro muku	it is not face-to-face.

NOTES SHEET 13B

76. *Butsukoku Zenshi shū, Musō Kokushi shū, Gakkai Zenshi shū*; *Usuyuki monogatari*. Curiously, this poem is often attributed to Ōishi Chikara, son of Kuranosuke, of *Chūshingura* fame, as his death poem (1703 at the age of 16).

77. *Tama-tsukuri monogatari* (early Edo period).

78. Source unidentified.

あふことは
かたのゝはらく
そこ
わかれ
ちて
つゆと
きえぬる
ことの
し

むさしのは
月のいつへき
山もなし
くさよりいてゝ
くさにこそいれ

山てらのいりあひのこゑ
いりあひ
あふとも
それと
うら
うら
むし

a/79

なつのよの	natsu no yo no	In the length of time
あふきとるまの	afugi toru ma no	required to take a fan
ひさしさに	hisashisa ni	in a short summer night,
はちにて月を	bachi nite tsuki wo	I seem to have invited
まねきけるかな	manekikeru kana	the moon with my plectrum!

b/80

すミよしの	sumiyoshi no	As I gaze out
松のこまより	matsu no ko-ma yori	from between the trees of pine
なかむれは	nagamureba	on Sumiyoshi,
月おちかゝる	tsuki ochi-kakaru	O, the mountains of Awaji Island
あハちしまやま	ahajhi-shima-yama	behind which the moon is about to set!

c/81

おほ井かハ	ohowi kaha	I hear them sending
いそのいかたを	iso no ikada wo	the raft of cedar
くたすなり	kudasu nari	down the Ōi River,
しつのおのこの	shidzu no onoko no	with the poor man
ゑいやこゑして	weiya kowe shite	shouting "Hey!"

NOTES SHEET 14A

79. No source was found for this poem. It seems to echo, however, a scene from the "Hashihime" (The Lady at the Bridge) chapter of *Genji monogatari*. During a visit to the Eight Prince (Hachi no miya) who lives in reclusion at Uji, Kaoru, one of the heroes of the Uji chapters, spies on the prince's two lovely daughters, Ōigimi and Nakanokimi, playing a *biwa* and a *koto* respectively and unaware of being watched. The tale's description of this scene, rendered below in Tyler's translation, includes the gesture of summoning the moon with a plectrum (Tyler, *The Tale of Genji*, 837):
The Captain cracked open the door that seemed to lead through the fence and peered in through prettily moonlit mist to where the women sat, beyond the rolled-up blinds. A single page girl was on the veranda, thin and looking awfully cold in her rumpled costume. One of the women within, partially hidden behind a pillar, had a biwa before her and was toying with the plectrum. Just then the moon which had been clouded, burst forth brilliantly. 'You can call out the moon-with this, too,' she said, 'though it is not a fan.' Her face as she peered outside was wonderfully fresh and appealing.
The *Genji* scene in turn references, according to Royal Tyller, poem no. 587 in *Wakan rōeishū* (Collection of Chinese and Japanese Poems to Sing, early 11th century, by Fujiwara no Kintō), in which the poet, Chisha Daishi, summons the moon with his fan. Another reference to the *Wakan rōeishū* poem is found in the Noh play *Hanjo* (Lady Han), where the poem is interpreted in Buddhist terms, with the mountains representing worldly illusion and the moon becoming a symbol of enlightenment.
80. *Minamoto Sanmi Yorimasa shū* (with third line *miwataseba*); *Mumyōshō*; Noh play *Yoro-bōshi*.
81. *Hisōshō*, 168, with the note that "*iso*[*ki*]" is another word for cedar.

ゐ池のよみ
めかき
さる風
ほつさふ
ちらめて
月と
田移き
けらるみ

すみよしの松のこ海
ちりあらしさ月
もちつらるあからさ田
かやな

若井 つい
いさよいうと
くるそ
さり
志ゆみ

ふみこのたや
して
い魚

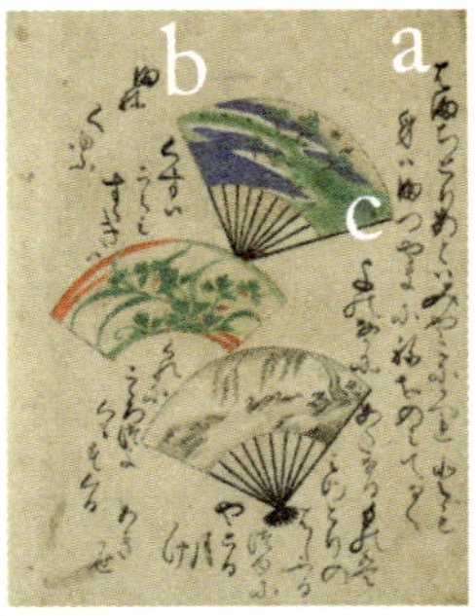

a/82

はまちとり
あとハみやこに
かへれとも
身ハまつやまに
ねをのミてなく

hama-chidori
ato ha miyako ni
kaheredomo
mi ha matsu-yama ni
ne wo nomi te naku

O beach-plovers!
Although your traces may return
to the capital,
I wait here on a pine-covered mountain,
crying my lone plaint.

b/83

くすハうらミ
すゝきハまねく
ゆふくれに
こゝろつよくも
すくるあきかせ

kuzu ha urami
susuki ha maneku
yufugure ni
kokoro tsuyoku mo
suguru aki-kaze

The kudzu is bitter and
the pampas beckons
in the twilight
but its heart is strong–
the passing autumn wind.

c/84

よのなかに
あたなるものは
ミつとりの
はしふるつゆに
やとる月かけ

yo no naka ni
adanaru mono ha
midzu-tori no
hashi furu tsuyu ni
yadoru tsuki-kage

The short-lived beings
of this world are like
the moonlight that lodges
in the dew that falls from the beak
of a water-bird.

NOTES SHEET 14B

82. *Heike monogatari* (*Engyō-bon*); *Genpei jōsuiki*, *Shasekishū*, *Hōgen monogatari*. All texts relate how retired emperor Sutoku, in exile in Sanuki composed this poem on the occasion of sending a set of scriptures he had copied to the capital. The "traces" of the plovers are a metaphor for writing; *matsu* means both "pine" and "to wait"; *mi* both "body" and "myself". Most texts have the last line as *ne wo nomi zo naku* – the Prague version seems to be a copyist error.

83. *Shōkaku Kokushi shū* (Musō Soseki, 1275–1351), 50, with line 2 "*wobana ha maneku*" (the pampas beckons) and line 4 "*suguru aki kana*" (oh the passing autumn).

84. A variation on a poem by Dōgen (with the second line *nani ni tatoen* ("to what shall we compare it?"); also included, in the same form as the Prague version, in the apocryphal *Kanke goshū*.

はまちとりあとはみやこにかよへとも
身はまつやまにねをのみそなく

よみあにめくるみるこゝろの
なかなる流れにやとる月け

くすい
うらこ
すゝきい
ゆふ
くれ
くれふ

これに
こゝろなよ
らてそ
あさる
せ

a/85

こほりいる
いけミつにすむ
をしとりも
ミのならハしの
うきねなるらん

kohori iru
ike-midzu ni sumu
woshi-dori mo
mi no narahashi no
uki-ne naruran

Entering the ice,
do the mandarin ducks, too,
who live in lake-water,
have a fitful sleep despite
being so used to it?

b/86

こひしくハ
たつねてもこよ
わかやとハ
ミハのやまもと
すきたつるかと

kohishiku ha
tadzunete mo koyo
waga yado ha
miha no yama-moto
sugi tatsuru kado

If you long for me,
come, if even only for a visit;
my house is the one
with the gate of rising cedar
at the foot of Mt. Miwa.

c/87

わかこひは
よとのかハせの
つなきこい
ミをもこゝろも
まかせさりけり

waga kohi ha
yodo no kahase no
tsunagi-goi
mi wo mo kokoro mo
makasezarikeri

My love is like
the carp swimming upstream
in the rapids of Yodo River:
neither my body nor my soul
have I surrendered!

NOTES SHEET 15A

85. Source unidentified.

86. This poem is a version of KKS 982: *waga iho ha / miwa no yama-moto / kohishiku ha // toburahi-kimase / sugi tateru kado* (My dwelling is / at the foot of Mt. Miwa– / if you long for me / do come to visit / the gate where the cedars stand). The poem is also quoted in the Noh play *Miwa*.

87. Apparently based on *Fuboku waka shō* (category: animals), by Fujiwara no Tomoie (1182–1258): *yo no naka ha / yodo no ikesu no / tsunagi-gohi // mi wo kokoro ni mo / makase yaha suru* (The world is like / carp swimming upstream / in a fish-farm at Yodo: / would they surrender / their bodies to their feelings? (–certainly not).

[illegible]

[illegible]

[illegible]

[illegible]

a/88

はせを葉に
とき〱かせの
おとつれて
さひしさまさる
やまてらのにハ

basewo-ha ni
toki-doki kaze no
otodzurete
sabishisa masaru
yama-dera no niha

The banana-leaves
sometimes the wind
does visit–
ah, the garden of the mountain temple
where the loneliness increases!

b/89

うつらなく
まのゝいりゑの
くらかせに
おはなかなミの
たゝぬひもなし

udzura naku
mano no iriwe no
kura-kaze ni
obana ga nami no
tatanu hi mo nashi

There is not a day
that the waves of pampas-grass do not rise
in the dark wind
of the inlet of Mano
where the quails do cry.

c/90

さつきまつ
はなたちはなの
かほかけは
むかしの人の
そてかそする

satsuki matsu
hana-tachibana no
ka ho kageba
mukashi no hito no
sode [no] ka zo suru

When I smell the scent
of the mandarin orange blossoms
that await the Fifth Month,
they have the scent of the sleeves
of someone from long ago.

NOTES SHEET 15B

88. Source unidentified.

89. KYS 239, "In the time of the Horikawa retired emperor, when we drew for topics in his presence, and I got the topic of pampas;" with the third line "*hama-kaze ni*" (in the beach wind) and the last two lines "*obana-nami yoru / aki no yufugure*" (twilight in autumn / when the pampas-waves draw near). Poet: Minamoto no Shunrai (Toshiyori, 1055–1129).

90. KKS (Summer) 139, anon.

うけたまはりて御めくてうあれくるみに
おもひよりあきの
たぬひとや

さはきき御める
たちまちめし
あけくねは

大せいの
まゐに
こく
みせめ
おとつきて
さひしき御
さる御てらめ
めい

もちる
そへて
くれめ
せいはれ

a/91

ほの〱と
あかしのうらの
あさきりに
しまかくれゆく
ふねおしそおもふ

hono-bono to
akashi no ura no
asa-giri ni
shima-gakure-yuku
fune o shi zo omofu

Faintly, faintly
through the morning mist
in the bay of Akashi,
my thoughts follow the boat
that becomes island-hidden.

b/92

あか月の
うきわかれにハ
こりすして
あふハうれしき
よひのたまくら

akatsuki no
uki wakare ni ha
korizu shite
afu ha ureshiki
yohi no ta-makura

I do not learn
from our unhappy partings
at daybreak –
ah, my happy arm that serves
as your pillow when we meet at night!

c/93

おなしくハ
花のもとにて
はるしなん
そのきさらきの
もち月のころ

onajiku ha
hana no moto nite
haru shinan
sono kisaragi no
mochi-tsuki no koro

If it's all the same,
I will die in Sping
at the foot of the blossoms,
during the full moon
of that Second Month.

NOTES SHEET 16A

91. KKS (Parting) 409, anon. Attributed to Kakinomoto no Hitomaro.

92. *Butsukoku Zenshi shū*, 19, "On the meaning of samsara." This is a private poetry collection edited by Kōhō Kennichi (1241–1316), a son of emperor GoSaga.

93. ShKKS (Misc.), "From poems on cherry-blossoms", Saigyō, with the first line "*negahaku ha*" (if I had my wish), and "*hana no shita*" rather than "*hana no moto*." The latter appears in such texts as *Saigyō monogatari*. "The full moon of that Second Month" refers to the day the historical Buddha was believed to have passed into Nirvana.

ほの/\と
あかしの
うらの
あさきりに
嶋かくれゆく
ふねをしそ思ふ

願くは花
のしたにて
春しなむその
きさらき
のもち
月の
ころ

よつ月のうれ
かい
いつれこそ
しくれ
あふゝ
たまくら
よひ
おもき

a/94

やまたもる	yama-da moru	The figure indeed
そふつのミこそ	sofudzu no mi koso	of the scarecrow who guards the field
かなしけれ	kanashikere	is sad!
あきはてぬれは	aki-hatenureba	Since autumn has reached its end
とふ人もなし	tofu hito mo nashi	there is none who comes to visit.

b/95

しのふやま	shinobu-yama	Ah, Mount Shinobu,
しのひてかよふ	shinobite kayofu	I would gladly find a way
みちもかな	michi mogana	in secret to frequent her,
人の心の	hito no kokoro no	that I might further explore
おくも見るへく	oku mo mirubeku	the recesses of her heart.

c/96

もみち葉の	momijhi-ba no	The deep color
こきハわかミの	koki ha wagami no	of the autumn leaves
おもひにて	omohi nite	is my longing;
うすきハ人の	usuki ha hito no	the faint color,
なさけなりけり	nasake narikeri	her compassion.

NOTES SHEET 16B

94. ShKS XII: 1608, by Prelate (Sōzu) Genbin (734–818). "*Sofuzu*" could mean both "scarecrow" and "Prelate"; "*aki*" means both "autumn" and "to tire of".

95. *Ise monogatari*, episode 15: "Back then he called on some insignificant fellow's wife in the province of Michinoku and was surprised to find her quite unlike what he'd expected" (trans. Mostow & Tyler).

96. *Hanyū no monogatari: momijhi-ba no / usuki ha hito no / nasake nite // koki ha wagami no / omohi narikeri* ("The paleness of / the maple leaves / is her compassion / the dark is my own / longing thoughts").

志のふやま志のひて
かよふみちもかな
ひとのこゝろの
おくもみる
へく

やまにかる
そふなれ
こゝろそ
なか
けまし
あきて
ぬまさん
とふ
人も
あり

よみち葉は
こゝろもしらは
おもひそめて
うらみすれは人は
あさけ
なり
けり

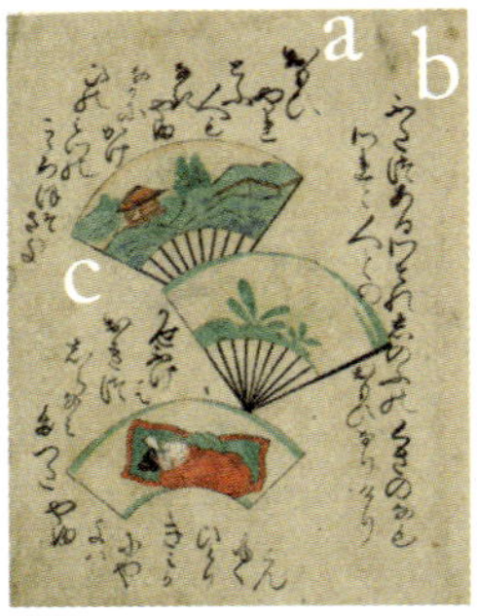

a/97

おもひやれ
とふ人もなき
やまなかに
かけひのミつの
こゝろほそさよ

omohi-yare
tofu hito mo naki
yama-naka ni
kakehi no midzu no
kokoro-bososa yo

Have sympathy!
for my loneliness which is like the trickle
of water in the wooden pipe
amidst the mountains
where there are no visitors!

b/98

ふたつある
わすれしのふの
くさのなも
われと人との
おもひなりけり

futatsu aru
wasure shinobu no
kusa no na mo
ware to hito to no
omohi narikeri

The names of the plant
are two:
longing- and forgetting-grasses–
so our same "feelings" differ,
hers and mine.

c/99

かせふけは
おきつしらなミ
たつたやま
よハにやきミか
ひとりゆくらん

kaze fukeba
okitsu shiranami
tatsuta-yama
yoha ni ya kimi ga
hitori yukuran

When the wild wind blows,
out upon the sea white waves
rise–Mount Tatsuta!
can you, by night, truly mean
to cross those hills all alone?

NOTES SHEET 17A

97. GSIS 1041 (Misc.), "Sent when she was living in Chōraku Temple, when someone asked about her," Jōtōmon-in Chūjō (a lady-in-waiting to the former Empress Fujiwara no Shōshi, under whom Murasaki Shikibu served), with the third line "*yama-zato ni*" (in this mountain village). "Loneliness" is literally "narrow-heartedness", and matches the thin stream of water through the wooden pipe.

98. Source unidentified. Cf. *Ise monogatari*, episode 100, which also concerns the supposed similarity between "longing-grasses" (Polypodium lineare) and "forgetting-grasses" (Memerocallis aurantiaca Bak.).

99. KKK (Misc. II) 994; *Ise monogatari*, episode 23; Noh play *Izutsu*. The first two lines are a "preface" (*jo*) to the word "*tatsu*", which means both "to rise" ("the white waves rise") and is part of the place-name Mt. Tatsuta (trans. Mostow & Tyler).

うらみあるゝされしのふれくさのかと
かまてくさの
おもひなりけり

あしや
まとふ
くも
あれやぬ
あうふのかけ
よそにかれ
こゝろはそらに

ゆめにけ
あきはて
さくらなく
あつこやぬ

ん
めく
ひとり
きゝら
ふや
よい

a/100

もののいへは
ちゝハなからの
はし〱ら
なかすはきしも
いられましかな

mono iheba
chichi ha nagara no
hashi-bashira
nakazu ha kishi mo
iraremashi kana

Since he spoke,
my father was buried under
the pilings of Nagara Bridge –
If he did not sing, the pheasant too,
would not be shot!

c/101

わかこひは
ふたミのうらの
かひしけミ
まきゑににたる
まつのむらたち

waga kohi ha
futami no ura no
kahi shigemi
makiwe ni nitaru
matsu no muradachi

My love is like
the shells lying thickly
on Futami Bay,
and the groves of pine-trees
look like gold-leaf lacquer-ware.

b/102

きれはうし
きらねはこのま
かけくらし
はなにはまけよ
はるのよの月

kireba ushi
kiraneba ko no ma
kake-kurashi
hana ni ha makeyo
haru no yo no tsuki

If I cut them, it's sad;
if I don't cut them, then it will
be hidden by the trees–
Surrender to the cherry-blossoms!
O moon of the spring night!

NOTES SHEET 17B

100. *Fujikawa gohyaku-shū*; *Shintōshū* (both with minor differences). The poem alludes to a story about a man being chosen to be a *hito-bashira* ("person-pillar"), an ancient form of human sacrifice used when constructing structures such as bridges. After his death, his daughter became mute, but composed this poem on seeing her husband shoot a pheasant.

101. KYS 544 (Misc.), "Composed on Futami Bay in the province of Ise", Ōnakatomi no Sukehiro (1028–1103), with the first line "*tamakushige*" for a more sensical poem: "Thick are the shells / at Futami Bay / calling to mind the lid of a jewelled box // and the groves of pine-trees / look like gold-leaf lacquerware". Futami can also mean "see again" and is used in love poems. Quoted in the Noh play *Matsukaze*.

102. Source unknown.

さきまえうしろめたこそにみゆけらし

たなみ
みゆけよ
しるの
よのほ

まれつを
ちうい
ちらくらの
あふさん
あかしと
いらせ
きしつる

しるしにて
これうちの
かひなけれ
みゆかく
小

み
たな

みゆれ

むかし
なら

a/103	きりのはも	kiri no ha mo	The fallen leaves of the paulownia
	ふミハけかたく	fumi-hakegataku	have also become difficult
	なりにけり	narinikeri	to walk through,
	かならす人を	kanarazu hito wo	although I am not waiting
	まつとなけれと	matsu to nakeredo	for someone who said he would surely come.
b/104	こやのいけ	koya no ike	The irises
	あやめにましる	ayame ni majiru	mixed with the flags
	かきつはた	kakitsubata	in the lake by the hut–
	花ゆへにこそ	hana yuhe ni koso	it is due to the flowers
	あらハれにけり	araharenikeri	that it has become apparent.
c/105	たつたかハ	tatsuta-gaha	Tatsuta River:
	もみちみたれて	momijhi midarete	the autumn leaves seem in disarray
	なかるめり	nagarumeri	yet flow on–
	わたらはにしき	wataraba nishiki	were one to cross the brocade
	なかやたへなん	naka ya tahenan	would surely break in two.

NOTES SHEET 18A

103. SKKS 534, "An autumn poem offered up in a hundred-poem sequence," Imperial Princess Shokushi (Shikishi). The picture shows a love-letter amongst the paulownia leaves.

104. *Man'yo waka shū* 445; *Fuboku shō* (Book 6: Spring): from a hundred-poem sequence of the Shōji era [1199–1201]; Retired Emperor GoToba; with the last two lines as "it has become known to others" (*hana yuwe hito ni / shirarenuru kana*).

105. KKS 283, topic unknown, anonymous.

ミりはても
うはけも
かくく
すりぬなり
なるとも
くと思へと
おけまき
かて

こやれは
あやめにかは
かはれたるこ
しめにこそある
進ふなり

色はたた
もみちつい
みちれて
なりるなり
ゆきらそめ
しき
なや
色へ
なん

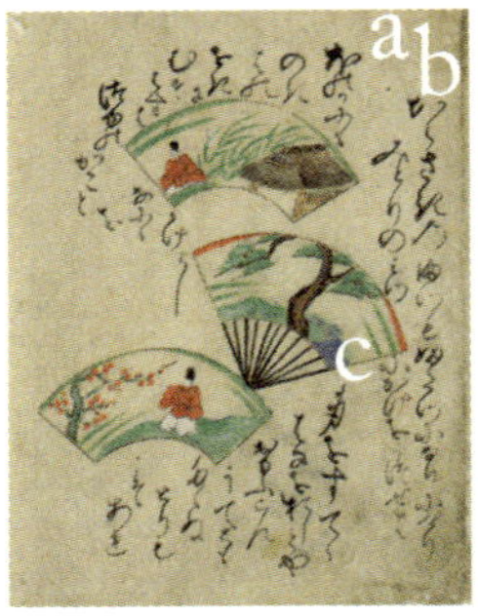

a/106

ほのかにも
のきはのをきに
むすはすは
つゆのかことを
なにゝかけまし

honoka ni mo
nokiba no wogi ni
musubazu ha
tsuyu no kagoto wo
nani ni kakemashi

Had I not at least
tied a knot around
the reed by the eaves,
what excuse would I have now
to voice my dewdrop complaint?

b/107

からさきの
まつもふたつに
なりにけり
みとりのミつに
かけをうつせは

karasaki no
matsu mo futatsu ni
narinikeri
midori no midzu ni
kage wo utsuseba

The pine of Karasaki
has become twain,
since it casts
its reflection
in the green water.

c/108

身をすてゝ
はなをおしとや
おもふらん
うてともたゝぬ
とりもこそあれ

mi wo sutete
hana wo oshi to ya
omofuran
utedomo tatanu
tori mo koso are

Even if they discard their lives,
will they regret the flowers,
do you think?
There are indeed birds
who do not rise, even though struck.

NOTES SHEET 18B

106. *Genji monogatari*, "Sakaki" (trans. Tyler); FYS 1093. Again, a tied love-letter appears amidst the reeds.

107. Source unidentified.

108. *Kokon chomonjū*, episode 153. In this tale, two Chinese are listening to a Buddhist sermon and see a *kei*-bell cast with a design of an eight-leaf lotus with peacocks on either side. The first man says something in Chinese in admiration of the flower; the other notes that even if the bell is struck, the peacocks will not fly away. A third man, overhearing the two, makes a linked-verse poem of their utterances, translated into Japanese.

ひさしきの中にいふかなり
みなりのこゝろかけてはなれせん

あはれみて
のこれ
まれ
ひとは
するも
消えつゝ
かくこと
とを
おもひて
うけもし

男すてて
くるしとや
まふらん
うてさて
あくるは
とりしも
こそ
あま

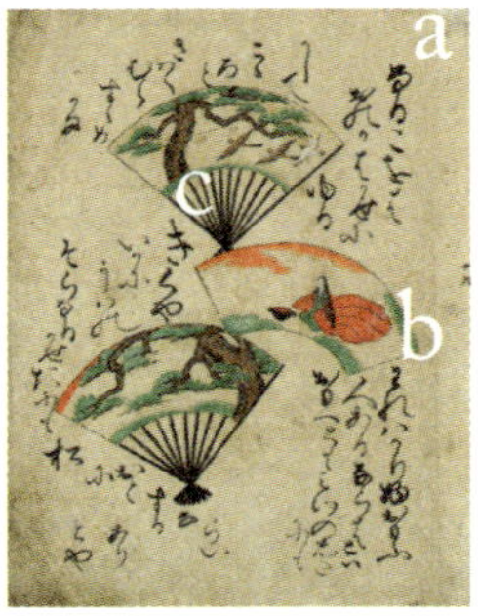

a/109

なるこをは
おのかはかせに
ゆるかして
こゝろとさハく
むらすゝめかな

naruko wo ba
onoga hakaze ni
yurukashite
kokoro to sahagu
mura-suzume kana

Bird-clappers in fact
by the wind of their own wings
set in motion–
frightening themselves,
the flock of sparrows!

b/110

われハかり
物おもふ人
あるならは
とはおもへとも
ミつのしたにも

ware bakari
mono omofu hito
aru naraba
to ha omohedomo
midzu no shita ni mo

Although I think,
"If there was someone
at all as miserable
as I am. . . ." And beneath the water
there is another.

c/111

きくやいかに
うハのそらなる
かせたにも
松におとする
ならいありとや

kiku ya ikani
uha no sora naru
kaze dani mo
matsu ni oto suru
narai ari to ya

Do you hear it?
Even the wind in uncertain skies
now, by habit,
sighs "Await his visit!"
as it rustles pines.

NOTES SHEET 19A

109. *Senshūshō* (1265–1282) 20; *Shasekishū* (1279–1283) 82: "Poems With a Deeper Significance: A verse by the Great Minister of Kamakura [Sanetomo]". "This poem has deep significance. In the Lotus Sutra it is said that 'all things in their essential nature are ever unconditioned and quiet' (Ch. 2). An ancient has said that things are by nature at rest, and that man puts them into turmoil. This is like the sparrows who activate the clappers and throw themselves into confusion" (trans. Morrell).

110. *Ise monogatari*, Episode 27, with many grammatical differences.

111. SKKS 1199, "Love as Expressed through the Wind," Kunaikyō; Noh *Sumida-gawa*; *otogizōshi Komachi sōshi* (trans. Huey, *ShinKokinshū*).

あなこなん
花のたのむ
ゆめ

りて
こゝろ
とろ
さて
むら
すゝめ
へる

きくや
いふ
うみ
そらのみ
せたかて
松

ふね
すみ
あら
い
あり
とや

これからぬむ
くめのあらたさい
おくとこのたる
かし

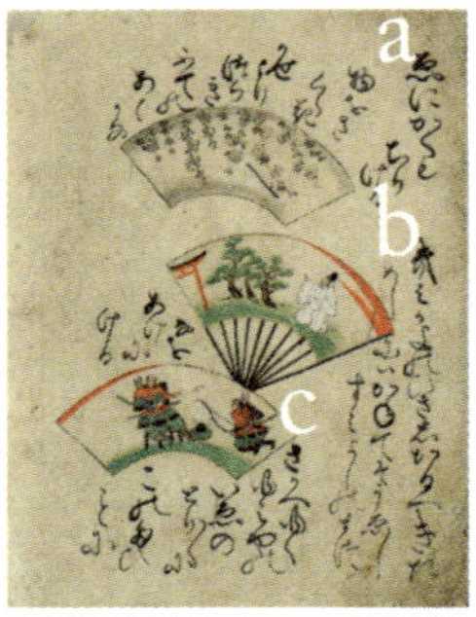

a/112		
ゑにかくも	we ni kaku mo	Even painted as a picture
ちりける物を	chirikeru mono wo	they scatter,
さくら花	sakura-bana	the cherry-blossoms–
かせよりつらき	kaze yori tsuraki	the traces of the brush
ふてのあとかな	fude no ato kana	are more heartless than the wind.

b/113		
きミかよの	kimi ga yo no	As an example
ひさしかるへき	hisashikarubeki	of how long
ためしにハ	tameshi ni ha	my lord shall live,
かねてそうゑし	kanete zo uweshi	there are the pines of Sumiyoshi
すミよしのまつ	sumiyoshi no matsu	planted from long ago.

c/114		
さかへゆく	sakahe-yuku	The prospering
ゆミやのいゑの	yumiya no iwe no	houses of arrow and bow
とり〱に	tori-dori ni	–each and every one–
このたひことに	kono tabi koto ni	this time especially
なをあけにける	na wo agenikeru	have they become famous.

NOTES SHEET 19B

112. Souce unidentified.

113. SKS 170, "Composed when Retired Emperor Sanjō made a pilgrimage to Sumiyoshi", anon., with the fourth line *kami no uwekemu* ("was it because the gods planted them?"); Noh *Takasago*.

114. Source unidentified.

思にかくも
ちり
けり
梅よさ
くら
花
さ
色
り
内ら
さ
そて
ぬ
おし
る

我そらよ風しきあかりくきた
わしみぬ吹て
すくち風
ちう思

あけ
ゐと
けるぬ

さくり
りくや
思の
とらか
これ
とぬ

a/115

あきハなを
ゆふまくれこそ
たゝならね
おきのうはかせ
はきのしたつゆ

aki ha nawo
yufu-magure koso
tada narane
ogi no uha-kaze
hagi no shita-tsuyu

In autumn is it
indeed most moving
at twilight –
the wind blowing over the reeds,
the under-dew of the bush-clover.

b/116

きくたにも
やさしかりける
つまこひて
ふもとになきつ
しかのとをこゑ

kiku dani mo
yasashikarikeru
tsuma kohite
fumoto ni nakitsu
shika no towo-gowe

Ah, the distant voice of the stag
crying in the foothills
as he longs for his mate,
who suffers
just hearing it.

c/117

うくいすの
はなふミちらす
ほそはきを
おふなきなたて
さふときらはや

uguisu no
hana fumi-chirasu
hoso-hagi wo
ofu-naginata de
safu to kirabaya

The skinny legs
of the bush-warbler
that trample and scatter the blossoms –
How I want to cut them, left and right,
with a great halberd!

NOTES SHEET 20A

115. WKRS, 229, Lesser Captain Yoshitaka.
116. Source unidentified.
117. The Noh play *Kagetsu*, with the last line *oho-naginata araba koso* ("if only I had indeed a great halberd").

あくかるゝや
ふりしよるらん
めきには
ゆふく
ゆふかせの
ふきこそ
たかねの
のきはの
うへに
すゝれ
まく
つゆ

さかりけはまつひ
はなよりのこゝろ
うくいそれ
こゑ
ゆき
ち
らそ
わそ
くれ
と

おもふ
あき
みに
てきかふと
ことつたや

a/118

すミよしの	sumiyoshi no	Since it is an august reign
まつにふちある	matsu ni fujhi aru	with wisteria in the pines
みよなれは	miyo nareba	of Sumiyoshi,
かミもこゝろを	kami mo kokoro wo	the hearts of the gods, too,
かけてこそ見れ	kakete koso mire	dote on it as they gaze.

b/119

月見れは	tsuki mireba	When I see the moon,
まつみやこゝそ	madzu miyako koso	it is first of all the capital
こひしけれ	kohishikere	that I long for,
まつらんとおもふ	matsuran to omofu	even though there is no one
人ハなけれと	hito ha nakeredo	who who thinks to wait for me there.

c/120

うつのやに	utsu no ya ni	The crying
あたりてしかの	atarite shika no	of the deer hit
なきつるは	nakitsuru ha	by the striking arrow–
ゆミはり月の	yumi-hari-tsuki no	it looks indeed like it was shot
いるかとそ見る	iru ka to zo miru	by the bow-like crescent moon.

NOTES SHEET 20B

118. Source unidentified.

119. SZS 521: "Sent when he was in Owari Province, having property there, and someone sent him a letter saying, 'Have you forgotten all about the capital?'".

120. Source unidentified.

月みるまはゆゝしてみやこにそこひけま
ゆ〳〵しらんと
まふくにかけまゐらせい

ともちらぬ
まつのふちら

おわ
みよ
あれもて
かゝるも
こゝろを
かけてそえ
みえまし

ゆき
ちり
月のかけ
ちそ
みなる

うちぬ
やふ
おもひて
志らぬ
さく
けりな

ESSAYS ŌGI NO SŌSHI

Fig. 1. **A fan-shaped picture with a court life motif from the Heian period novel *The Tale of Genji*** (*Genji monogatari*) in the Nara-e style (*Nara-e ōgi*), ink and color pigments on paper, 17.5 x 47.5 cm, 17th century. (Photo credit: National Gallery, Prague, Vm 2965)

The so-called Nara-e ōgi *("Nara-picture fan") was a new type of folk picture derived from the Yamato-e style and executed in a routine manner for townspeople at the beginning of the Edo period. One from a set of 20 fan-shaped pictures from the Hloucha Collection in the National Gallery, Prague.*

SUMMING UP THE JAPANESE POETIC TRADITION

Helena Honcoopová

The mainstream of Japanese poetry

Japan is a land of a great poetic tradition that has substantially influenced the character of Japanese culture. While the classical culture of Europe started from Greek drama and epic poetry, the Japanese dwelt on lyrical poetry which permeated all its other classical literary forms, such as narratives (*monogatari*), diaries (*nikki*) and even travelogues (*kikō*), religious legends (*engi*), and war chronicles (*gunki*). The typical literary form of the Heian period (794–1185), the narrative *monogatari*, was nothing other than a sequence of lyrical episodes based on a simple "Japanese poem", or *waka.* The most famous example of this type of poetic prose, dating from the 10th century, *The Ise Stories* (*Ise monogatari*),[1] is a collection of 209 poems and associated narratives in 125 episodes describing the amorous life of the handsome and elegant courtier Ariwara no Narihira.[2] The matrix novel of Japanese literature, which was written in the early 11th century by a court lady, Murasaki Shikibu, *The Tale of Genji* (*Genji monogatari*),[3] contains as many as 795 poems exchanged largely in communication among the main characters. The oral version of the war chronicle between the Taira and Minamoto clans, *Heike monogatari,* dating from the 13th century, includes 97 *waka* poems, regardless of the cruel battlefield scenes described within the long narration.[4] All these great stars of Japanese literature were surrounded by lesser lights in the heaven of past literary achievements. From these the first drama evolved as late as the 14th century in the form of the Noh theatre, which was also based on lyrical librettos with many integrated poems. To sum up, poetry pervaded all classical literary genres. And besides that, there was the mainstream of poetry itself in private and public collections, compilations, and anthologies. And the basic unit in all these forms was a little poem called *waka.*

Waka 和 歌 is a concise unrhymed poem of 31 syllables, consisting of five lines with a measure of 5-7-5-7-7 syllables. Because the way of reading or declaming the poems was melodic, the term *uta* 歌, or "song," was simultaneously used. Another term, *tanka* 短歌 ("short poem"), was used to distinguish this form from the archaic long poem, or *chōka* 長歌. *Waka*, *uta* and *tanka* are synonymous words.[5] The unit usually combines a subjective expression of feeling and a poetic image or metaphor, usually taken from nature. The poem further splits into two hemistiches, upper and lower (*kami no ku* 上の句, *shimo no ku*下の句) typically divided by a pause, twist of thought, or a caesura called *kire* (切れ). The rhythm of 5–7 syllables became the basic pulse of Japanese prosody and permeated all later literary forms.

Waka became established as the main poetic form already in the oldest Japanese poetry anthology, the *Collection of Myriad Leaves* (*Man'yōshū*, 万葉集), which gathered Japanese poetic production from ancient times (the oldest poems date from 357 AD) until the year of its compilation (around 762), when Japanese literature still preferred Chinese as the chief literary medium. The *Man'yōshū,* with over four thousand *waka* in twenty books, became a model for later anthologies of poetry written in Japanese. The *Man'yōshū* was still written in Chinese characters used phonetically (so-called *man'yōgana* 万葉仮名), from which the simplified Japanese syllabary *kana* (仮名 or "borrowed names"), gradually evolved during the 9th century. This simple script, called "feminine writing" (*onnade* 女手) at the time, was suitable for writing down glosses, diaries, narratives and Japanese poetry (Fig. 3). *Waka* uses Japanese words and almost no compounds of Chinese origin and is calligraphed in elegant vertical columns of linked curving lines with a very limited repertory of abbreviated Chinese characters included. The square, masculine, complicated Chinese script (*kanji* 漢字) was, in short, used for learned writings produced by men (*otokode* 男手) (Fig. 2), and the slim, slender, feminine and simple Japanese script (*kana*) was used for emotional expression. This division of roles between the two scripts was expressed in the saying: "Chinese wisdom – Japanese soul" (*Kara-jie / Yamato-damashii* 唐智恵 大和魂). The act of writing beautiful letters of *kana* on coloured strips of paper, often decorated with abstract paintings and gold and silver flocks or dust (砂子 *sunago*), was an object of aesthetic appreciation.

Collections of Japanese poetry during the "golden age" of their compilation in the Heian period were written on paper scrolls (*kansubon* 巻子本, *makimono* 巻物). Horizontal scrolls were the only medium for writing Japanese literature before the Japanese type of sewn book binding was introduced in the 16th century. Compilations of Japanese poetry were as a rule assembled every roughly fifty years upon imperial order, forming a chain of twenty-one *anthologies on imperial order* (*chokusenshū* 勅撰集).[6] Between the years 905–1439, these anthologies were regularly and officially collected by groups of highly esteemed poets in the imperial Bureau of Poetry (*uta-dokoro* 歌所, *waka-dokoro* 和歌所) and recorded over 33,000 poems – the best poetic production of Japan created over five centuries (see Appendix C).

The first of these imperial anthologies was the *Kokin* (*waka*) *shū* (*Collection of Poems of Ancient and Modern Times* 古今和歌集), dating from 905. Its structure became the ideal form for all the other imperial anthologies. It had forewords (one in Chinese, one in Japanese) and twenty books, divided into two parts, the first one based on descriptions of nature, the second on subjective emotions. The first six books covered the passage of the seasons (*shiki no uta* 四季の歌) from early spring to winter, with most poems in the books of Spring and Autumn (two books each) – the seasons abounding in melancholic atmosphere, typical of Japanese poetry. After four books of poems on the topics of Congratulations, Partings, Travel, and Acrostics, the second, more intimate, part began with books on Love capturing the development of a typical love affair of the Heian period, when the aristocrats enjoyed sexual freedom and polygamy. Five books of Love poetry (*koi no uta* 恋歌) started from the first glimpse of the desired woman and continued through letter exchanges, first meetings, partings, negligence and forlorn feelings of solitude after the departure of the man for a different destination. The closing five themes of the twenty books were Laments (*aishō no uta* 哀傷歌) (mostly on deceased persons or lost positions), Varia on miscellaneous topics (*zakka* 雑歌), and Irregular poems (*zattai no uta* 雑躰歌). The anthology ended with two books of poems from the *uta-dokoro*, the Bureau of Poetry. The last parts were exchanged for books with poems on Buddhist and Shintō themes in later anthologies, as Japanese society grew more religious.

The knowledge of and skill in composing and communicating in poetry belonged among the highest achievements of the so-called "fine people" (*yokibito*) – the aristocracy connected with the imperial court in the capital of Kyōto. All educated members of the ruling class, the aristocrats and clergy, had to learn how to compose, write in fluent calligraphy and recite (in a semi-singing, pitched voice) poetry. *Waka* became the main vehicle of both official and intimate communication. Desires were expressed in poetry; complaints were hidden in poetic images, lovers communicated by exchanging skilfully written poetic slips of decorated paper with expressions of deep feelings concealed in natural imagery. All kinds of fancy paper were used for calligraphy: paper decorated with torn and patched scraps of coloured paper, golden or silver dust or painted with abstract or natural details in the background (Figs. 2–5). The most common sizes of these poetry papers gradually developed into the square *shikishi* (色紙, approx. 20 x 18 cm) and vertical *tanzaku* (短冊, approx. 36 x 6 cm). The letters of poems were sometimes hidden within the design, so as to create a riddle, as, for example, the vertical columns of elegant *kana* letters dripping among reeds on a lake-shore. These pictorial puzzles were called "reed-hand" (*ashide* 葦手) and were part of the courtly games and amusements (Fig. 4).

As early as the 10th century, the practice of composing poetry was well developed; many poetic contests (*uta-awase* 歌合わせ) took place in palaces and became a form of social amusement. Two parties, Left and Right, would sit across the room and compete in composing poems on the same topic, while a noted

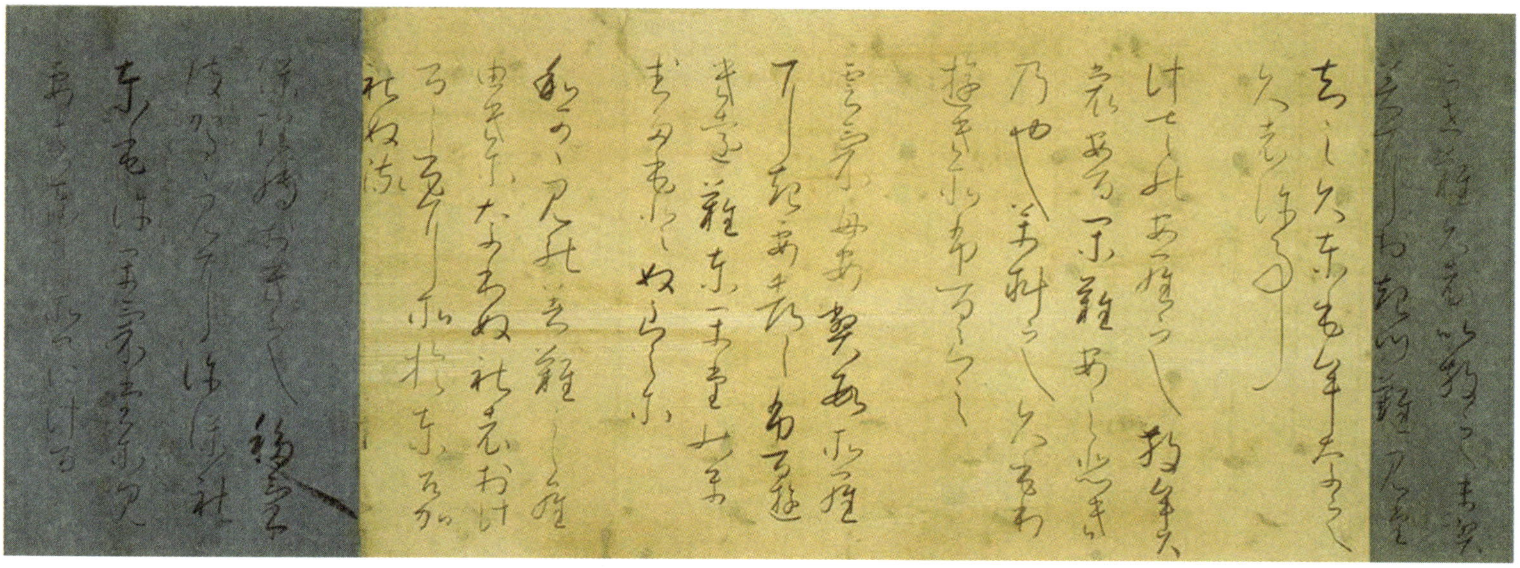

Fig. 2. **Ono no Michikaze** (894–966): **A part of the Preface to Akihagi** (Akihagi-jō). One hand-scroll, ink on colored paper, 24.0 x 842.4 cm, 10th century.
(Photo credit: Tōkyō National Museum, B-2532, C0065143, P D photo, National Treasure)
An example of otokode *– the "male style" of writing. This calligraphy in the cursive script* sōsho *from the Heian period is inscribed on colored strips of paper, which were used chiefly for writing* waka *poetry.*

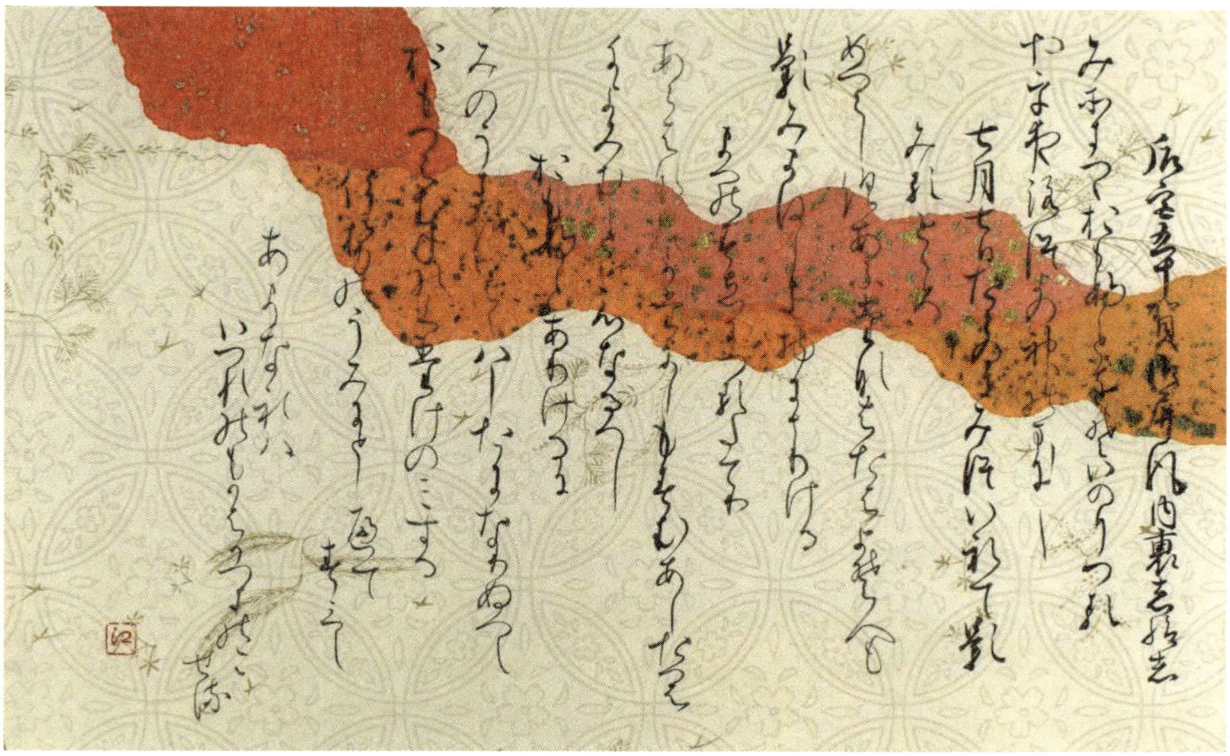

Fig. 3. **Sokin Saitō** (born 1923): **A part of the Ise Collection** (Ise shū). Calligraphy in black ink on colored paper with underpainted decoration, mounted as a hanging scroll, 22 x 35.5 cm, mounted as a hanging scroll, 86 x 46 cm, 2002.
(Photo credit: National Gallery, Prague, Vm 6375)
An example of onnade *– the "female style" of writing of Japanese* kana *syllabary and Chinese characters, a modern variation on Heian script by a contemporary female calligrapher.*

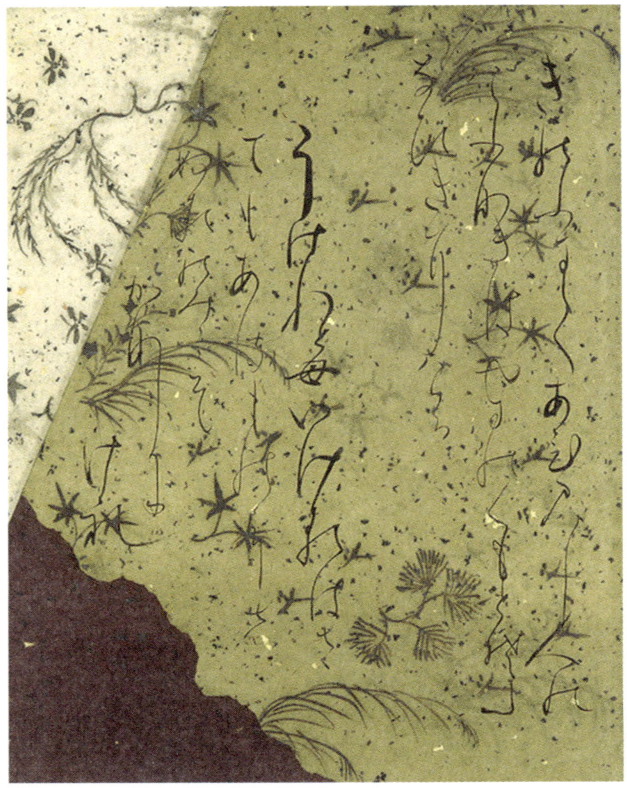

Fig. 4. Anonymous 12th century calligrapher: **Two poems by Ki no Tsurayuki** (872–945), the so-called Ishiyama-gire ("Fragment from Ishiyama"), originally a part of the Thirty-six Poets Anthologies (Sanjū rokunin kashū), album leaf, calligraphy on paper, 21.2 x 16.1 cm, 1112. (Photo credit: The Freer Gallery of Art, Smithsonian Institution, Washington, Purchase F1969.4)
An example of so-called "reed-hand" (ashide) *type of writing. Calligraphy in elegant kana letters are written on assembled dyed paper decorated with natural motifs (such as reeds, twigs, leaves of maples, pines and willows, birds, insects etc.) which are drawn in silver, gold, or faint colors on the background, sprinkled with golden flakes* (nashiji).

poet, acting as a referee or judge (*hanja* 判者), decided which party would end in a win, lose or draw. These contests had from one hundred to over a thousand rounds (*ban, tsugashi* 番) – the famous *Competition of One Thousand and Five Hundred Rounds* (*Sengohyakuban uta-awase*) was held in the times of the retired emperor GoToba in 1201.[7] Very often, the winning party was a courtier in a higher position at court. Thus, for instance, the outstanding poet and poetry theoretician Fujiwara no Teika, who reached only the fifth court rank, would lose to the less gifted Fujiwara no Yoshitsune[8] who was the Regent of the imperial court. Although poetry contests might have originally been playful, the act of composing poetry was serious and participation in these poetry meetings and contests, as well as inclusion in imperial anthologies, was highly prestigious.

Everybody tried to train his abilities by composing sequences of poems on given topics (題 *dai*),[9] so as to be able to compose on the spur of the moment at poetry meetings and in games. To be an able poet opened the way to promotion in the social hierarchy of the nine ranks at the court and thus was of vital importance for noblemen of low birth but high talent. Even Buddhist monks could participate in poetic contests; some men even chose to enter the priesthood in order to be able to attend these meetings, as they were of too low a birth to be accepted among the high nobility otherwise. This situation was commented upon wittily by the monk Yoshida Kenkō (1282–1350), the author of "Essays in Idleness" (*Tsurezuregusa* 徒然草, ca.1330–32). To be a good poet meant to be socially successful.

Waka reached its perfection during the late Heian and early Kamakura period with the eighth imperial anthology, *New Collection of Poems of Ancient and Modern Times*, (*Shinkokin* (*waka*) *shū* 新古今和歌集, 1205), edited upon the order of the retired emperor GoToba[10] by the famous poets of the time, Fujiwara no Shunzei (aka Toshinari 藤原俊成, 1114–1204) and his son Fujiwara no Teika (aka Sadaie, 藤原定家, 1162–1241), among others. Father and son became the most venerated arbiters of modern forms of poetry of the *Shinkokinshū* age. Their views on poetry were carried on through Teika's son Tameie (藤原為家, 1198–1275) into the future, though *waka* entered a period of decline during the Kamakura period (1185–1339), marked by the rule of the shoguns and their military clans whose main concern was warfare.

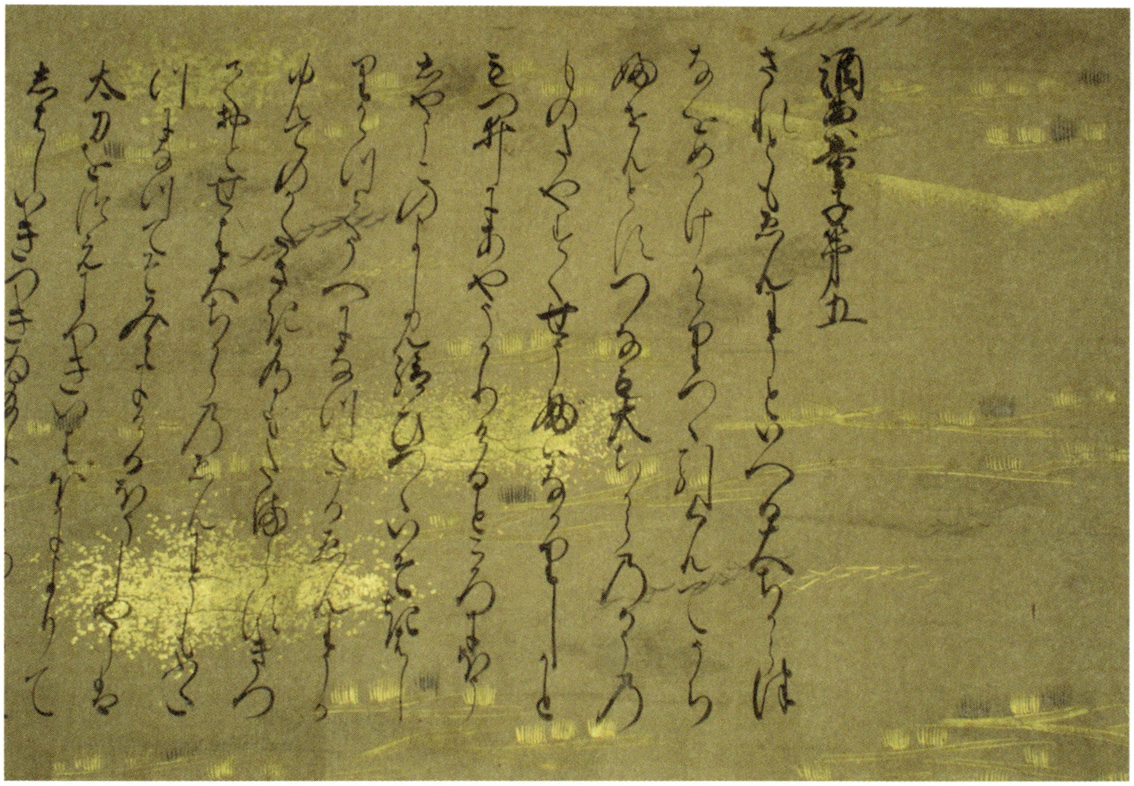

Fig. 5. **Asakura Jūken** (calligrapher of the 17th century): **Introduction to the fifth scroll of Shuten Dōji**, ink on *ganpi* paper decorated with natural motifs in silver and gold (*gindei, kindei*), 32.5 x 1517 cm, a 17th century copy of an *otogi-zōshi emaki* illustrated originally by Kanō Motonobu (1476–1559). Five hand scrolls.
(Photo credit: Private collector, Prague)
Shuten dōji *is a legendary monster, the 'drunken acolyte' of Mount Ōeyama, who abducted women from the capital of Kyōto. He was vanquished by Minamoto no Yorimitsu (984–1021) and his four brave warriors.*

However, poetry composing did not lose its appeal throughout the middle ages, even though the art of poetry had been surpassed by the skills of the warrior. The hedonistic lifestyle of the gentle court aristocracy was exchanged for the hard life on battlefields in the incessant struggles for power. In this atmosphere, the beliefs in the merciful Buddha Amida spread widely among the population, while more sophisticated Zen philosophy and higher learning was cultivated in large Zen temple complexes that provided for the intellectual life of the samurai class, introducing the concept of the fragility of life, which could be easily lost.

Methods of linking poetry in renga

As noted above, Japanese literature was conveyed through the simple form called *waka*. After centuries of writing *waka* with the same poetic diction and with the same repertory of images and words, and on the same topics, poets would end up in the terminal station called low entropy in modern terms. Because composition of *waka* became widespread and familiar, it gradually grew stale and trite and attempts were made to make it more interesting through integrating it, not only into stories, but also into the longer form of so-called "linked poems" or "chain-poetry" (*renga* 連歌). This tendency towards composing poems in linked poetry prevailed from the Muromachi period (1339–1568). Several poets, who would compete in *uta-awase* in previous ages, would meet to unite their imagery and combine their poetic efforts by creating a poem of thirty six or one hundred stanzas in turns, one by one. *Renga* would start from the so-called *hokku* 発句, the initial verse of 5-7-5 syllables, and on went the chain with each poet adding either 7-7 verses or starting a new unit with a 5-7-5 verse sequence. The poem could be read as 5-7-5// 7-7 or as 7-7 // 5-7-5, extending its links to both the preceding and following verses.

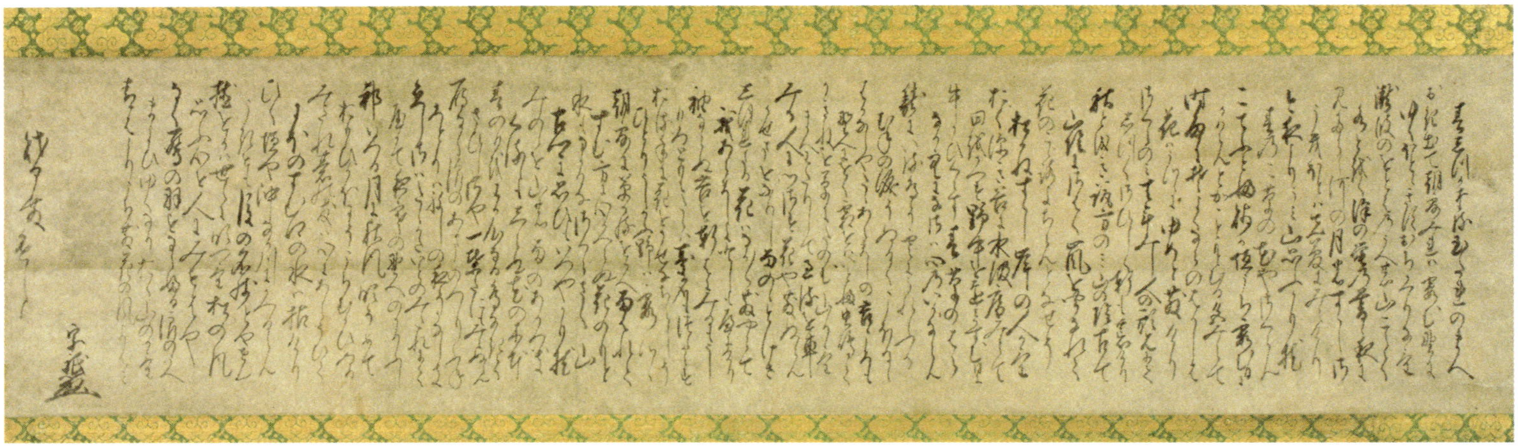

Fig. 6. **Monk Sōgi** (1421–1502): **Calligraphy of a renga poem "Haru shizuka naru tamatare no mae,"** ink on paper mounted as a hanging scroll, 25.1 x 105 cm, 1481.
(Photo Credit: National Institute of Japanese Literature, 99–22. nijl)
A rare example of an original kana *handwriting by a noted* renga *poet and a great expert on poetry, Monk Sōgi.*

The pioneering figure in *renga* composition was Nijō Yoshimoto (二条 良基, 1320–1388), an heir of the Teika tradition and the editor of a collection of *renga* poems, *A Collection from Tsukuba* (*Tsukuba shū* 菟玖波集), from 1356. The greatest 15th century master of *waka* and *renga* was the Zen monk Sōgi (宗祇, 1421–1502), who edited *A New Selection of the Tsukuba Collection* (*Shinsen Tsukuba shū,* 新撰菟玖波集) a hundred years later in 1470 (Fig. 6). Sōchō (1448–1532) was Sōgi's biographer and his pupil and follower in *renga,* as well as in his wanderings through the countryside.[11] And because even this form was becoming obsolete and repetitive, humour and irony were slowly changing *renga* into the more humorous *haikai no renga* 俳諧の連歌.[12] The fashion of long humorous poems culminated in the 16th century in *New Selections of the Dog's Tsukuba Collection* (*Shinsen Inu Tsukuba shū,* 新撰犬筑波集, ca 1524–1532) by Yamazaki Sōkan (山崎宗鑑, 1465–1553).[13]

The rules of composing *renga* became very strict, demanding a fluent change of seasons, employment of a seasonal word (*kigo*), placing the symbols of the seasons, such as *sakura* or the moon, at specific locations in the sequence, inserting famous local names (*uta-makura*), shifting from a noble environment to a common life setting, from lofty to earth subjects, from poems with ornamental, decorative diction to poems written in plain style, from verbal to nominal expression, from old-fashioned to modern language, and so on. Also the focus of attention should change constantly from distant views and far-fetched connotations (*so* 疎) to close-ups and immediate connections (*shin* 親).[14] The changing point of view from a large whole to a detail had a parallel in a constant and natural flow of spectacular poems (so-called "decorative poems" – *mon no uta* 文の 歌) and plain poems (so-called "background poems" – *ji no uta* 地の歌). Thus the permanent change of the angle of vision, the distant and close associations and the juxtaposition of noble and simple poems became the set rules underlying the composition and integration of linked verse. Firmly fixed places for stanzas on the moon and flowers (*hana no za, tsuki no za,* 花.月の座) had to be observed in the *renga* chain. The common length of *renga* was 100 stanzas (*hyakuin* 百韻連歌) and for *haikai no renga* 36 stanzas (*kasen* 歌仙). The rules would even dictate how many poems were recorded on the obverse and the reverse of each sheet of paper, whether to write them in large or smaller letters, in which density and so on. Thus *renga* became an extremely complicated structure, and only real masters could create long sequences of lasting value. Yet, *haikai no renga* composition was also greatly amusing and challenging, and *renga* composition parties became widespread. *Renga* teachers and masters were much in demand throughout the country, as there were many *renga* poets among commoners.

The fashion of integration was followed by a tendency toward abbreviation. *Renga* had its posterity in *haikai no hokku* 徘徊の発句 – the initial verse of the *renga* sequence. This verse form had 3 lines and only 17 syllables. This short form became very popular in the 17th century. Thus the development of the short poem *waka* led to its further abbreviation, as for instance in the following *haikai no hokku* by the 15th century masters Shinkei (1406–1475)[15] and Shōhaku (1448–1528):[16]

kumo ha naho	It is to the clouds
sadame aru yo no	one looks for a world of certainty
shigure kana	in the cold drizzle
tsuki idzuku	The moon is elsewhere
sora no kasumi no	as the sky is overspread with haze
hikari kana	glimmering with light

During the Edo period (1600–1868), the creation of short three-line verses reached its peak in the elegant and light poems (*fūga*, *karumi*) of the wandering monk-poet and greatest master of *haikai no renga* Matsuo Bashō (松尾 芭蕉, 1644–1694), one of the great literati of the Genroku era.[17]

The next development of poetry led to humorous variations of its basic forms. The five-verse *waka* was transformed into the "witty verse" (*kyōka* 狂歌), while the shortened form of three-line *hokku* found its comic counterpart in *senryū* 川柳. Their age came at the end of the 18th century when the craze for *haikai no hokku* led to a great expansion of poetry clubs, poets and poetry publications. *Hokku* and *senryū* were renamed *haiku* 徘句 much later at the close of the 19th century by the poet Masaoka Shiki.[18] The tendency towards abbreviation of *waka* took place shortly after the historical phase in Japanese poetry when the so-called *Books of Fans* (*ōgi no sōshi*) came into fashion as textbooks for classical poetry.

The Prague version of *Ōgi no sōshi*

Books of Fans (*ōgi no sōshi* 扇の草子) are a genre that appeared just about the time of great change at the end of the 16th century, in the phase when an old and obsolete tradition of serious poetry was changing into a light-hearted and humorous variation in the hands and hearts of the *machishū* 町衆 – the town inhabitants, the lower social orders. It was one among several minor genres at the time of transformation from the mediaeval to early modern society. The genre of *Books of Fans* is not generally known, standing slightly apart as it does from the mainstream of the poetic tradition, hidden in the shadow of the late Muromachi and Momoyama periods, at the close of the turbulent century of the States at War period (*Sengoku jidai* 戦国時代). It is essentially an educative genre, a textbook of the basic poetry repertoire in the short form of *waka* with fan-shaped pictures. The textbook is aimed at young noblemen or the offspring of samurai, and rich townspeople who desired to get acquainted with their native poetic tradition as early in their life as possible. Through the study of this book, youths in their teens could obtain the essential air of literacy, as it offered them a minimum (around one hundred) of the most familiar poems of their time.

In 2003, a Japanese scholar, Makoto Yasuhara, published her detailed research into the hitherto almost unknown genre of *ōgi no sōshi*. She compared about fifty extant versions containing poems illustrated with pictures in fan-shaped cartouches. She tried hard to pin down the original sources of the total of 456 poems included in ancient works dating from the 16th and 17th centuries. Each of the extant *Ōgi no sōshi* has a slightly different selection of poems, which means they are not copies of a single source, and Yasuhara ennumerated as many as 19 model versions of the genre (*denpon* 伝本). Yet all are joined by more or less skilfill fan-shaped illustrations (Figs. 7, 10, 27a, b). Yasuhara came to the conclusion that the Prague version of the Book of Fans, which contains forty pages with three fans and poems on each page (that is, 120 poems), is the most extensive and complete manuscript remaining in the world.[19]

Even though the texts of the *Books of Fans* were written in an easily legible feminine handwriting style (so-called *hentaigana* with several variations of *kana* letters for each syllable), using few Chinese characters, the books were not primarily meant for girls. They were too bold for a young lady.[20] There are poems that aimed to teach the young men proper decorum of behaviour toward women, how to woo them, and how to behave as the love-affair developed. The poems also prepare the reader for life as a warrior, or introduce him to the pleasures of hunting and the hardships of traveling to far-away provinces. And it offered its readers also a wide variety of poems – varied not only by their motifs or themes, but also with regards to their authors, to the time of their origin or to their tone, poetic decorum and diction. Side by side, there are poems with noble, discreet and lofty imagery (based on the classical poetic ideals of elegance *miyabi* 雅, tranquil beauty *yūen* 優艶, melancholy *aware* 哀れ, mystery *yūgen* 幽玄, true emotion *ushin* 有心, emotional overtones and ethereal charm *yojō yōen* 余情妖艶, etc.) and next to them we can find onomatopoeic and nursery-rhyme-like verses with word puns, and even riddles and acrostics. Thus the quality of poems within the remnant copies of *ōgi no sōshi* is uneven. This seems to be a rule of all of *ōgi no sōshi* for minors as the repertory of poems is quite similar. However, the integration and ordering of poems is different in each extant example and Books of Fans are definitely not copied from a single original model.

The Prague version of *Ōgi no sōshi* is not signed; it was originally bound in the Japanese style in one volume in a plain, grey semi-hard paper cover with a hand-written inscription *Ehon waka shū* (*Illustrated Book of Poetry* 絵本和歌集), and there is no other inscription. The 120 poems are written three poems per page in free flowing *chirashi-gaki* calligraphy, so that it is not so easy to follow the lines. We know nothing about the author or owner of this volume. There are several poems scattered throughout the volume that speak about an arrow. The last one of these poems (no. 114) is a congratulation, wishing long life of prosperity to "the houses of bow and arrows", which is a synecdoche for a samurai family.

sakahe-yuku yumiya no iwe no tori-dori ni kono tabi koto ni na wo agenikeru	The prospering houses of arrow and bow -each and every one- this time especially have they become famous.

This may suggest that the collection was composed especially for a noble house that had an arrow in its family emblem (*kamon* 家紋). But this is mere speculation. Also the poems often speak of Sumiyoshi, which is the most frequent of "famous-place poems" (*meisho no uta* 名所の歌), appearing in four poems (49, 80, 113, 118). For this reason we may suppose that the *Book of Fans* could have been produced for a family living in the Yamato region in Sumiyoshi near Naniwa (Ōsaka) and we may imagine their "house of bow and arrows" around there.

kimi ga yo no hisashikarubeki tameshi ni ha kanete zo uweshi sumiyoshi no matsu	As an example of how long my lord shall live, there are the pines of Sumiyoshi planted from long ago.

Many of the poems are connected with the so-called "pillow-words" (*uta-makura* 歌枕), inserting a clear image of a certain beauty spot by naming a certain mountain, bay, or stream. The device of employing local names definitely enlivens the imagery of native Japanese, but these names are almost impossible to translate, as foreign readers cannot imagine the described locations, let alone their literary connotations. For this reason they are mostly left as names without translating their meaning. An exception is made in case of poem no. 55 which speaks of the River of Silence and the Bridge of Whispers.

Fig. 7. Anonymous painter of the 17th century: **A sheet with a single fan-picture** (*ōgi-e*) illustrating calligraphy of a *waka* poem, ink, colours, liquid and leaf gold on paper, 23 x 17 cm, one sheet of a fragmentary *ōgi no sōshi* of fours sheets, early 17th century.
(Photo credit: Private collector, Japan)
The poem by Fujiwara no Takamitsu (Shūishū, 435) reflects on the topic "Upon observing the moon when he considered retiring to a temple":

かくはかり
へかたく見ゆる
世の中に
うら山しくも
すめる月かな

kaku bakari	Though it may seem
hekataku miyuru	hard and worthless to live
yo no naka ni	in this vain world
urayamashiku mo	I envy the moon which shines clear
sumeru tsuki kana	behind the mountain range.

kumano naru	If only I could pass
oto-nashi kaha ni	the silent Otonashi River
watasabaya	of Kumano
bingo no tomo no	by the Sasayaki Bridge of whispers,
sasayaki no hashi	companion of Bingo Province!

The interesting aspect here lies in the fact, that, besides a single mention of Mount Fuji and a single one of Futami Bay and two of Musashi Plain, which all lie far towards the east of the capital (Kyōto, Miyako), only locations in and around the ancient Yamato region nearby the capital are mentioned in the pillow-words (such as Akashi, Suma or Naniwa Bay, Tatsuta, Ōi or Yodo River, Shinobu or Kasuga Mountain, Awaji Island). If the compilation was a hundred years younger, more local names alongside the eastward Tōkaidō Road would certainly appear in the poems, as the road became very frequented, starting from the early Edo period and the first travelogue *Tōkaidō meishoki* by the *kanazōshi* writer Asai Ryōi (浅井了意, ca. 1612–1691), containing many old and new poems, appeared around 1660.

A majority of poems in the Prague version of *Ōgi no sōshi* are on nature. Most poems contain a seasonal word (*kigo* 季語). There are many poems on trees and flowers: pine-trees (*matsu*), blossoming cherries (*sakura*), plums (*ume*), red maple-trees (*momiji*), wistaria (*fuji*), willow trees (*yanagi*), bamboo (*take*), paulownia (*kiri*), bush-clover (*hagi*), yellow wild roses (*yamabuki*), chrysanthemum (*kiku*), reeds (*ōgi*) and many less familiar flowers. There are also poems on animals and birds: stags, horses, boars, oxen, tigers, herons, falcons, cocks, and various water birds with symbolic functions. All of these motifs appear also in the fan-shaped illustrations where green and blue hues dominate the colour scale with red, white, pink and yellow highlights. The next most frequent pictorial and poetic motif is the moon (both full and bow-shaped). After that comes water, mist, rain and snow imagery (the rising and falling elements of Japanese poetics). Though seasonal words are arranged according to the passage of time in most poetry collections, there is no evident order in the passage of the seasons through the Prague *Ōgi no sōshi* – Summer follows Winter and Spring turns into Autumn in a rather abrupt manner. The swift change of seasons is much closer to *renga*, where the need for variety surpasses the respect for gradual seasonal development.

As for the other major theme of classical poetry, Love, the poems on this subject are not as frequent as nature lyrics, even though Japanese love poetry often dresses up in natural imagery and symbols. Most love poems show the appropriate decorum of nostalgia of waiting in vain for the lover to come, or forlorn feelings of having been deserted and deprived of love. Some love poems are comical, like the poem about thundering paper clothes on a secret night visit to the bed of a girl (no. 58), or the one about a country maid promising to kill a rooster who chased away her lover (no. 60). The volume also includes a poem on homosexual love among monks (no. 78). Last, there are poems of congratulations, long-life wishes, or reflective Buddhist and Shintoist poems, which appear in the closing parts of the volume. There is no poem on filial piety or other Confucian principle, which speaks for a pre-Tokugawa origin of the volume.

Some poems in Prague *Ōgi no sōshi* are straightforward, some highly allusive, some plain and even funny, or at least amusing. They may be considered even as forerunners of *kyōka*, the witty verse. Poem no. 28, for instance, on the topic of a single boar running to the forest instead of a group of sixteen boars, is a word pun on the boars' name *shishi* 獅子, a repetition of the numeral four (*shi-shi* 四四).

shishi naraba	With boars,
jifuroku tsurete	four times four,
yukubeki ni	should make sixteen.
kuku ni moruru ka	says multiplication, but have they escaped?
hitori hashiru ha	–there is only one running.

Poem no. 30 depicting a peasant woman who is waiting under a pine tree for the gust of wind to get her some pine-needles to make fire obviously makes fun of the conventional image of a court lady waiting by the pine-tree for a lover. Pine (*matsu* 松) is homonymous with waiting (*matsu* 待つ), and pining and waiting are often connected in a figure of speech called "double-meaning words" (*ken'yōgen* 兼用言, or *kakekotoba* 掛け言葉). A high-born lover from the court is often compared to a wind or storm from the skies, or from the top of a mountain, which descends to make his low-born lady happy. Thus the following poem is a clear-cut parody of such obsolete imagery and can be labelled as an early parody on *waka,* or the "witty poem", *kyōka* 狂歌.

shidzu no me ga	The humble woman
matsu no ochi-ba wo	grows used to raking up
kaki-narete	the fallen pine needles-
asu no takigi ni	for tomorrow's firewood,
arashi wo zo matsu	she waits for the storm.

The most difficult part in accessing the *Ōgi no sōshi* volume was faced when trying to identify the original sources or the authors of the poems. Out of the 120 stanzas, 16 poems are unidentified – both their source and authors remain unknown.[21] That means that about 80% of the poems could be identified. 27 are anonymous poems from identified sources, each from a different one (only the collections *Kokinshū, Shūishū, Shinkokinshū and Fuboku waka shō* account for multiple anonymous poems). Most poems come from different collections, which are listed in the General index (Appendix E). What strikes us as unusual is that *Ise monogatari* is by far the most popular source – as many as nine poems from this oldest *uta-monogatari* have been included in Prague version of *Ōgi no sōshi.* Other collections, both imperial and private, and all the other classical narratives provide material for lesser numbers of poems. For instance there are only four poems drawn from the famous *Genji monogatari* (nos. 6, 24, 79, 106) and two from *Heike mo-*

Fig. 8. Calligraphy by **Hon'ami Kōetsu** (1558–1637), painting by **Tawaraya Sōtatsu** (ca. 1570–1643): Calligraphy of a poem on decorated background, mounted as a hanging scroll, ink on paper decorated with gold and silver; 20 x 17.8 cm, 1606. (Photo credit: Metropolitan Museum of Art, 1975.268.59)
The cooperation between Kōetsu and Sōtatsu led to highly decorative poetic pieces of art on single leaves and on horizontal scrolls. The two laid the foundation for the artistic tradition called Rinpa (after the genius painter and lacquer-maker Ogata Kōrin), which gave new flavour to ancient Yamato-e themes at the close of the 17th century. The poem, from the Shinkokinshū (no. 397), is by Kamo no Chōmei (1155–1216):

ながむれば
千々に物思ふ
月に又
我が身ひとつの
嶺の松風

nagamureba	I stare at the moon,
chijhi ni mono omofu	dwelling in thousands of thoughts.
tsuki ni mata	The wind comes in low
wagami hitotsu no	from the pines on the mountain top
mine no matsukaze	as if to console me alone.

nogatari (nos. 68, 82). The majority of the resource collections pre-date the Edo period, even though there are a few exceptions (*Kohon ikyoku shū*, 1666, no. 39; *Shūgai kasen*, 1665, no. 42; *Tama-tsukuri monogatari*, early 17th century, no. 81). The inclusion of three poems found in collections dating from the 17th century, however, does not indicate that the poems may not actually date from earlier times. As for quotations from *renga* collections, there are two poems from the *Tsukuba shū* (nos. 7, 45). At least 19 poems are quoted also in the contemporary (16th century) Noh drama.

There are fifty-five poets included in the *Book of Fans*, most of them represented by singular masterpieces. As for the famous poets (if we exlude the dubious authorship of Ariwara no Narihira in case of the nine poems quoted from *The Ise Stories*), the monk Saigyō and the court lady Murasaki Shikibu (*Genji monogatari*) are represented by four poems. The god of poetry, Sugawara no Michizane, and Minamoto no Nakamasa (*Fuboku waka shō*) by three poems each. The compiler of the *Kokinshū*, Ki no Tsurayuki, the Zen poet Musō Sōseki, the Reizei tradition poet Shōtatsu, the great patron of poetry retired emperor GoToba and his court lady Kunaikyō all show up twice. All the other famous poets' names appear under a single poem.

The Composition of the Prague *Ōgi no sōshi*

Though very complex methods of integration when composing a poetry anthology were known at the time, the composition of the Prague version of *Ōgi no sōshi* seems to be random at first sight. In fact, it uses the very same methods of linking the verses into a sequence as the linked poetry *renga*. These include the principles of fluent changes from the distant (*so*) to the close-up (*shin*) focus and association of the topics.[22] This flow of focus (zooming) becomes clearly evident in the adjoining fan-shaped illustrations showing panoramic views (with for instance a temple in the Yoshino mountains in spring) next to details (of for instance, the reeds with hanging strips of poetry flowing in the wind). There is also the interchange of ornamental (decorative poems, *mon no uta*), and plain poems (background poems, *ji no uta*) that were used in composing *renga*.[23]

Because all pages are numbered and the order is not haphazard, the principles *of uta-awase, ōgi-awase, kai-awase* or other competitions used in pairing poems on similar topic can be discerned on opposing pages. Starting from the presumption that these links might have been employed here, too, we have to look across the page in the way the book had been originally bound in the Japanese manner as a book with the outer rims of the sheets sewn inside the middle ridge (*fukuro toji sasshibon*). We cannot see these links immediately, as the book was disassembled, but if we compare the left side (B) on one sheet with the right side (A) of the following one in the manner the book was bound from back to front, the links become more evident. When comparing the poems and trying to find out some underlying principle for their integration into the *Book of Fans* volume, one can notice that there were evident pairs of poems across the pages that are matched both by phrases, imagery, grammatical phrases or some other link (for example, a pair of well-known poems, so called *mon no uta*). Many pages are connected through the themes of the moon, red maples, green pine trees or white cherry tree flowers, which are interwoven throughout the complete cycle and always depicted in the adjoining fan-shaped pictures *ōgi-e.*

Distinct pairs of poems that might be similar to comparing poems in an *uta-awase* can be found on opposing pages. This hypothesis is supported by graphic aspects of the book, because there are always three fans with ribs placed quite irregularly on each page-spread and three fans remain plain, without mounting. The ribs may suggest the winning (or losing) poem of a pair. The cross-page pair links are quite obvious on the double-page 8B+9A where two poems (48, 51) deal with the topic of the pass of Shiga, playing on the usual interchange of white *sakura* flowers and white snow. Another equivalent pair comparing the moon above two famous places (*meisho*) Musashino and Sumiyoshi (Poems 77, 80) can be seen on a double-page 13B+14A. Multiple images of water birds and fish connect the poems on the double-page 14B+15A. The next double-page (15B+16A) offers four very famous classical poems, so that the link is more or less literary, but two of them (90, 91), both from *Kokinshū,* are famous for their onomatopoeic qualities ("*satsuki matsu*", "*hono-bono to*"). Phrase connections are evident between the pair of poems using "*tofu hito mo nashi/naki*" (16B+17A). The following double-page (17B+18A) offers a parallel of a bay lined by white shells (*kai shigemi,* 101) and a river lined by red momiji (*momiji midarete,* 105). The next double-page (18B+19A) shows a parallel of two poems using the image of reflection in the water ("*midori no midzu ni / kage wo utsuseba*" 107, "*midzu no shita ni mo*" 110). Placed among the more-or-less "congratulation and celebration" type of poems, which befit the end of a poetry cycle, there are two "sadistic" poems (from the category of mixed topics or Varia) on the next double-page (19B–20A). The first one is about a "cruel" brush which scatters *sakura* blossoms even on the screen painting (Poem 112) and the other about the "furious" poet who wishes to use a halberd to kill the warbler that tramples the plum blossoms (Poem 117).

Difficult to associate are pairs linked by historical literary connotations beyond the text, like the pair on the very first double-page (1B+2A) where the Nonomiya shrine visit of prince Genji to his former lover Lady Rokujō, and her daughter, the future Ise Priestess, is recalled by the carriage of flowers (Poem 6). On the next page (Poem 8, quoted from the Noh play *Matsuyama-kagami*) a daughter is remembering her mother by looking into a mirror, as the child took after her deceased parent. Both poems are linked by a Mother-Daughter relationship. Such and similar links are to be found on each of the twenty double-pages throughout the volume. In trying to pair similar poems across the page, the student might have been challenged to solve an additional puzzle and enjoy the book in the way of a game, as his predecessors did during an *uta-awase.*[24]

We may therefore conclude that rather than the principles used in classical poetry compilations, such as in the *Shinkokinshū*, the principles of integrating *renga* poetry were employed in composing the *Ōgi no sōshi* book. Yet the principle of comparing two poems, used in the *uta-awase* of classical times of poetry of the Heian period, has been employed in the compilation of *Ōgi no sōshi* as well. The person who made the selection of the Prague *Ōgi no sōshi* volume must have been well-versed both in the classical poetic tradition and in composing linked poem *renga* or the humorous *haikai no renga* sequences.

The overall quality of *Ōgi no sōshi* poetry falls short of the standard of official, professional poetic anthologies created by noted poets and poetry-contest judges. The anonymous compiler prepared a wild mixture of both ancient and recent, archaic and modern, serious and funny, noble and vulgar styles. The lower level of poetry included in *Ōgi no sōshi* may be the reason why this genre of educative poetry compilations has been almost forgotten.

(Endnotes)

1 *Ise monogatari* 伊勢物語 was written over time by several authors of the 10th century. Its latest English translation with commentaries was published recently by Mostow and Tyler (see Selected bibliography).

2 Ariwara no Narihira (在原 業平, 825–880) was one of the *Six Poetic Immortals* (*Rokkasen* 六歌仙), a group of six poets who started writing Japanese poetry in the second half of the 9th century after a period of over two hundred years when Chinese poetry was the preferred medium of poetic expression. The *Rokkasen* were first named by Ki no Tsurayuki 紀貫之 in the Japanese preface of the *Kokinshū* (905). The *Rokkasen* are named in the preface in the following order: Sōjō Henjō, 僧正遍照, Ariwara no Narihira, 在原 業平, Bunya no Yasuhide, 文屋康秀, Kisen Hōshi 喜撰法師 (called the Happy Monk from the Uji Mountain, Uji-san no Sōki, 宇治山の僧喜), Ono no Komachi 小野小町, and Ōtomo no Kuronushi 大伴黒主. Out of these six most famous poets, only four appear in the Prague version of *Ōgi no sōshi*.

3 *Genji monogatari* (源氏物語) was written in 54 chapters by the court lady Murasaki Shikibu (紫 式部, c. 978 – c. 1014 or 1025).

4 The earliest written version of *Heike Monogatari* 平家物語 dates from the 14th century (1371).

5 The term *waka* in modern Japanese theories covers both *tanka*, the short poem, and *chōka*, the archaic long poem, which has been preserved mostly in the *Man'yōshū*.

6 A different term in use for the poetry compilations upon imperial request is *The Twenty-One Anthologies – Nijūichidaishū* (二十一代集).

7 *Sengohyakuban uta awase* 千五百番歌合, the *Poetry Contest in 1,500 Rounds*, held under the auspices of GoToba-in in 1201, brought together 15 famed poets of the competing Mikohidari and Rokujō Schools both on the Left and Right sides. Its composition is described in detail in Huey, Appendix D (see Selected bibliography).

8 Fujiwara (or Kujō) Yoshitsune (九条 良経, 1169–1206), held the position of *Sesshō*, Regent, between 1202–1206.

9 *Dai* (題), the "topic" or "inspiration" is mentioned at the beginning of each poem in anthologies, preceding the author, if known. Anonymous poems are labelled as: *Dai shirazu, yomibito shirazu*. ("Topic unknown, poet unknown").

10 Retired emperor GoToba (後鳥羽院, 1180–1239; ruled 1183–1198) was a pivotal personality in the unprecedented blossoming of *waka* during the *Shinkokinshū* period at the beginning of the 12th century.

11 A well-known *renga* by three poets–Sōgi, Sōchō and Bonchō–was *Minase sangin hyakuin*, 1488. For a translation of Sōchō's diaries, see H. Mack Horton, *The Journal of Sōchō*, Stanford University Press, 2002.

12 *Haikai no renga* is sometimes called also *renku* 連句 – "linked stanzas".

13 *Shinsen inu Tsukuba shū* was published in a woodcut printed edition a hundred years later in the middle of the 17th century when the fashion of *renku* reached its peak. It was followed by *Shinzoku inu Tsukuba shū* by Kitamura Kigin in 1667.

14 Konishi Jin'ichi: *Sōgi* (*Nihon shijin* series no. 16), Tōkyō: Tsukuba shōbō, 1971, p. 177.

15 English translation by Earl Miner, see Miner, 1979, p. 33 for Shinkei.

16 English translation by Earl Miner, see Miner, 1979, p. 41 for Shōhaku.

17 The three genius writers of the Genroku period at the turn of the 17th and 18th centuries are the poet Matsuo Bashō, the novelist Ihara Saikaku and the playwright Chikamatsu Monzaemon.

18 Masaoka Shiki 正岡子規 (1867–1902) is regarded as one of the four greatest *haiku* poets: Bashō, Buson, Issa and Shiki.

19 As for the number of poems in other remnant versions of Books of Fans, the most complete are the following versions named after the present-time holder: a private holder (*kojin-zō*) 108, Nihon mingeikan 103, Nezu Museum 100, Keiō University Library 90, Harvard University 80. The late woodblock-printed version kept by Tōyō bunko – Iwazaki bunko has 80 poems.

20 Girls were educated through a different type of more practical books called *onna setsuyōshū*, preparing them for the roles of perfect wives, teaching them how to take care of a husband and his family, how to behave toward guests, how to prepare tea or make flower arrangements, how to wrap up presents, how to take care of children, etc.

21 The unidentified Poems are: 10, 16, 28, 48, 49, 78, 85, 88, 98, 102, 107, 112, 114, 116, 118, 120.

22 Similar terms originate in the three styles of calligraphy *sho* 書, with *shin* 真 being formal, *gyō* 行 being semi-formal and *sō* 草 being informal. Yet *renga* theory used different concepts and characters – see page 104.

23 For a closer explanation, refer to: Miner, E., *Japanese Linked Poetry* (Princeton University Press, 1979), p. 72, and Appendix with translated *renga* sequences.

24 More details on the structure of the Prague *Book of Fans* are explained in the following study by J. Mostow.

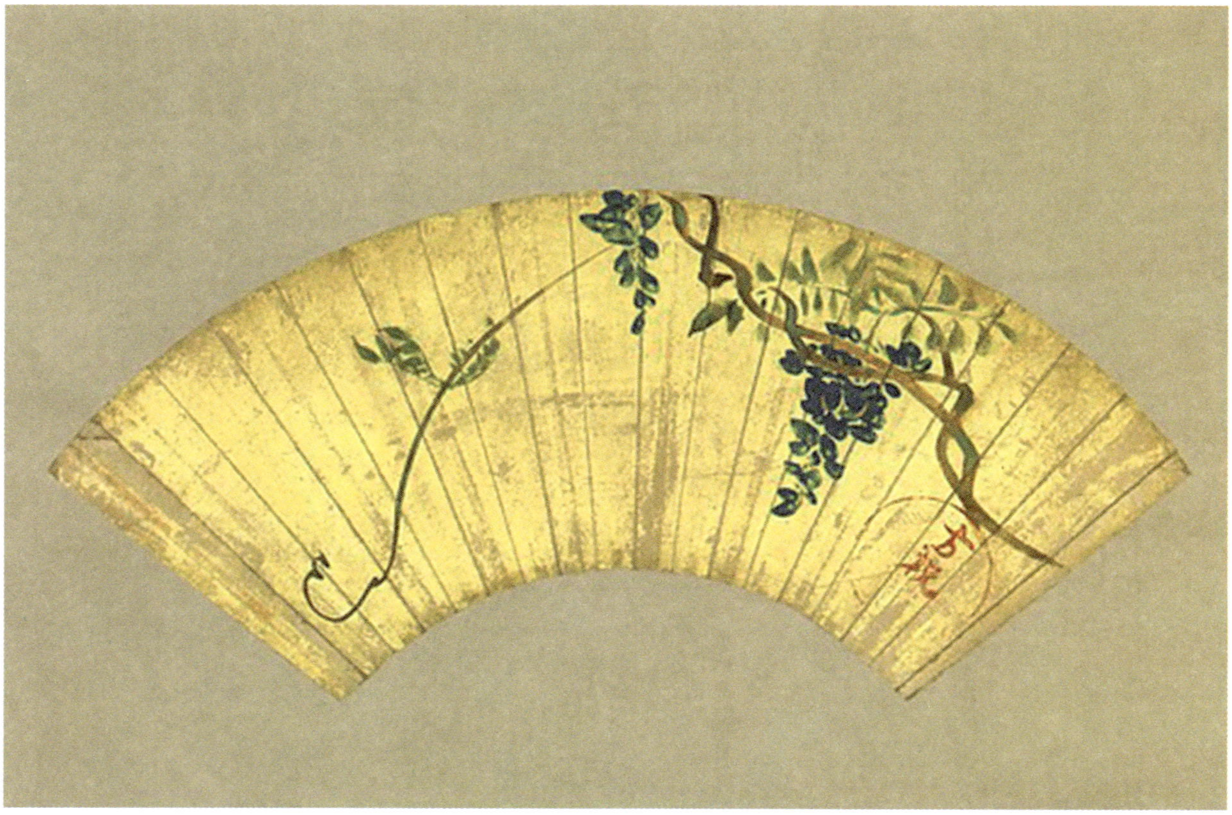

Fig. 9. **Ogata Kōrin** (1658-1716, attributed to): **A fan with a blossoming wisteria**, ink, color pigments and gold on paper, mounted as a hanging scroll, seal: Kōrin, 17.2 x 52.7 cm, late 17th/early 18th century. (Photo credit: Metropolitan Museum of Art, New York, 29.100.526, bequest of Mrs. H. O. Havemeyer, 1929)

FOLDING-FAN PICTURE BOOKS: INTERWEAVING TEXT AND IMAGE

Makoto Yasuhara

The term "Books of Fans" (*ōgi no sōshi*) does not refer to a single work, but rather to a group of texts that display a particular kind of image. That is, it refers to a group of works that are composed as multiple sets of poems and pictures in which a *waka* is inscribed alongside a folding fan picture that illustrates the poem's meaning. The genre could more accurately be called "folding-fan picture books".

Presently, there are fifty extant texts (picture scrolls, picture books, picture albums) (Fig. 10). Their production dates back to the time between the late sixteenth to early seventeenth centuries, which was a period of historical transition in Japan from a time of domestic wars (Sengoku jidai, 1467–1603) to an era of peace (Edo period, 1615–1868).

"Folding-fan picture books" is a distinctive group of texts for which there is no close analogue in other cultures and in which three elements exist in combination: visual art (folding-fan pictures, *ōgi-e*), literary art (*waka* poetry), and elegant, free-flowing calligraphy (*chirashi-gaki*). Since there are no records that indicate the contexts and practices in which this art form was embedded, the ways in which it was received are not known.

However, there are documents that provide some important indications of its reception. These are tales (*otogi-zōshi*), such as the *Jippon ōgi*[1] and the *Haikai emaki*, and diaries, such as *Jitsugyō ki* and *Muromachidono nikki*[2], from the second half of the sixteenth century. In these works, we find descriptions of situations in which people were shown fans with pictures and guessed what kind of *waka* poems the pictures were based on. In light of this evidence, it can be inferred that this was a literary art enjoyed in a playful context.

In Japan, "literary art" and "play" were closely associated. Their affiliation can be traced back to the ninth century – the early Heian period. The primary agents of culture at the time were aristocrats. Heian aristocrats delighted in a game called "poetry contests" (*uta-awase*) at their private residences and at the imperial palace. *Uta-awase* were elegant games in which participants were divided into a Left and a Right team, sat facing each other, and composed *waka* poems on a common topic. A judge would then determine which side's poem was superior. Later, the records from such games would be collected and appreciated as literary art.

The origins of folding-fan picture books can be found in such poetry contests. The "folding-fan contest" (*ōgi-awase*) can be situated within this lineage. In this game, carefully designed folding-fan pictures that featured *waka* poems were set out for judgment. The competition was thus more comprehensive than *waka* poetry contests in the sense that they took into consideration both pictures and poems.

However, from the end of the twelfth century (Kamakura period, 1192–1333), as the primary agents of culture shifted from aristocrats to samurai, there were fewer people who could compose *waka* poetry. As a result, poetry contests ceased to be practiced. About four hundred years later, a kind of game similar to folding-fan contests once again began to be practiced, which is when the folding-fan picture books were most likely produced – a period of Japanese history not unlike the Renaissance of Europe in the specific sense that its emergence coincided with a rebirth of the classical canon.

Fig. 10. Anonymous painter of the 17th century: **Scroll with fan-shaped pictures and waka poems**, detail (*Ōgi no sōshi emaki*), ink, colors, liquid gold (*kindei*) and white (*gofun*) on paper, 18.1 x 383.2 cm, early Edo period.
(Photo credit: National Institute of Japanese Literature: nijl 99.73L)
The right-most fan illustrates a poem by Emperor Kōkō (830–887, Hyakunin isshu, 15, translated by J. Mostow) reads:

きみがため
はるののにいでて
わかなつむ
わがころもでに
ゆきはふりつつ

kimi ga tame
haru no no ni idete
waka-na tsumu
wa ga koromo-de ni
yuki ha furitsutsu

For my lord's sake
I went out into the fields of spring
to pick young greens
while on my robe-sleeves
the snow kept falling and falling.

The middle fan is paired with a poem by Sarumaru Tayū (lived in the second half of the 9th century, Hyakunin isshu 5, translated by J. Mostow) reads:

おくやまに
ももちふみわけ
なくしかの
こえきくときそ
あきはかなしき

oku-yama ni
momijhi fumi-wake
naku shika no
kowe kiku toki zo
aki ha kana shiki

When I hear the voice
of the stag crying for his mate
stepping through the fallen leaves
deep in the mountains–then is the time
when autumn is the saddest.

The third poem joining the left fan is one of the three introductory poems of the Prague version of Ōgi no sōshi on the Japanese harp - koto (OS 2). It was written by Princess Kishi (949-986) and included first in the imperial collection Shūishū (451):

ことのねに
みねの松かせ
かよふらし
いつれのおより
しらへそめけん

koto no ne ni
mine no matsu-kaze
kayofurashi
idzure no o yori
shirabe-someken

The wind through the pines
on the peak closely resembles
the sound of the zither–
from which slope or string
does it begin to play?

In the old capital of Kyōto that was being reconstructed after its destruction in the domestic wars of the sixteenth century, the aristocratic class was revitalized, the samurai class set aside their swords and began pursuing peace, and, importantly, the urban class suddenly emerged on the cultural scene. This class in particular, which began to maintain the economic and spiritual stability of the country, also began to actively devote their time to cultural initiatives. It is from out of this milieu that new cultural forms such as Kabuki and Ukiyo-e were born, on the one hand, and, on the other, traditional literary forms such as *monogatari* and *waka* were once again carefully studied.

Most of the *waka* poems on the folding-fan picture books are famous classical poems that had become well-known by the early seventeenth century. Thus, the folding-fan contests, which constituted the context of the folding-fan picture book's creation, differed from that of four hundred years earlier: instead of a competition based on the merits of the *waka* poetry, the game became a way to study traditional culture through the medium of *waka* poetry.

As the name "book" (*sōshi*) in the term "Books of Fans" suggests, these objects took the form of reading books (*yomi-mono*). However, the term obscures the origins of these objects in "play". At first, each folding-fan picture was drawn on actual fans that folded. That pictures were drawn on a thing that moves was intended to give the impression to its users of a folding-fan contest. Second, it can also be inferred that the fact that the written characters were freely distributed on the page without restriction—a traditional way of writing for the purpose of visually communicating the artistry of *waka* as a written thing—had the effect of giving the impression of the written characters gently flowing on waves or in wind along with the folding fan.

Traces of the playful origins of folding-fan pictures can still be discerned in the objects themselves. Although we can generally draw a distinction between pictures that express the content of the *waka* poem and those that visualize a scene in a *monogatari* narrative, both often depict some thing or event not comprehensible by reference to the text alone. Most mysterious among them are hints intended to help guess the *waka* poem that appear as words that blend into the picture itself in a rebus-like fashion.

For example, there is the following classical *waka* based on the legend of Tanabata, according to which, on the night of Seventh Day of the Seventh Month, magpies spread their wings in perfect alignment to form a bridge by which the divine lovers Hikiboshi and Orihime cross the Milky Way to meet once a year.

kasasagi no	When I see the whiteness
wataseru hashi ni	of the frost that lies
oku shimo no	on the bridge the magpies spread,
shiroki wo mireba	then do I know, indeed,
yo zo fukenikeru	that the night has deepened.

The folding fan picture that corresponds to this *waka* poem does not depict magpies (*kasasagi*) but rather an umbrella (*kasa*) and a heron (*sagi*) of the same size above a bridge. In a style that might be called surrealist, the picture is thoroughly unrealistic and even humorous. The key to deciphering the riddle of the picture is the sound of the word *kasasagi* which is spuriously deconstructed in visual form according to the sounds *kasa* (umbrella) and *sagi* (heron). In the Prague version, however, the pictorial rebus is further reduced to a white heron on a bridge (Poem 18).

This form of visual play in which words are broken down into distinct parts and those parts are visually transferred in the form of separate pictures is called "*hanji-e*" or "*hanji-mono*", that is "pictorial puzzles" or "visual riddles". A famous example of this form is Utagawa Kuniyoshi's (1797–1861) triptych "Fifty-Three Cats of the Tōkaidō" (*Myōkaikō gojūsan-biki*), which is a pun on the "Fifty-Three Stations of the Tōkaidō" (*Tōkaidō gojūsan-tsugi*) series by Utagawa Hiroshige (1797–1858).[3] The Tōkaidō is the route of fifty-three stations that connected Edo and Kyōto. In Kuniyoshi's pictures, the stations are not represented by inscrip-

Fig. 11. **Utagawa Kuniyoshi** (1787–1861): **Triptych *Fifty-three Cats of the Tōkaidō*** (*Myōkaikō gojūsan-biki*), a humorous variation on the popular series Fifty-three stations of the Tōkaidō (*Tōkaidō gojūsan-tsugi*) by Utagawa Hiroshige (1797–1858) dated from 1833–34, color woodcut, publised by Ibasen, Edo, two censors' seals, 1848.
(Photo credit: William Pearl, kuniyoshiproject.com)

Fig. 12. Anonymous painter of the 17th century: **Two illustrations of a *Nara-ehon* entitled *The Sumiyoshi Tale*** (*Sumiyoshi monogatari*), ink, colours and gold leaf on paper, 32.4 x 23.2 cm, dated into the Kan'ei era (1624–1643).
The classical Heain period narrative of a princess who was chased out of Kyōto to Sumiyoshi by her jealous stepmother, was recreated as a "companion book" (otogi-zōshi) type of book with fifty pages. The style of illustrations clearly derives from Yamato-e scrolls.
(Photo credit: Private collector, Tōkyō)

tions but rather by pictures of cats (Fig. 11). These visual puzzles, which reached their peak at the end of the Edo period in the nineteenth century, have their roots in folding-fan picture books. Thus, this group of works has special relevance and value in regard to later pictorial traditions.

Lastly, a few words on the distinguishing characteristics of the pictorial style and format of the folding-fan pictures in the Prague collection. The characteristic feature of this version of *Ōgi no sōshi* that cannot be found in other texts is the presence of several monochrome ink images among the majority of pictures decorated with vibrant greens, reds, and blues. Since there are similar examples of this sobre and colourful interplay in the genre of "folding-fan screens", in which folding-fans were affixed and drawn on folding screens (*byōbu*), it is possible that these folding-fans were drawn in order to resemble a folding screen.

The style of the images belongs to a kind of illustrative picture form found in illustrated tales (*otogi-zōshi*) called "Nara picture books" (*Nara-ehon*) or "Nara picture scrolls" (*Nara-emaki*) that were widely produced around the turn of the seventeenth century (Fig. 12). This genre was produced by an anonymous group of urban painters called "*machi-eshi*" which constituted a distinct school separate from other lineages of painters, such as the Tosa School (renowned for *Yamato-e*), and the Kanō School (renowned for *Kanga*). As a result, the producers and period of production of *ōgi no sōshi* folding-fan picture books and the *otogi-zōshi* stories contained therein are unknown in most cases. The most appealing feature of the Prague version is the way in which it exemplifies the *Nara-ehon* form and its simple pictorial style. Although the "illustrated books from Nara" also contain intricate images that make use of gold and silver, in contrast to other texts that give a rigid impression of an aristocratic sensibility, these texts are done in a style that may be perceived as crude, but most certainly charming. They overflow with a human warmth and vitality.

The Prague pages were originally in the format of a bound book. That they were loved by their owner and frequently read can be discerned from the creases in the center of the pages and the traces of finger marks at the bottom. Since, in this way, these texts were appreciated not as works of art but as material objects, they convey the enjoyment that they inspired in the people of the time. In the case of the Prague sheets, the following scene comes to mind: the owner – perhaps a young girl of the middle class – looked at these books almost daily in her room and joyfully pursued her study of *waka* poetry while recalling memories of when she participated in folding-fan competitions. Folding-fan picture books, a genre that has been obscured by time, mostly forgotten, and, consequently, enshrouded in mystery, still awaits further elucidation from the point of view of the disciplines of art history, literature, and cultural history.

(*Translated by Ethan Bushelle*)

(Endnotes)

1 *The Ten Fans* (*Jippon ōgi* 十本扇) is an anonymous 16th century narrative of the *otogi-zōshi* genre.

2 *The Diary/Tale of Muromachi Estate* (*Muromachi-dono nikki/monogatari* 室町殿日記) concerning the history of the Ashikaga family shoguns in the period of Civil Wars (ca.1467–1603) was written by Naramura Naganori 楢村長教 in the 16th century and exists in several hand-written copies (*shahon*). One, dated 1686, is kept by the National Library of Australia. A modern annotated version of *Muromachi-dono nikki* by Sasakawa Sachio (*SS kaisetsu kōchū*) was reprinted in Rinsen Shoten, Kyōto, 1980. (http://trove.nla.gov.au/work/12480450?versionId=14746833).

3 The Tōkaidō was a 488 km long historical road connecting the imperial capital of Kyōto with the shogun's administrative centre of Edo (東京, Tōkyō). Hiroshige illustrated the 53 stations along the road (*Tōkaidō gojūsan tsugi* 東海道五十三次) with lively genre pictures between 1833–34 and Kuniyoshi, who loved to draw "funny pictures" (*giga*), designed a single triptych with his favorite cats as humorous symbols of all the post stations in 1848.

Fig. 13. **Kanō Sōshū** (1551–1601): **Kiyomizu-dera Temple from the set of fan-pictures Famous Places in the Capital and Legendary Figures** (*Kyō meishozu senmen*), fan painting *senmenga*, ink, colors and gold on paper, 19,2 x 50,4 cm, late 16th century. (Photo credit: Museum of Fine Arts, Boston, originally William Sturgis Bigelow Collection, 11.6380.3)

This set of rare, gilt, precisely painted fan paintings had been attributed to Kanō Shōei (1519–1592) in Boston, yet Japanese researchers identified the painter as Shōei's son and the younger brother of the illustrious Kanō Eitoku, Kanō Sōshū (1551–1601), who specialized in saiga (smaller, meticulously painted pictures). In 1580s, Sōshū was employed by Hideyoshi for whom he painted, among others, The Thirty-six Poetic Immortals on wooden boards, now preserved in Hōkoku Shrine, Kyōto.

RENGA, NOH, AND THE STRUCTURE OF THE PRAGUE *ŌGI NO SŌSHI*

Joshua S. Mostow

The *ōgi no sōshi* genre is manifested in a great variety of media, including scrolls (*emaki*), illustrated codices (*e-zōshi*), screens (*byōbu*), and printed books (*hanpon*). The extant examples also vary tremendously in quality, cost of materials, and skill of execution. Moreover, despite some overlap and similarities, each extant work is unique in its selection of poems and may differ considerably in its manner of illustrating those poems (except in the case of the printed version, of course).

The research of Tomoko Sakomura has demonstrated that the *ōgi no sōshi* is essentially a pedagogical genre, aimed at young students of Japanese poetry. Many of the extant versions, like the Prague version, show a decidedly masculine orientation (for example, poems 7, 9, 11, 78, 114, and others), and the sole information on any owner of an *Ōgi no sōshi* identifies one Toramatsumaru, a young boy in the late sixteenth century.[1]

Ōgi no sōshi, Renga, and Noh

Waka (Japanese court poetry), Noh libretti, and *renga* ("linked verse") served as the bases of cultural literacy in the late medieval and early modern eras of Japan. And *renga*-masters (*renga-shi*), mostly itinerant, were perhaps the most common of instructors. Such masters would travel the country, not only providing the opportunities for *renga* composition sessions and instruction, but might also lecture on *waka*, or literary court romances such as *The Ise Stories* (*Ise monogatari,* ca. 950) or *The Tale of Genji* (*Genji monogatari*, ca. 1008). They, and itinerant Noh troupes, could also provide instruction in the important practice of *utai*, or the amateur chanting of Noh libretti. Such libretti themselves had an intimate connection to *renga*, as they were a tissue of citations from Japanese – and sometimes even Chinese – poetry, joined together by some of the same techniques of verbal and metaphorical association that provided the basis of *renga*.

Sakomura has also noted the "dramatic increase in the production" of collections of poetry in which the poems were classified by thematic categories (*ruidaishū*) in the mid-Muromachi and early Edo periods – the precise time that sees the emergence of *ōgi no sōshi*.[2] These anthologies collected poems from a wide range of canonical sources and then listed them under poetic topics (*dai*), such as "heaven (*ten*), mountain (*yama*), water (*mizu*), love (*koi*), and insects (*mushi*)" (ibid.). One of the largest of such collections was the *Fuboku waka shō* (夫木和歌抄 *The Japanese Collection*[3]), from the late Kamakura period, which contains 17,350 poems arranged in 596 categories.[4] Many of the poems in the Prague version also appear in the *Fuboku waka shō*.

It is difficult, however, to imagine itinerant *renga*-masters touring the country with such large compendia, or the complete collection of the twenty-one imperially-commissioned anthologies (*chokusenshū*), under their arms. No doubt they had many of these verses committed to memory, and no doubt they learned many of the poems from sources other than the *ruidaishū*. And of course, several of the poems included in *ōgi no sōshi* can be found in a variety of places: some poems from *The Ise Stories* also appear in the first imperially-commissioned *Kokinshū*, for example. The research of Yasuhara Makoto has shown the sometimes bewildering range of sources to which *ōgi no sōshi* poems can be traced.[5] But at least in regards to the Prague version, a surprising percentage of its poems can also be found quoted in Noh libretti. This gives a whole new, aural, aspect to the appreciation of the *ōgi no sōshi* genre, and one can imagine the viewer of this work breaking out into "song" on encountering particular poems. This might range from the near complete and straight-forward quotation of a verse, such as Poem 40, in the play *Kazuraki* (the quoted poem is in italics):

> Kaheru sugata ya *yamabito no*
> *Kasa mo takigi mo uzumorete*
> *Yuki koso kudare tani no michi wo*
> Tadori tadori kaheri-kite
>
> *The mountain dweller homeward treads on her way,*
> *Her hat and brushwood all covered white with*
> *Snow that is falling thick down the steep valley path;*
> Struggling along, they make their way toward her home.[6]

to the poems being more intricately woven into the brocade of the libretto, as in Poem 86 and *Miwa* (here in italics in the transcription and quotation marks in the translation):

> SHITE: yama-moto chikaki tokoro nari
> sono uhe *waga ihori ha*
> *miha no yama-moto kohishiku ha* to ha yomitaredomo
> nani shi ni ware wo ba toburahi-tamafu-beki
> naho mo fushin ni oboshi-mesaba
> toburahi-kimase
> JI: *sugi tateru kado* wo shirushi nite
> *tadzune-tamehe*
>
> SHITE: My house is in the village of Miwa, close to the foot of the mountain – just as the verse says, "my cottage snuggles against the foot of the mountain, if you long to see me, do come", and should you have doubts about the whereabouts, ask for
>
> CHORUS: this sign, "cedars standing at the gate".
> Please do come and visit.[7]

We have here, then, the most complete pedagogical package possible: the young student would learn these poems by reading them written and associating them with the images depicted in the fans, and for many of the verses he could chant them, seeing them imbedded in a dramatic context. Indeed, if he was being taught to be an amateur performer of Noh, then he might also know the "dance-steps" for these particular passages (Fig. 14). He had, in other words, verbal, visual, auditory and kinetic associations for many of these verses.

The Organization of the Prague Version

As stated earlier, the organization of each extant *Ōgi no sōshi* is unique, and to my knowledge no scholar has attempted to examine the structure or organization of any of these works. One might well imagine that the order of the poems included in these works was random or arbitrary. The Prague version, however, makes very clear at its beginning that thought has gone into the ordering of the poems as the very first three of the poems are all about the Japanese floor-harp (*koto*, often translated as "zither"), and all three fans have pictures of *koto* painted on them. This would suggest that the ensemble of three poems and fans on each page are supposed to be seen as having some basis of association.

Fig. 14. Anonymous painter of the 18th century: **The spirit of poetess Izumi Shikibu dancing in front of monks at the Tōhoku-in Temple**, a scene from the Noh play *Tōboku*, a sheet from an album featuring Noh and Bugaku dances (*Bugaku gachō*), ink and colors on thin paper, 27 x 38 cm, 18th century.
(Photo credit: National Gallery, Prague, Vm 2981)
This file of Noh designs is a carefully drawn and richly colored copy of an earlier scroll. It bears numbers and German notes inscribed straight onto the 22 sheets of thin, translucent paper, which has been cut to sections and pasted on cardboard.

Of course, "linking" in *renga* is actually more about the discontinuities between verses (*ku*), and no *renga* sequence would ever feature three verses on an identical topic.[8] However, the category of *mono-zuke* ("linking by things [or names]") is a recognized one.[9] The use of such techniques for pedagogic purposes that would not be found in regular poetic practice can also be seen in the *Forty-Two Debates Among Things* (*Shijūni no mono-arasoi*)[10] that produces thirty-one syllable poems of a rather un-*waka*-like nature[11] (Fig. 15).

Links from the last poem on the bottom of one page to the first poem on the top are evident, as in the case of Poems 42-43, linked by the repetition of the word *onodzukara*. Accordingly, even in the subsequent less-obvious pages of the Prague version, it appears that each page of three poems is to be seen as presenting inter-related verses. The sequence of Poems 10-11-12 (on sheet 2B) is one clear example, as all deal with seeming contradictions: blue flowers emerge from iron-dark earth (Poem 10); although the snail too has "horns," he is no match for a calf (Poem 11); and although cherry-blossoms are among the lightest of things, they weigh down the mountain-man with his bundle of brushwood (Poem 12). The sequence of Poems 52-53-54 seems to be centered around the concept of shelter: the lack of it in Poem 52, the cage of Poem 53, and the eaves of Poem 54. Likewise the sequence of Poems 43-44-45 on sheet 8A seems linked by a dual combination of grammar and logic: Poem 43 creates a dyad of the moon and the water (*midzu mo omohazu / tsuki no tadzunezu*, "the water does not think it; the moon does not ask for it") and Poem 44 insists that what can be done inside Paradise can be done outside as well, while Poem 45 is about how the very names of plants change depending on geography.

Fig. 15. **Tosa Mitsunobu** (1434–1525) (?): **Detail from a scroll illustrating Forty-two Debates among Things** (*Shijūni no mono arasoi*), horizontal handscroll *emaki* combining painting and calligraphy, 15.8 x 1166.5 cm, seals: Tosa, Kikusui, copy from the late16th century.
(Photo credit: the British Museum, inv.no. 1960,0409,0.3)

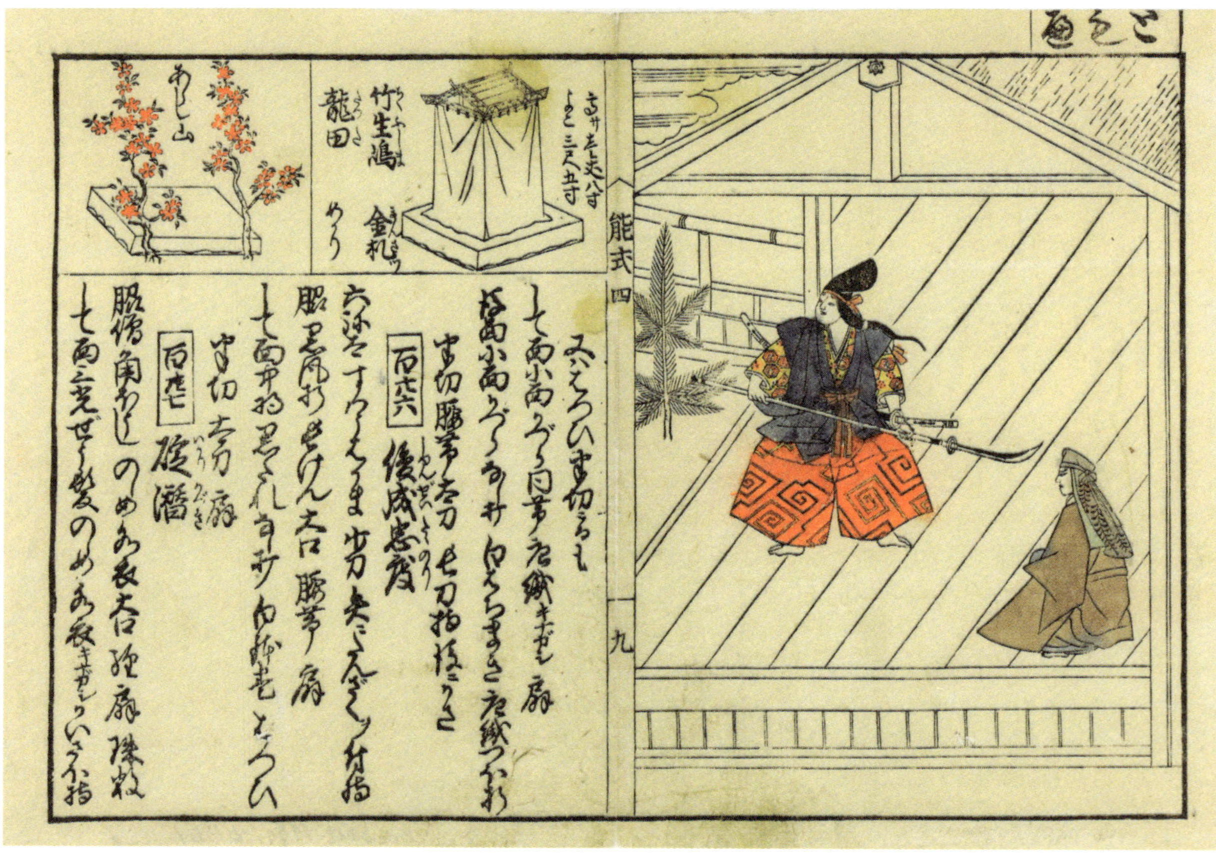

Fig. 16. Anonymous graphic artist of the 17th century: **Noh play Tomoe**, illustration of a fragmentary book, labelled on the edge as Diagrams from the Noh Plays (*Nō no zushiki*), 4th volume, 6 double-pages, black and white woodcut, hand-coloured, 21 x 15 cm, not dated (17th century).
(Photo credit: National Gallery, Prague, Vm 3813)
Tomoe Gozen (1157?–1247) was a female warrior (onna bugeisha) well-known from the Heike monogatari *war chronicle as a loyal and brave companion of her lord and lover, Minamoto no Yoshinaka. She has been often depicted in Japanese art as a beauty riding a horse in full armour. The stage props of Noh plays are drawn in the upper part of the illustrated compendium of Noh plays printed in the 17th century.*

Fig. 17. Anonymous Kanō School painter of the late 17th century: **Detail from from an *otogi-zōshi* tale hand-scroll entitled *Ibuki Dōji emaki*,** showing a group of kidnapped court ladies in the palace of a monster named Shuten Dōji or Ibuki Dōji on the Ōe (or Ibuki) Mountain near Kyōto. 2nd image of the second scroll of three, ink, colors and gold on paper, 31.2 x 834.7 cm, late 17th century.
(Photo credit: The British Museum 1881,1210,0.270 l.)
The Yamato-e stylization of figures was at first adopted by both the Kanō and Tosa Schools during the 16th century, so that, i.e., Kanō Motonobu (1476–1559) was the author of the Yamato-e style model version of Shuten Dōji emaki, *copied many times in later years, even though it was the Tosa School which officially carried over the Yamato-e tradition into the 17th century.*

Linking seems possible both through the repetition of words and similarity of situation. So, for example, in the sequence of Poems 67-68-69, the first two poems seem linked through the repetition in the phrases *ko no ma yori* ("from between the trees") and *ko no shita-kage* ("the shade beneath the trees"), while the connection between Poems 68 and 69 would seem to be that they both concern a traveler.

Often the link between two of the poems is quite obvious – and reinforced by the pictures – and it is the association of the third that is more challenging. So, for example, in the sequence of Poems 79-80-81, the fans for the first two poems both depict a full moon. The poem on the cedar rafts of the Ōi River seems unconnected to either of the earlier two, but perhaps there is an association between the woman "inviting" the moon with her plectrum, and the narrator of the third poem hearing the river-boat men shout "Hey!"

Sometimes understanding the link requires knowledge beyond the poems themselves. For example, in the sequence of Poems 64-65-66, the first two poems are connected by the "cries" of the frogs in the first with the "crying" of the rooster in the second. The link between the second and third poems is that both are drawn from the literary court romance *The Ise Stories* (*Ise monogatari*, ca. 950). In the sequence of Poems 91-92-93, the first poem is a famous one attributed to Hitomaro, with its distinctive phrase *shima-gakure-yuku* ("going and becoming island-hidden"):

hono-bono to	Faintly, faintly
akashi no ura no	through the morning mist
asa-giri ni	in the bay of Akashi,
shima-gakure yuku	my thoughts follow the boat
fune wo shi zo omofu	that becomes island-hidden.

Fig. 18. Painting by **Tosa Mitsunori** (1583–1638), calligraphy by **Konoe Nobuhiro** (1599–1649): **The poetess Nakatsukasa**, one album sheet of The Thirty-six Poetic Immortals (*Sanjūrokkasen*), ink, color pigments and gold flakes (*sunago*) on silk, 31.1 x 22.2 cm, copied around 1800.
(Photo credit: The British Museum, inv. no. 1881,1210,0.370)
The poem about the autumn wind is translated in the caption to another portrait of the court lady Nakatsukasa for Fig. 37.

Poem 92 seems to be a straight-forward love poem, and the fan-painting in fact shows a couple in bed, thus linking it to the poem of parting by Hitomaro. However, in the *Butsukoku Zenshi shū* (*The Collected Poems of the Zen-master Butsukoku*), in which this poem also appears, its headnote states that the topic of the poem is "on the meaning of *samsara*". This then makes the logical link to the final verse, Poem 93, which conveys the monk Saigyō's desire to pass away on the same day as the historical Buddha. The sentiment here is similar to that in the sequence of Poems 82-83-84: in the first, the exiled Emperor Sutoku laments that while the plovers can return to the capital, he must remain alone; in Poem 83, the wind passes by and ignores the enticing *kudzu* and pampas. This can clearly be taken as a metaphor for a monk resisting the enticements of the flesh in favor of religious progress. This moralistic interpretation is confirmed by Poem 84, a variant of a poem by Dōgen, which likens the ephemerality of life to moonlight reflected in a drop of water falling from the beak of a water-bird.

But it would appear that the third poem of the set can also be linked to the first verse, rather than the second. In the sequence of Poems 85-86-87, the first is about mandarin ducks entering the icy water and having a fitful sleep (*uki-ne*). The cause of such fitful sleep was usually thought to be the absence of a beloved, and Poem 86 is a famous love poem. Poem 87 is also a love-poem, but its "carp swimming upstream" obviously echo the mandarin ducks of Poem 85. Likewise in the following sequence, the first two poems are linked by the wind blowing through the banana-leaves in the first and through the pampas grasses in the second. While this second poem could be interpreted as a love-poem, it is not explicitly one, and so the inclusion of Poem 90, about "someone from long ago," seems most related to the "loneliness" of Poem 88.

In conclusion, then, we see how the *ōgi no sōshi* genre helped the young poet familiarize himself with the topics of Japanese poetry and their codified usage without the strict rules of *renga*. Along with many canonical verses are a variety of humorous or very un-courtly poems, which would have kept a young man's attention. As suggested, *Ōgi no sōshi*, and especially the Prague version, was a well-nigh complete poetic education and important introduction to the worlds of *waka*, *renga*, and Noh.

(Endnotes)

1 Tomoko Sakomura, *Pictured Words and Codified Seasons: Visualizations of Waka Poetry in Late Sixteenth- and Early Seventeenth-Century Japan* (unpublished Ph.D. dissertation, Columbia University, 2007), pp. 108–109, citing Makino Kazuo, "Nanto ni okeru 'ōgi (e) no sōshi' nado", *Kokubungaku* 41, no. 4 (1996): 130–137.

2 Sakomura, p. 39.

3 The characters "fuboku" 夫木 are derived for a Chinese name for Japan, Fusō 扶桑. Earl Miner, Hiroko Odagiri, and Robert E. Morrell, eds., *The Princeton Companion to Classical Japanese Literature* (Princeton UP, 1985), s.v. "*Fuboku (Waka) Shō*".

4 Sakomura, pp. 39–40.

5 Yasuhara Makoto, "*Ōgi no sōshi*" *no kenkyū: asobi no geibun* (Tōkyō: Perikan-sha, 2003).

6 Chifumi Shimazaki, trans., *Restless Spirits from Japanese Noh Plays of the Fourth Group* (Ithaca: Cornell East Asia Series, 1994), pp. 92–93.

7 "Miwa," trans. Monika Bethe, in Karen Brazell, ed., *Twelve Plays of the Noh and Kyōgen Theaters* (Ithaca: Cornell University East Asia Papers, no. 50), p. 29.

8 For a concise introduction to *renga*, see Esperanza Ramirez-Christensen's review of Earl Miner's *Japanese Linked Poetry* (1979), "The Essential Parameters of Linked Poetry", *Harvard Journal of Asiatic Studies*, vol. 41, no. 2 (Dec. 1981), pp. 555–595.

9 For its use in the structure of a variant form of *Ise monogatari*, see Katagiri Yōichi, "Ihon Ise monogatari emaki ni tsuite", *Kokugo kokubun*, no. 299 (1959), pp. 39–42.

10 An extant small scroll example in the British Museum from the late 16th century is described in detail on the BM website under 1960,0409,0.3, AN478158. It uses the translation *Poetry contest on forty-two themes, or A Poetry Contest of Forty-two Matches*. The BM text quotes all the 42 pairs of compared objects.

11 For a discussion of the *Forty-Two Debates* genre, see Sakomura, *Pictured Words*, pp. 179–272.

Fig. 19. **Ogata Kōrin** (1658–1716): **A fan with a motif of a flying goose**, a fan-painting (*senmenga*), ink and colors on paper, 26.5 x 60.5 cm, mounted as a hanging scroll in grass-green silk, seal Inryō (one of Kōrin's pseudonyms), ca. 1700. (Photo credit: Arcimboldo Gallery, Prague)

COMMENTS ON THE ILLUSTRATIONS

Helena Honcoopová

Japanese painting uses the same utensils as calligraphy (brush, ink and paper)[1] and for this reason it has always been close to the world of letters, that is, literature. As early as the ancient Heian period (794–1185), Japanese poetry was illustrated by so-called poem-pictures (*uta-e* 歌絵). The tight connection between literature and painting is obvious in many early works of art, which also contain lines of verse. Due to the established repertory of poetic motifs connected with pictorial symbols, *uta-e* or poem-pictures were able to allude very subtly to famous poems. Thus, for instance, the full moon image from the next page (Fig. 20) points quite directly to a well-known poem by Minamoto no Michikata (1189–1238) (*Shoku Kokin waka shū,* 425) even though it contains no calligraphic inscription (as translated in the Museum caption):

musashino ha	On Musashi Plain
tsuki no irubeki	there is no peak
mine mo nashi	for the moon to enter–
wobana ga suwe ni	white clouds catch
kakaru shira-kumo	on the tips of the pampas fronds.

The same painting may allude also to a variation (*honkadori*) on the old poem by an anonymous poet which is included in the Prague *Book of Fans* (no. 77):

musashino ha	There are no mountains
tsuki no idzubeki	from which the moon can rise
yama mo nashi	on Musashi Plain–
kusa yori idete	it rises from the grasses and
kusa ni koso ire	into the grasses, indeed, it sets.

In the hedonistic surroundings of the court nobility where every single human was very familiar with the poems of the past, pictures alone could easily evoke certain poems. This connotative potential was used in *uta-e* as well as in *ōgi-e* contests.

Numerous examples of poem-pictures that illustrate this volume have been drawn from various resources worldwide. Nevertheless, the commentary focuses on two sets of four hundred years old and still unpublished[2] full-scale images that represent the oldest strata of Japanese secular paintings in Czech collections. The naive pictures of seated poets in ancient court attire, whose murky faces look at us from the figures 37–42 (plus the frontispiece) represent six poets of the renowned suite of *Thirty-six Poetic Immortals* (*Sanjūrokkasen* 三十六歌 仙).[3] This assembly of poets has been a major topic of Japanese figural art in numerous depictions, imitations, copies, variations and parodies ever since their first selection in the early 11th century. The six illustrations of seated poets (*kasen-e*) have many aspects in common with the illustrations of Prague version of *Ōgi no sōshi* (*ōgi-e*). They date from about the same period (late Muromachi to early Edo) – most probably from the Momoyama period (1568–1615). Yet, the poets' pictures may date slightly prior to the pictures of the fans, to about 1560–90.[4] Both are painted on the same type of on handmade "Japanese paper" (*washi* 和紙) with the same set of painting utensils (*enogu* 絵の具). Both painters used the yellowish, skin-like type of paper made of the *gampi* plant (*gampishi* 雁皮紙),[5] ink, thick natural opaque color pigments and white powdered shell paste (*gofun* 胡粉). Moreover, the six sheets from the *Sanjūrokkasen* set have details painted in liquid gold (*kindei* 金泥) and are executed in an unusually large size (51.8 x 36.8 cm). Remarkable calligraphy of the *waka* poems by a single hand of an unknown calligrapher joins both the *ōgi-e* and *kasen-e*. The poems are not written in the proper verse order, but the lines are "scattered" (*chirashi-gaki* 散らし書き) so as to encode the poem as a puzzle. Both the fan-pictures and the seated poet-pictures represent the same style of "Japanese painting" (*Yamato-e* 大和絵,). The following comments will therefore focus on the rare Prague versions of the fan pictures *ōgi-e* and the poet-portraits *kasen-e* and their position within Japanese artistic context.

I. Yamato-e

The domestic style of painting, *Yamato-e*, originated in the Chinese painting of the Tang dynasty (618–906) (*Kara-e* or *Kanga* 唐絵、漢画) but changed remarkably due to assimilation to the strong local tradition in the Yamato land (the ancient name of Japan) during the Heian period. *Yamato-e* depicted the life of the Japanese aristocracy in Kyōto palaces, gardens, monasteries, during their rituals, festivities, games, pilgrimages and journeys. It showed the courtiers in their natural surroundings as small figures seen from a high perspective, or a bird's-eye view (*chōkan zuhō* 鳥瞰図法)[6], so that we "read" the pictorial space usually from the right upper corner downwards and towards the left (which was the natural direction for reading the Japanese texts). The interior of palaces were from shown as if through a "blown-off roof" (*fukinuki-yatai* 吹抜屋台), or "withdrawn roof" (*hikinuki-yatai* 引き抜き屋台), and the figures were seen seated or standing beside walls, blinds and screens of the buildings that were drawn in straight lines without any sign of perspectival convergence (Fig. 23). Japanese art preferred eccentric, asymmetrical compositions along a diagonal axis. The surrounding elements (gardens, ponds, streams, or mountain landscapes in the background) were added into the shallow pictorial space in the manner of theatrical sets (Fig. 15). The edges of the composition or empty space were often obscured by horizontal streams of trailing clouds (*suyari* すやり) or misty clouds (*suyari gasumi* すやり霞). The clouds eliminated unimportant details and divided the space into individual scenes. These clouds were seldom white and especially in the later development within the imperial Tosa School paintings they were often painted in a low, ornamental relief with *gofun* paste and gilt on top of the relief (*moriage* 盛上げ). Horizontal clouds represent another typical feature of *Yamato-e* painting (Figs. 12, 13, 15, 17).

The robes of the courtiers were the focus of each painting, their outline being drawn in angular lines, with bodies and limbs covered by layers of luxurious colorful textiles (silk, brocades, embroideries), showing only the hands with a courtly attribute (of a fan or a scroll or an official baton), crowned by an oval head with a high black-lacquered hat (*eboshi* 烏帽子) in the case of courtiers or with long flowing black hair in the case of court ladies. The faces of the courtiers, to the contrary of the detailed robes, were rendered rather simply – an oval face in semi-profile was marked by high painted eyebrows (the mark of high standing), two lines for the slanting eyes and a hook for the nose (*hikime kagihana* 引き目鉤鼻), completed with tiny bud-lips. Because the hair and the robes were more important than the face, the habit of showing sitting or standing ladies from behind or partly hidden behind a screen, evolved quite early and stayed with Japanese art until today as a typical feature of the *Yamato-e* style[7] (Figs. 18, 21, 22).

Yamato-e used a thin and even, firm, flexible and flowing ink outline[8] filled in with flat layers of thick, opaque color pigments – a technique that was called "built-up paintings" (*tsukuri-e* 作り絵). The pigments made of plants and minerals mixed with animal glue (*nikawa* 膠) used a basic palette of greens, blues, ochre and red. Faces were painted with white paste (*gofun* 胡粉) made of minced shell and oyster powder. The robes and fabrics were filled in with rich color layers and decorated with black ink ornamentation drawn in minute details. On deluxe paintings, the final finish – the ornamentation of the robes – was often made of finely cut-out leaves of thin gold plate (*kirigane moyō* 切金摸様). Contrarily, when the *Yamato-e* style was

Fig. 20. Anonymous painter of the 17th century: **Folding screen with a full moon on Musashi Plain** (Musashino byōbu), ink, gold, silver and colors on gilt paper, 152.6 x 355.6 cm, 17th century. (Photo credit: Metropolitan Museum of Art, New York, inv. no. 67.235)

Fig. 21. Anonymous 15th century painter: **Poetry Contest on *The Tale of Genji*** (*Genji monogatari uta-awase emaki*), detail no. 14 of a *kansubon* scroll, ink and colors on paper, height 18.4 cm, dated 1487, Muromachi period. (Photo credit: National Institute of Japanese Literature, nijl 99–121)
This poetry contest was linked to the 54 chapters of The Tale of Genji *and the scroll belongs among the so-called "small paintings" (ko-e 小絵) of the Muromachi period based on earlier Kamakura paintings.*

used for making popular narratives of the *otogi-zōshi* type, the cheapest "clay pigments" (doro enogu 泥絵の具) were used instead of the durable "mineral pigments" (iwa enogu 岩絵の具). During the Kamakura period, narrative *emakimono* on religious, legendary or even humorous subjects were often painted in black and white outline (*hakubyō-e* 白描絵), sometimes colored only sparingly with subdued colors (Fig. 32).

The colorful *Yamato-e* style was used then for illustrating secular literature – such as poems (*uta-e* 歌絵) or tales (*monogatari-e* 物語絵) – written in Japanese. Specifically, Japanese literature up to the 15th century was written and illustrated in handscrolls (*makimono* 絵巻物、*kansubon* 巻子本). There is written evidence that sliding walls (*shōji* 障子) and folding screens (*byōbu* 屏風) of Kyōto palaces were decorated with beautiful landscapes of the famous places of Japan (*meisho*-e 名所絵), or with pictures showing the passage of seasons (*shiki-e* 四季絵), or sets of paintings following annual festivities of nobility "in the order of months" (*tsukinami-e* 月並み絵). Yet none of the large mural paintings with secular motifs from ancient periods survive, simply because the wooden palaces could not endure for a millennium. Therefore, the common forms of early paintings in the *Yamato-e* style today are illustrated picture scrolls *emaki* (*or emakimono* 絵巻物) and fan pictures (*ōgi-e* 扇絵).

The court aristocracy perpetuated the old rituals by both practicing and patronizing the courtly arts of Japanese-style poetry and Japanese-style calligraphy, both of which are inextricably linked with *Yamato-e.* The imperial Bureau of Painting (*edokoro* 絵所) was located at the palace from the 9th century onward. Its painting production, however, was limited to the imperial family. The wider nobility relied on monastic workshops. Ever since the Nara period (710–894), monastic sculpture and painting workshops had been in Nara (with the center in Kōfukuji temple 興福寺), specializing in making sutras, mandalas and Buddhist icons. From the late Heian period on, these workshops, called "painting studios of the southern capital" (*nanto edokoro* 南都絵所), had been organized into guilds, as the suffix – *za* 座 was added to the workshops names.[9] Though these workshops were chiefly busy with creating religious objects, secular paintings in the *Yamato-e* style were also produced there as side-products during the Kamakura and Muromachi periods (Fig. 23). For this reason, scrolls with illustrated secular stories were called "picture-scrolls from Nara" (*Nara-emaki* 奈良絵巻). Starting from the late Muromachi period, illustrated popular stories of

Fig. 22. Anonymous painter of the 17th century: **Princess Kishi** (Saigū nyōgo, 949–986), ink and colors on paper, 23.2 x 19.9 cm, mounted 119 x 38.5 cm, 17th century. (Photo credit: Masaki Art Museum, Ōsaka)

The finely inscribed poem from the Shūishū *collection (VIII. no. 451) is also included in the Prague version of Ōgi no sōshi as no. 2. (Translation by J. Mostow).*

ことのねに
みねのまつかぜ
かよふらし
いずれのをより
しらへそめけむ

koto no ne ni
mine no matsukaze
kayofurashi
idzure no o yori
shirabe-someken

The wind through the pines
on the peak closely resembles
the sound of the zither-
from which slope or string
does it begin to play?

the "book-companion" type (*otogi-zōshi* 御伽草子), bound in book form (*sasshibon* 冊子本) were labelled as "picture-books from Nara" (*Nara-ehon* 奈良絵本) (Figs. 12, 24). The *Nara-ehon* provided easy reading for women and thus were often labelled as "trousseau books" (*yomeiri-bon* 嫁入り本). The themes of *Nara-ehon* comprised, for instance, fairy tales (*Urashima Tarō, Issun Bōshi*), religious biographies (*Kannon no honji, Amida no honji*), histories (*Sakura no Chūjō, Tomonaga*), legends (*Tanabata*) or fantastic stories (*Tsuchigumo, Tengū no dairi*). There were also books dealing with poetry, such as *Ōgi no sōshi*, the already mentioned *Forty-two Debates among Things* (*Shijūni mono arasoi*) (Fig. 15), or the *Story of a Contest of Fans* (*Ōgi-awase monogatari*, aka *Kachō Fūgetsu*). The last title gives us a chance to see the context of *ōgi-awase*, as it tells a story about a competition between fans illustrated with the figure of a courtier. The competing parties dispute whether the handsome man is Ariwara no Narihira (the hero of *Ise monogatari*) or Hikaru Genji (the hero of *Genji monogatari*) and two lovely shamanesses, Kachō and Fūgetsu, solve the puzzle by proving it is Genji.[10]

In the flow of secularization of painting in the late Muromachi (1336–1567) and Momoyama (1568–1615) periods, a variety of popular pictures were painted also for inferior social strata, lower nobility and rich townsmen (*machishū* 町衆), often on folding screens or on fans. New painting workshops (*eya* 絵屋) or fan shops (*ōgiya* 扇屋), that catered to a rising urban clientele, were established in Heian-kyō (Kyōto), in Naniwa (Ōsaka), in the port of Sakai, and other large towns. These urban painting studios mushroomed

Fig. 23. **Tosa Mitsunobu** (1434–1525): **The History of Seikōji Temple** (*Seikōji engi emaki*), scroll 2, a pair of scrolls with Yamato-e illustrations, ink and colors on paper, height 33 cm, dated 1487.
(Photo credit: Tōkyō National Museum, C0009541)
Legends and histories of temples and shrines from the mediaeval period evolved into the Nara-ehon *of the early modern times. This led to perpetuating the classical Yamato-e style of painting. The detail depicts a genre-scene from town-folk domestic life with servants cooking in the inner rooms. The painters of the imperial Tosa School developed the Yamato-e style to illustrate not only the classical literature but also contemporary tales and narratives in the form of scrolls* (emakimono) *and "companion books"* (otogi-zōshi).

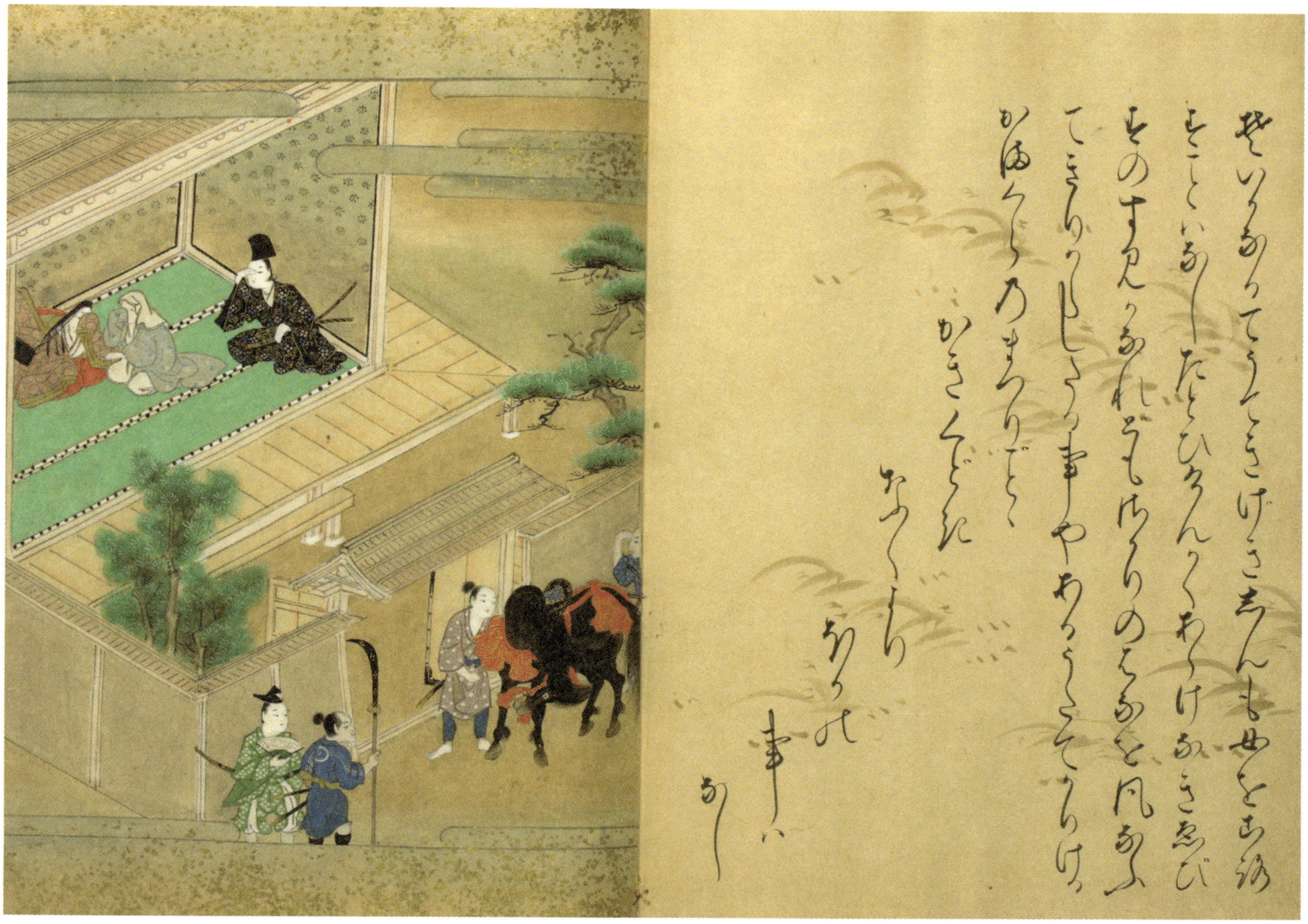

Fig. 24. Anonymous painter of the 16th century: **A double-page from a *Nara-ehon Shizuka, otogi-zōshi***, first volume of two, last double-page no. 26, 32 x 21 cm, Muromachi period.
(Photo credit: National Institute of Japanese Literature, nijl 99-32-1,2)
The popular tale narrates the very moving story of the shirabyōshi *dancer Shizuka Gozen, the favorite lover of Minamoto no Yoshitsune, who left her with her children in the Yoshino mountains when escaping the wrath of his brother, the first Minamoto shogun, Yoritomo. Shizuka was kept captive and imprisoned in Kamakura and because she refused the proposals of Yoritomo, he killed her new-born baby. The picture shows the brave woman weeping sadly in Kamakura.*

from the time of the resurrection of the war-ruined country in the late 16th century. The new "town painters" (*machi-eshi*), who were either recruited from former monastic studios or started their work without much training, created simple cheap paintings on loose sheets of paper (*ichimai-e* 一枚絵), in a card form (*shikishi* 色紙) or on fan-shaped papers (*ōgi-e*). It was not until the mid 16th century that genre scenes first appeared, capturing various amusements of the townsmen in the form of screens. The large folding screens with "luxurious pictures" (*yūraku-zu* 遊楽図) depict both ancient architectural jewels and bustling daily life in the capital city of Kyōto. During the Momoyama and early Edo periods *Scenes from Inside and Outside the Capital* (*Rakuchū rakugai-zu* 洛中洛外図) became popular, marking the birth of genre painting, called "the pictures of manners" (*fūzoku-ga* 風俗画). The wide panorama townscape on a pair of six-fold screens depicting the familiar mountains, rivers, bridges, temples, palaces and avenues of Kyōto, is divided by golden horizontal clouds. We can observe crowded streets overflowing with colorfully dressed tiny figures of townsmen of all walks of life. On one of the pairs of screens (Funaki version) from the Tōkyō National Museum we can trace a small fan shop with the inscription *ōgi-ya* on the entry curtain (Fig. 25).

II. Ōgi-e

Folding fans *ōgi* 扇 (or *sensu* 扇子) were a Japanese invention of the 7th century. The Chinese used compact, flat, oval or circular leaf fans (called *uchiwa* 団扇 in Japanese). *Ōgi* are made of ten to twenty thin, flat wooden pieces of cypress (or a bamboo rib construction) covered by stiff paper or silk, that can be easily folded. They are most often decorated with so-called "fan paintings" (*senmenga* 扇面画) or with calligraphy, often in one's own hand (*jihitsu* 自筆). Fans underwent a long development from a simple, large and clumsy *hi-ōgi* 桧扇 painted all over the wooden ribs to a wide *kawahori* 蝙 蝠 resembling the wings of a flying bat[11] before they developed into the elegant wide shape with many ribs. Besides the practical function (fanning was indispensable during the hot and humid summer season), fans acquired important and multiple cultural and ceremonial functions. During the Heian period, fans were used as a part of court ceremonial dress both by males and females. They became the medium of such courtly amusements as comparing fans (*ōgi-awase* 扇合わせ) or floating fans on the water (*ōgi-nagashi* 扇流し).[12] *Ōgi* acquired symbolic functions both in Noh and later also in Kabuki theatre where they were used chiefly for dancing, or in lieu of various stage properties. Fans were used for cooling, as well as fashion accessories, for playing games, for dancing, and even for fighting. To hit a foe with a fan was a cardinal offence in the Edo Kabuki tradition. Attacking an enemy with a fan was one grade less offensive than using a straw or a wooden sandal, less fatal, however, than using a sword.

The popularity of fans reached its peak during the Momoyama and early Edo periods when folding screens depicting fans floating on waves or fans embroidered on kimono in the "*Whose Sleeves?*" (*Tagasode* 誰が袖) type of puzzle-paintings embellished many households (Fig. 26). They were painted by professional painters of the Kanō School but also by town painters (*machi-eshi* 街絵 師). Production of *ōgi* was a typical female craft (Fig. 29), while painting was mostly executed by male painters. Well painted *ōgi* would be dismounted and stored or re-mounted as a hanging scroll. Because folding screens were used in every household, people used to embellish them with fan-shaped pictures (*senmenga*). Folding screens decorated with a colorful fan assortment on a golden background became a new feature in the 17th century, thanks to the exquisite decorative talents of Sōtatsu. Tawaraya Sōtatsu (俵屋 宗達, fl. ca. 1600–1643) worked for the textile workshop Tawaraya and started painting fans there, popular as *Tawaraya ōgi*. His schooling is unknown, yet he combined traditional Yamato-e themes and techniques with the bold designs, gold and silver of the Kanō School which reached prominence in the late 16th century when serving the new warrior rulers and decorating palaces and temples of the ruined capital city in reconstruction. Sōtatsu defined shapes of his natural and figural motifs with color rather than with ink outlines and used skilfully the casual effects of *tarashikomi* (溜込) – a technique of applying color layers on a wet background. In around 1620 he received the highest painting rank of *hokkyō* (法橋)[13] and was summoned to paint walls and screens for important buildings. Sōtatsu painted several screens displaying wide-open fans as in an *ōgi awase* contest (Fig. 28). For some fifteen years, he collaborated with the famous calligrapher and swordsmith Hon'ami Kōetsu (本阿弥 光悦, 1558–1637)[14], the master of the unique Takagamine art colony where many top artisans of the time created indigenous pottery, lacquer, calligraphies and paintings under his enlightened leadership. Sōtatsu and Kōetsu collaborated in creating unique pieces of art, which combined painting and calligraphy and established a completely new stream of Japanese decorative painting, much later labelled as the Rimpa School[15] (Fig. 8). The school was named after the genius artist Ogata Kōrin (尾形光琳, 1658–1716) who would paint fans as well as the Thirty-six Poetic Immortals among other creative works in large screen and textile painting. He brought the tradition founded by Sōtatsu and Kōetsu to mastery (Figs. 9, 19).

In the 18th century, painted fans acquired their sober black and white look in the hands of literati painters who preferred to embellish fans with ink painted pines, bamboos, plums, orchids, birds, etc. and, especially, with beautifully calligraphed letters (Fig. 64). The popularity of fans in the Edo period flourished anew with the quick development of cheap woodblock printing techniques. Printed fans with beauties, actors, or Kabuki scenes became commonplace during the Edo period. In modern times since the Meiji period, fans became a major export article to Europe. They also served as a most welcome present, which

Fig. 25. Attributed to Iwasa Matabei (1578–1650): **Ōgiya – a fan shop in a Kyōto street.** A detail from the left part of the Funaki version of a pair of six-panel-screens showing *Scenes from Inside and Outside of the Capital* (Kyōto) (*Rakuchū rakugai zu-Funaki*), ink, colors and gold on paper, 162.7 x 342.4 cm, 1615–1617.
(Photo credit: Tōkyō National Museum, C0008731)
These screens provide rich, reliable and exact visual material on the architecture, life and customs in Kyōto in early modern times. According to a recent research carried by Japanese scholars for the large exhibition of Rakuchū rakugai-zu *at Tōkyō National Museum in 2013 and at Kyōto City Museum in 2015, this small fan shop is located near the crossing of Gojō and Higashi no Tōin-dōri, where we can still find several ōgi-ya today.*

Fig. 26. Anonymous painter of the late 16th century: **Whose Sleeves?** (*Tagasode*), six-panel screen (one of a pair), ink, colors and gold on paper, 144.9 x 346.8 cm, late 16th century.
(Photo credit: Metropolitan Museum of Art, New York, inv. no. 29,100,493,494)
The kimono hanging on the lacquered rack in the upper-right corner is painted or embroidered with irregularly placed folding fans. This type of screen points to the remarkable popularity of fan design in the 16th century. The game of Tagasode (Whose Sleeves?) *was another quiz-like type of social amusement in the Momoyama and Edo periods when questions of fashion came to foreground.*

Fig. 27a., b. Anonymous painters from the early 17th century: **Two sheets from two fragmentary Books of Fans** (*Ōgi no sōshi*), ink, colors and gold on paper, 30.6 x 21.7 cm, early 17th century. (Photo credit: Private collector, Japan)
Such fragments of early ōgi no sōshi *exist in several instances, especially in Japan, but only a few Books of Fans have been maintained in their entirety.*

led to the increase of fan shop numbers, still plentiful in Japan. Fan workshops and stores are among the most popular tourist shopping destinations in Japan to this day.

Books of Fans (*Ōgi no sōshi*) were popular for several decades around the year 1600, as all the extant examples in scroll or book form date from about this time (Figs. 10, 27a, b). There is a woodblock printed version of *Ōgi no sōshi* published as late as the Kanbun era (1661–1673)[16] which means that the practice was not dead up to around the time when simple printed books written in *kana* (*kana-zōshi* 仮名草子) were slowly changing into more sophisticated secular stories (*ukiyo-zōsh*i 浮世草子) and profane literature was pushing the noble habits of the past away from the popular scene. According to recent research, the Prague version of the *Book of Fans* is the longest extant manuscript in comparison to the other fifty surviving examples of this type in various collections.[17] When brought to Prague, it was a book containing forty pages sewn into Japanese "envelope binding" (*fukuro-toji* 袋綴じ) in greyish, (now shabby) plain soft paper covers with a hand-written title slip "*An Illustrated Collection of Poems*" (*Ehon wakashū* 絵本和歌集). Now it is dismantled into twenty sheets numbered 1–20, containing double-pages with three poems and three fans on each page. It comprises 120 poems illustrated by 120 fan-shaped illustrations that probably refer to the *ōgi-awase* practice of the late 16th century, of which very little is known barring the presumption that the fan contest was modelled after the poetry contest, comparing two painted fans instead of two poems. The fans illustrated the contents of the associated lyrical poems by using a set of established visual symbols. The style of the painting of the fans was derived from *Yamato-e*, and was close to the then common *Nara-ehon* illustrations.

The early dating of the unsigned volume of the Prague version can be assessed not only from its quite simple and lively execution, but also from its size, which is much larger than books that were made in the 17th century. The Prague volume measures 31.1 x 23.6 cm[18] and this size corresponds with other books that were produced during the closing years of the 16th century, such as the *Kōetsu Sanjūrokkasen* (32.9 x 24.9 cm) from the Keichō era (1596–1615).[19] Starting from the *Kōetsu-bon* and *Saga-bon* of the early decades of the 17th century, the so-called "large book" (*ōbon* 大本) format was reduced to ca. 26 x 18 cm. In addition, the hand-painted *Nara-ehon* of the late 16th century have similar measurements of

Fig. 28. **Tawaraya Sōtatsu** (active ca. 1600-1643): **A six-panel screen with opened pictorial fans** (*Ōgi no byōbu*), ink, colors, gold and silver painted fans pasted onto golden-leaf-covered paper of a folding screen, 170.2 x 378.5 cm, early 17th century.
(Photo credit: The Freer Gallery of Art, Smithsonian Institution, Washington, D.C., Freer Collection F1900.24)
Detailed analysis of this screen with thirty opened fans is a subject of a study by Miyeko Murase (see Bibliography).

approximately 32 x 24 cm, however, the typical *Nara-ehon* of the early 17th century is usually a horizontal book of ca. 16 x 22 cm. We may therefore date the Prague volume to the final years of the 16th century or early years of the 17th century – from the Keichō (1596–1615) to the Genna era (1615–1624).[20] The earlier dating is most probable.

The repertoire of pictorial motifs inside of the three little fans (ca. 16 x 6 cm) on each page of this volume closely corresponds to the adjacent poems. As Japanese poetry has the character of subjective natural lyrics, most motifs bring together Man and Nature. The illustrations draw on various topics of the seasonal development in nature and are combined with little figures of the "subjects" – that is the poets who express their "heart" (*kokoro* 心) in finely selected "words" (*kotoba* 言葉). In forty-three pictures, we meet with courtiers, court ladies, but also monks, samurai in full armor, pilgrims with wide hats and walking staffs, mountain dwellers and even children. All figures are tiny with only schematic facial features, their identity characterized by their attire – the feature typical of *Yamato-e* painting. Mostly we see only one figure, but some pictures feature a couple (e.g., of two monks) or a group (e.g., of hunters). The fan depictions show figures in courtly surroundings open to nature. The figures are set in palaces with their "blown-off rooves" that allow us to "peep" inside the inner spaces from above, on verandahs, on bridges, in gardens with lakes and running streams, by country huts near ponds, in mountain monasteries, in front of Shintō gates (*torii*), etc. Only a few fans depict figures in an interior (such as a sleeping couple, or a love-sick woman in bed).

Over seventy fan-pictures present details of nature. Nature is expressed in symbols that correspond to the seasonal words in poetry (*kigo* 季語). Spring poetry is exemplified by blossoming plums (6x), cherries (14x) and wisteria (3x), willows (3x) and irises (2x); Summer by *tachibana* orange flowers (1x), or the wild yellow rose bush *yamabuki* (2x); Autumn by red maples (3x), reeds (9x) and chrysanthemums (1x). Winter is represented by snow (4x) and bamboo (4x). The chief symbol of autumn – the full moon – appears on the fans nine times. The most frequent motif, however, are twisted pines that keep green all year round (20x). There are also many animals depicted – stags, horses, cocks, carp, geese, pheasants, falcons, sparrows, and even a boar and a bull. Several fans show details of inanimate objects, such as the zither (*koto*), palanquin (*kago*), a bridge, a writing-brush, a fulling block, etc.

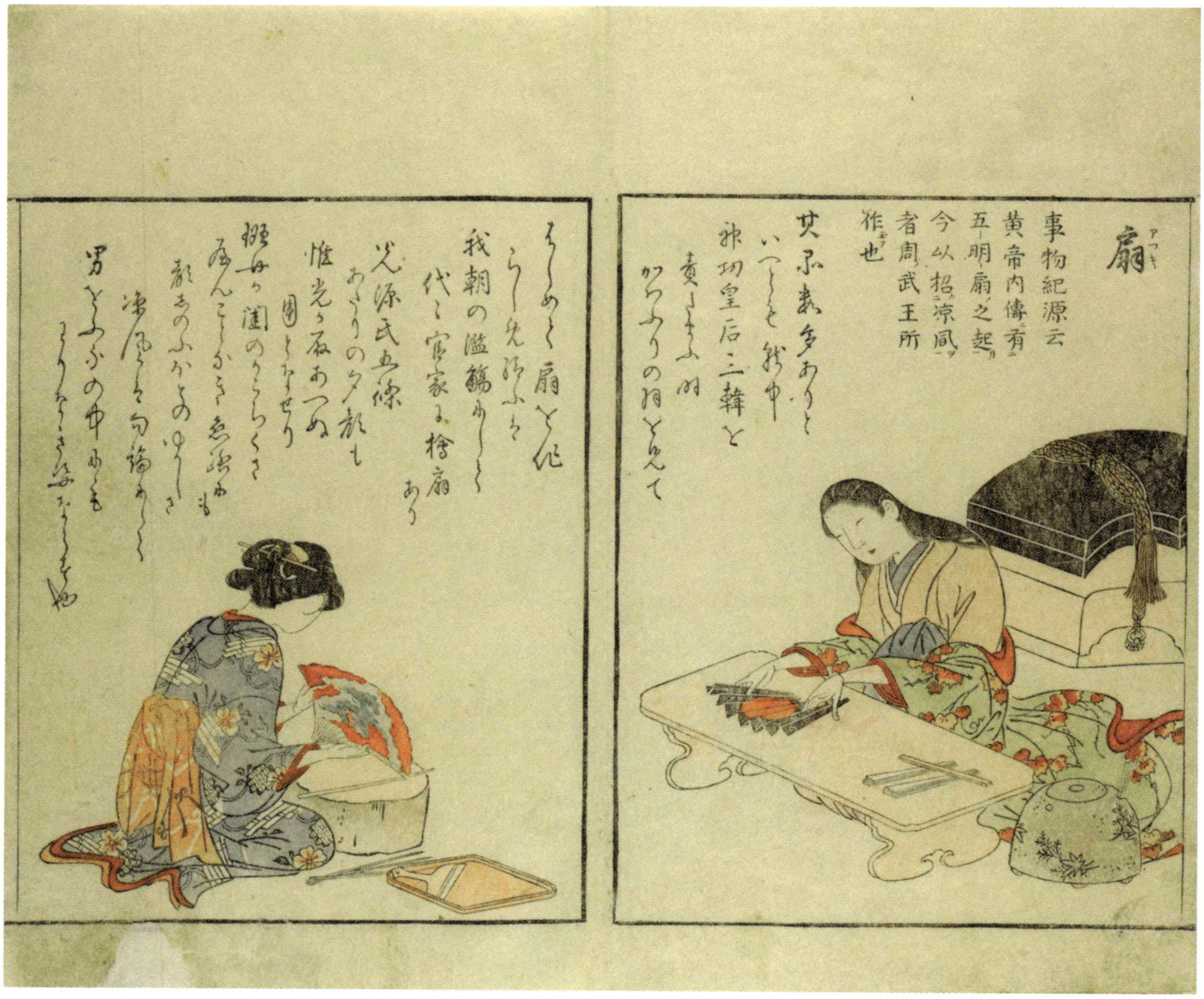

Fig. 29. **Tachibana Minkō** (active ca 1760–70): Girl artisans making fans, color woodcut illustration from the album of Classified Craftsmen in Color Illustrations (*Saiga shokunin burui* 、彩画 職人部類), one volume with 27 pp, color woodcut, painted with stencils, 27.9 x 18.5 cm, published Uemura Tōzaburō and Takatsu Isuke, Edo, 1770, second edition 1784. (Photo credit: National Gallery Prague, Vm 1291_18)
One of the earliest color-printed illustrated books (ehon) *includes fan-maker artisans represented here by townswomen.*

On many pictures there is an element of water involved (lakes, ponds, rivers, brooks, sea), so that the prevailing colors are the dark blue of water and the green of plants, with the striking red accents of flowers, autumn leaves and dresses, and the complementary *gofun* white of cherry blossoms, snow, clouds and noblemen's faces. The earth is ochre and the faces of common men and the wood of bridges and houses are painted pink. Five fans with details of nature use only monochrome ink painting, which was quite usual decoration on real fans painted only with ink (*sumi-e*). The obligatory horizontal clouds (*suyari*) of *Yamato-e* alongside the upper edges of the fans, that resemble spears (which is the literal meaning of *suyari*) rather than clouds, are drawn in reds, blues and greens instead of the usual gold.

The style of illustrations of the Prague version of *Ōgi no sōshi* perpetuates *Yamato-e* conventions in a rather mechanical, careless way, as if the fans were produced as the routine output of a small painting workshop by apprentices. The pictures are drawn quickly and rather recklessly, as if they were painted according to a model in many copies or in long series. There is no gilding used, no visible fine finishing effects (like spraying with golden or silver dust), as there is, for instance on the *Ōgi no sōshi* in Fig. 10. There is no miniature decorative final finish, no careful attention to detail that was typical of luxurious paintings, so that the painting utensils may be branded as of the cheap variety – "clay pigments" (*doro enogu*). All these aspects of the Prague version of *Ōgi no sōshi* speak for an origin in a small painting workshop rather than a monastery or a professional school studio. The technique of the painting shows that it was not made for a demanding upper class client but rather for a townsman (*chōnin*) in a town painting-studio (*eya*). Regardless of the fact that there are no golden decorations and the painting had been executed in a swift manner, the pictures in fans are very expressive, fresh, and charming.

The order of illustrations in no way follows any temporal axis (such as the changes of day and night or the passage of seasons from spring to winter), which was usual in classical poetry anthologies. On the contrary, the fans demonstrate a wild disorder of motifs both in variety and scale. This "tutti frutti" way of linking is suggestive of the intricate and subtle principles of association used in the integration of *renga* chain poetry. As in *renga*, the depictions within the *ōgi* frames move on as if taken by a film camera from large wholes (Mount Fuji, mountain monastery, sea bay, river) to closer views (hut, tree, blossoming bush, stag under a maple tree or a courtier under a cherry tree) and finally it focuses on details of varied natural or inanimate objects: strips of poetry hanging in reeds, writing utensils, the first budding grasses of the spring, a pair of mandarin ducks, etc. These abrupt changes (film cuts) of the scale of the pictures from grand panorama to close detail also show an analogy to *renga* integration with its concept of sudden shifts from distant (*so*) to close (*shin*) imagery.

There is one more important aspect of the fan illustrations that may bring a clue to the reading of the poems. On each double-page we can see six fans; three of them are mounted on ten thin ribs and three of them remain unmounted, on plain paper without ribs. The positioning of the ribbed fans within each page is quite irregular, which may suggest that the ribs may denote a poem which won in the imaginary *ōgi-awase* contest that took place between the poems presented on double-pages throughout the volume. This presumption is supported by the fact that the notorious poems by famous poets are all adjoining illustrations on fans with ribs. Ribs therefore may suggest the judgement "kachi" (victory) in an imaginary contest of a pair of poems across each double-page. The competing poems (Left and Right side) of each couple on the double-pages throughout the volume, however, are not placed at the same level on the page (upper, middle and lower poem in the vertical direction of each page). That adds to the intriguing demands on the reader of an *ōgi no sōshi* book, who has to find an associated poem among the three on the opposing page by comparing the six involved poems in a criss-cross manner, as described above on p. 110. The ribbed poems are evidently the better ones in the couples self-selected by the reader on the double-pages. There is only one exception to this rule of painting three fans with ribs and three without ribs per each double-page of the Prague version of *Ōgi no sōshi*. The double-page on pages 12B–13A displays four fans with ribs which may mean that two ribbed poems in a pair were esteemed as equal "draw" in the imaginary *uta-awase* which took place on the opposing pages. If we take a closer look at the two pages in question presenting poems 70–72 on page 12B, and 73–75 on page 13 A, we can find the following associated pairs of poems: nos. 70 and 73 talking about the necessity of selecting only one way in two, the pair 71 and 75 with the topic of "muddy waters", and the last pair of poems nos. 72 and 74 written by a monk on the topic of love. The ribbed poems indicate that Monk Saigyō (72) won in the love theme couple, the poem about lively crabs (75) won the contest between the "muddy waters" pair and both poems on "the necessity to choose between two possible ways of acting" (70 and 73) were considered equal and therefore their fans are painted with ribs. Thus reading and solving the puzzles posed by poems and illustrations of an *ōgi no sōshi* was both stimulating and enjoyable.

III. Kasen-e

Portraits of seated poets have established the iconography of "pictures of immortal poets" (*kasen-e* 歌仙絵 or *kasen-ga* 歌仙画) and have been perpetuated in the Japanese secular painting tradition ever since the oldest *Yamato-e*-style depictions. The term *kasen* means "Poetic Immortal" literally, as the Chinese character *ka* 歌 stands for "poem," while the character *sen* 仙 (consisting of pictograms for a man 人 and

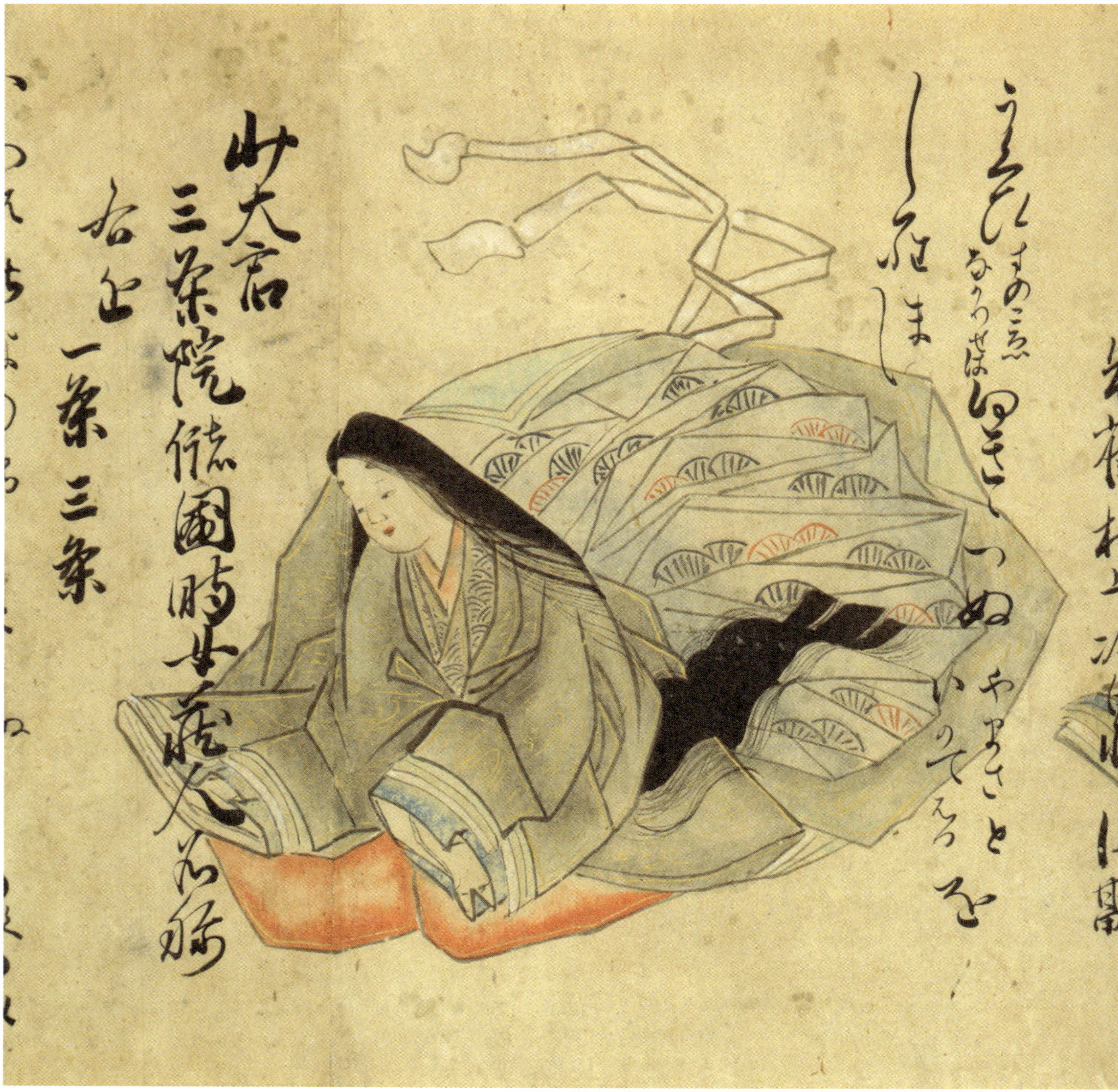

Fig. 30. Anonymous painter of the early 14th century: **The court ladies Ise and Nakatsukasa**, detail from a hand scroll of The Thirty-six Immortal Poets owned by Fujifusa (*Fujifusa-bon no Sanjūrokkasen emaki*), ink and colors on paper, orig. early 14th century, copy from the early 17th century.
(Photo credit: National Institute of Japanese Literature, 1.Yo 39 nijl)
An example of black and white drawing filled in in subdued colors and gold. The original scroll on classical poetry theme dating from the late Kamakura period was owned by Madenokōji Fujifusa (万里小路藤房), *one of the heroes of the Chronicle of the Great Peace (Taiheiki), the loyal noble official (Chūnagon) of Emperor GoDaigo who summoned the brave Kusunoki Masashige for imperial service at the Southern Court.*

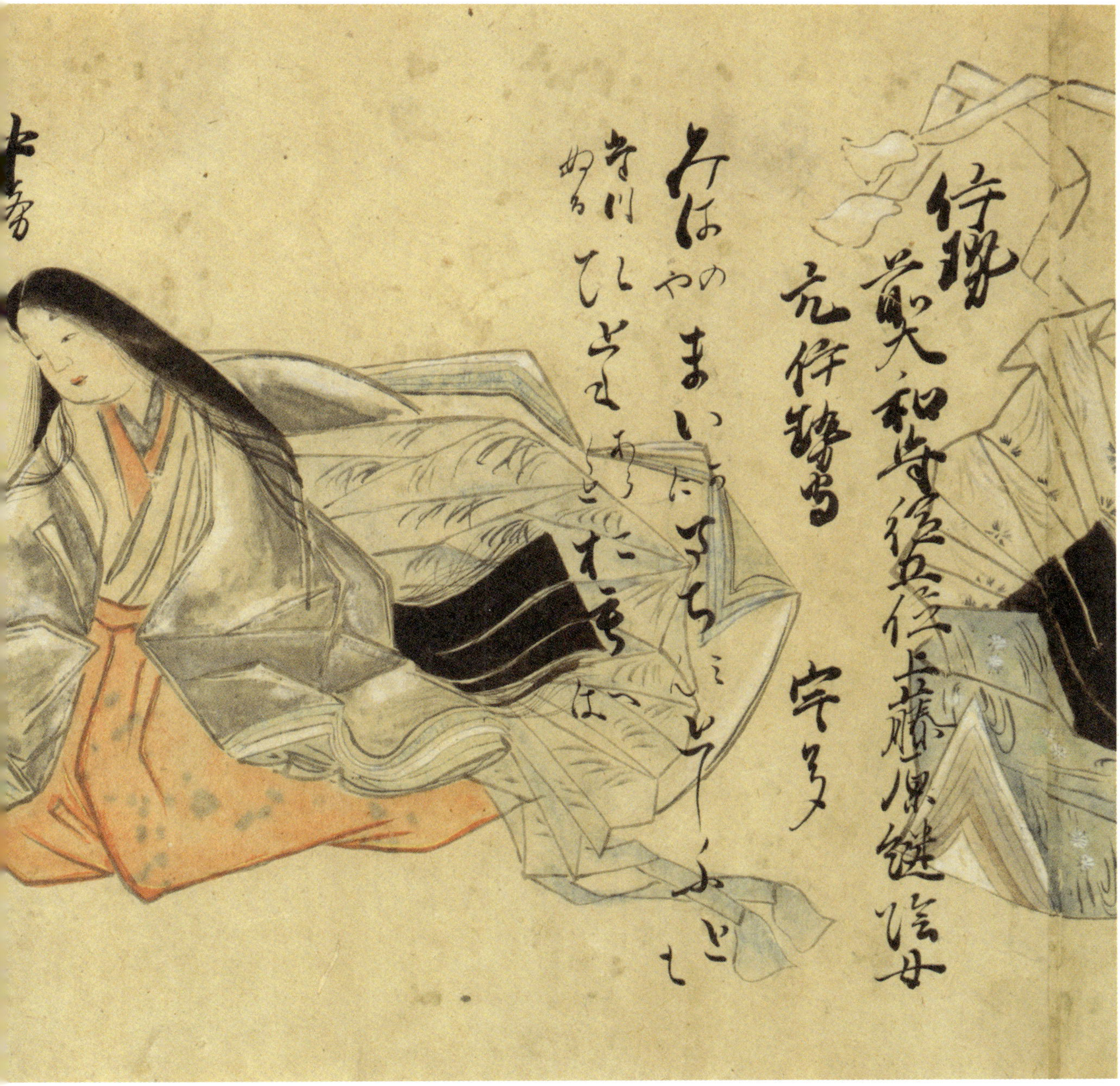

On the right, there is a poem by Lady Ise (KKS 780): on waiting for a lover.

みはのやま
いかにまちみむ
としふとも
たつぬるひとも
あらしとおもへは

miwa no yama
ika ni machimimu
toshi futomo
tadzunuru hito mo
araji to omoheba.

No matter how long
I keep waiting for love
under Mount Miwa
The man I long for
seems to never come to see me.

On the left is a portrait of Lady Nakatsukasa, the daughter of Lady Ise, with her poem on waiting for Spring.

うくひすの
こゑなかりせは
ゆききへぬ
山さといかて
はるをしらまし

uguhisu no
kowe nakariseba
yuki kienu
yamazato ika de
haru wo shiramashi.

If not the warbler
who would welcome with songs
the arrival of spring
in the mountain village
where the snow never thaws?

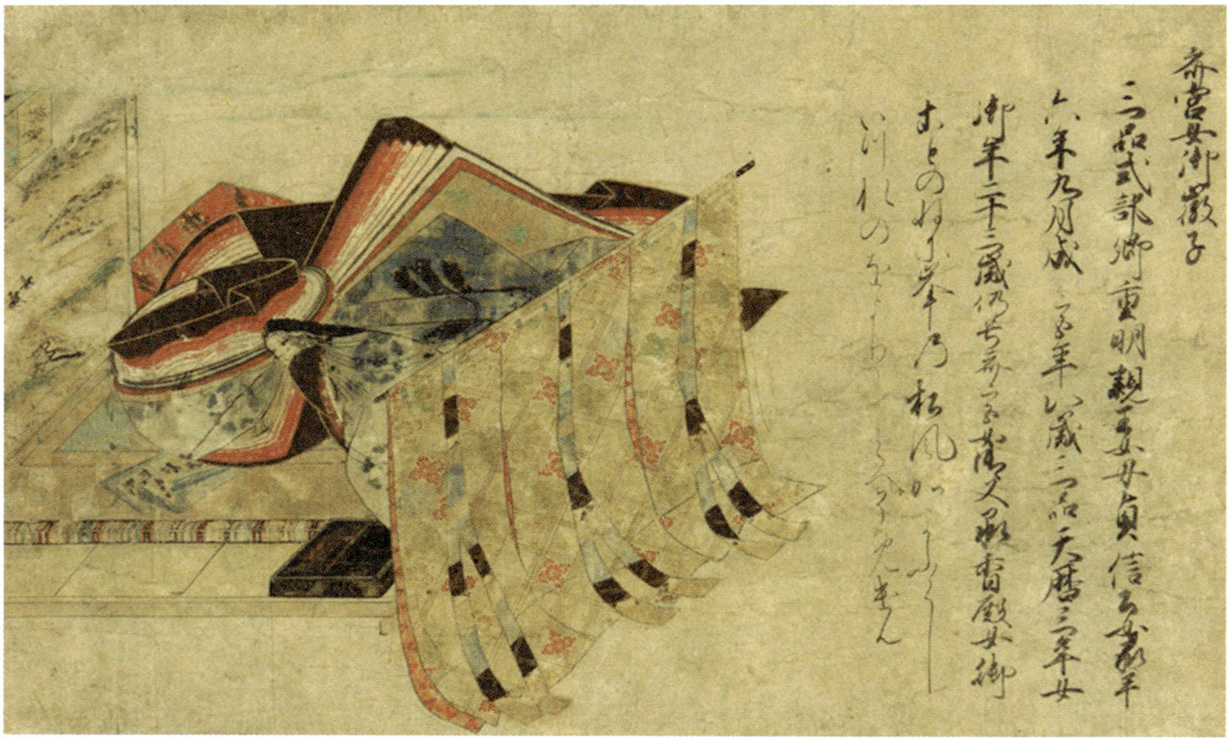

Fig. 31. **Fujiwara no Nobuzane** (1176?-1265?): **The poetess Saigū nyōgo (Princess Kishi, 949–986)**, a fragment of the Satake Version of Thirty-six Immortal Poets (*Satakebon Sanjūrokkasen*), colors on paper, mounted as a hanging scroll, height 36.7 cm, 13th century.
(Photo credit: The Freer Gallery of Art, Smithsonian Institution, Washington, F1950.24)
To the right, the short biography of Princess Kishi is written in Chinese characters. The kana-calligraphed poem about the sound of koto is quoted in the Prague Book of Fans as no. 2. The same poem is illustrated in Fig. 22 and 53.

a mountain 山) was used for mountain hermits, who could perform miraculous deeds and strove to achieve immortality.[21] The term *Six Poetic Immortals* (*Rokkasen* 六歌仙) denotes six famous Japanese poets of the 9th century who made their entry onto the poetic scene in Ki no Tsurayuki's Japanese Preface to the first imperially-commissioned *Anthology of Old and New Poems* (*Kokinshū*), compiled in 905.[22] A hundred years later, in 1009, the well-known court poet, theoretician and arbiter of court poetry rules, Fujiwara no Kintō (藤原公任, 966–1041)[23] selected the thirty-six famous poets who would soon be widely familiar as the *Thirty-six Poetic Immortals* (*Sanjūrokkasen* 三十六歌仙).[24] The selection had been first accomplished upon the imperial commission of Prince Tomohira[25] and contained only thirty poets, each represented by three poems, for a total of ninety poems. The learned prince, however, soon passed away and Kintō was free to include six more of his favorite poets and include ten of their poems,[26] so that the complete collection by thirty-six poets comprises 150 *waka* poems. Two hundred years later, the arbiter of modern poetry, Fujiwara no Shunzei (藤原俊成, 1114–1204) could not help writing a remake of the *Sanjūrokkasen*, limiting the number of poems to three for each poet, reshuffling the order of the selected poems, and reaching the final number of 108 poems encompassed by the collection. The Shunzei version thereafter served as a model for the majority of later copies of the thirty-six immortals of poetry.[27]

In the Heian period, poets were usually depicted in a seated, triangular shape, yet they could be occasionally depicted as standing. They were painted in hand-scrolls alongside their poems. Beautiful calligraphy was the major point of interest because calligraphy, in Heian aesthetic terms, was the mirror of a cultivated soul. In the space above or next to the seated figures, *waka* poems were calligraphed in *kana* and the poet's name and his or her court title and biography in Chinese *kanji* were included (Fig. 31). Both the *Six* and *Thirty-six Poetic Immortals* were habitually represented in the *Yamato-e* style – as figures sitting

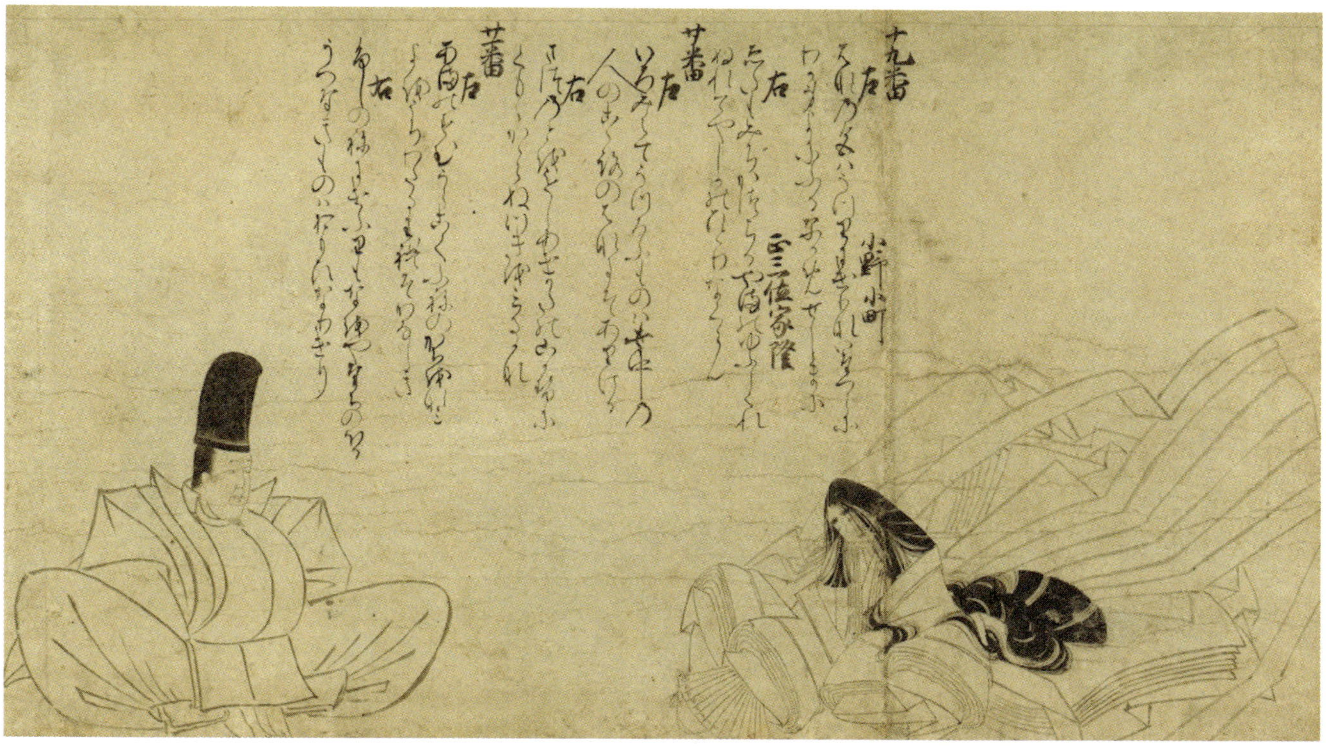

Fig. 32. Anonymous painter of the 14th century: The poets **Ono no Komachi** (c. 825–c. 900) and **Fujiwara no Ietaka** (1158–1237) in a poetry competition, a part of the scroll fragment Contest of Poems from Different Ages (*Jidai fudō uta-awase*), black and white drawing (*hykubyō-e*), ink on paper, mounted as a series of 25 sheets pasted on gold background, 3 poetry contest runs on each sheet, not signed, Kamakura period, 14th century.
(Photo credit: Tōkyō National Museum, Important cultural property, CO104439, PD photo)
Each fragment of this ancient scroll depicts a pair of competing poets – one from the ancient period and one contemporary, living at the court of the retired emperor GoToba-in (a great patron of poetry), who devised this imaginary competition form. There are three poetry contest rounds on each sheet – that is 75 poems out of the complete set of 108 poems. The art of Ono no Komachi, the 9th century beauty and great poet, at the Left side is measured against the art of the pupil of Fujiwara no Shunzei, Shōsanmi Ietaka, as he was known by his court title, competing for the Right side of living poetry masters. Their mutual combats are numbered as Rounds 19, 20, 21 (ban). Only the three poems by the beauty Komachi are well known to posterity nowadays (Hana no iro ha, Iro miede, Ama no sumu). One of her 45 love poems in imperial anthologies (Kokinshū 797) is calligraphed in the middle of the inscription above:

色見えで	iro miede	The only flower
うつろふものは	utsurofu mono ha	which keeps on changing color,
世の中の	yo no naka no	which whithers here
人の心の	hito no kokoro no	and blossoms elsewhere then,
花にぞありける	hana zo arikeru.	lives in the hearts of men.

in formal court robes with the signs of their court rank (hats and court batons in the hands of courtiers and twelve-layer robes, and long, loose hair in the case of court ladies). Sometimes they were seated on mats with ornamental edging in the so-called *agedatami*-type of *kasen-e* (Figs. 31, 33). The sitting posture of the poets, in a way, reflected physical necessity, especially for women whose robes were too heavy to stand up or move in for a longer spell of time. Another reason for sitting down was that poetry meetings and contests would last for days and nights.[28]

Recalling the habit of poetry contests (*uta-awase*) of the Heian period,[29] the thirty-six poets were divided into pairs labelled as Left or Right, and competed with poems composed on a given topic (*dai*) in one round (*ban, tsugashi*).[30] The Left and Right always form a firmly fixed couple with a balanced composition (Fig. 32). Very often the poems by the Left were written in columns from left to right, while the Right poets' lines were written in the standard Japanese way, from the right-hand-side towards the left. This method was used also in the Prague set of six *kasen-e*.

Fig. 33. **Kanō Naonobu** (1607–1650): **The poetess Kodai no Kimi from the set of The Thirty-six Poetic Immortals in Frames** (*Sanjurokkasen gaku*) from the Kompira Shrine in Shikoku, painting and gold on a wooden board (*hengaku*), 1648.
(Photo credit: Kotohira-gū Hōmotsukan, Shikoku, Japan, PD photo)
The highly allusive poem (Shūishū 1201) relates to the deity of the Iwabashi bridge whom nobody can behold without danger of drowning in the river beneath. Pilgrims therefore cross the bridge at night. The poet is afraid of daylight and her awe-inspiring lover who resembles the deity of Kazuraki:

いわはしの
よるのちきりも
たえぬへし
明るわひしき
かすらきの神神

iwabashi no
yoru no chigiri mo
taenubeshi
akuru wabishiki
Kazuraki no kami.

The night crossing pledge
of the Iwabashi bridge
drives me mad with fear
that the God of Kazuraki
may behold me in daylight.

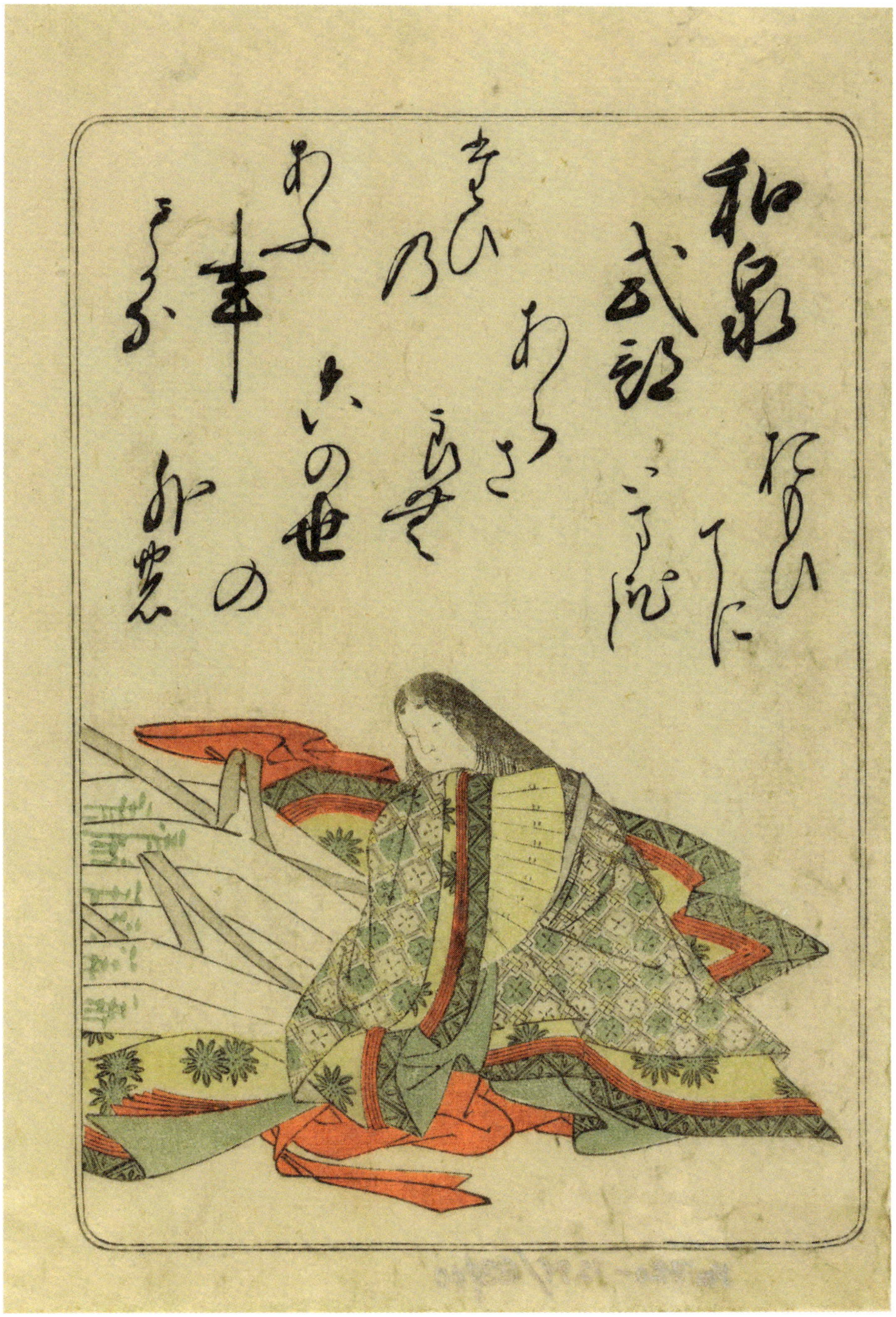

Fig. 34. **Katsukawa Shunshō** (1726–1793): **The poetess Izumi Shikibu**, a page from the album The Hundred Poets in the Eastern Weave Brocade (*Nishiki Hyakunin isshu Azuma ori* 錦百人一首あつま織), *nishiki-e*, published by Kariganeya Ginosuke and Seikichi, 28 x 18. 2 cm, 1775. (Photo credit: National Gallery, Prague, Vm 720)

The poem from Goshūishū (763) is calligraphed in Shoren-in style by Sayama Chikayuki:

あらさらむ
この世の外の
おもひでに
いまひとたひの
あふ事もかな

arazaramu
kono yo no hoka no
omohide ni
ima hitotabi no
afu koto mogana.

As days pass by
I approach my end.
All the more I long
even for a little while
to see you once again.

Fig. 35. Anonymous Tosa painter of the late 17th century: **The poetess Ono no Komachi**, *kasen-e* portrait from the album of Six Poetic Immortals (*Rokkasen*), painting in ink, colors and gold on silk with so called "pear-speckled ground" (*nashiji*) and calligraphy of six poems on decorated paper, bound in hard covers, 25.8 x 18.2 cm, late 17th century.
(Photo credit: National Gallery, Prague, Vm 1318)
The famous poem (Kokinshū 552) reads:

思ひつつ
ぬれはや人の
みえつらむ
夢としりせハ
さめさらましを

omohitsutsu
nurebaya hito no
mietsuramu
yume to shiriseba
samezaramashi wo

Deeply in love
I spend my days long
longing for you.
Last night I met you in my dream
I would not wake up if I knew.

This type of seated poet was derived from portraits of Hitomaro, a major poet in the first collection of Japanese poetry, the *Man'yōshū* from the 8th century. He had been regarded as the patron saint of poetry before the position of the God of Poetry was allotted to the 9th-century-poet Sugawara no Michizane.[31] Portraits of Hitomaro with a long white beard, dressed in ancient Chinese-like attire, were displayed during poetry contests in the 11th century. However, such early paintings have not survived (as paper does not generally keep undamaged for a millennium) and there is only fragmentary evidence. Early *kasen-e* were drawn in black and white, in plain ink (*hakubyō-e* 白描絵), outlining the figures in rather angular lines. The oldest remaining *kasen-e* of this black and white type dates from the 14th century and illustrates the *Contest of Poems from Different Ages* (*Jidai fudō uta-awase* 時代不同歌合), which was compiled by the retired emperor GoToba from his favourite poets across the Japanese tradition early in the 13th century (Fig. 31). One of the earliest extant scroll fragments from the so-called *Satake-bon Sanjūrokkasen*[32] dating from the 13th century shows the seated figure of the Princess Kishi with her short biography written in Chinese characters and the soft, fluent calligraphic lines of her poem in Japanese *hiragana* (called "female writing," *onnade* 女手 at the time) (Fig. 31). Because of the perennial cult of classical poetry, almost each monastery, shrine or noble household had its own copy of the *Thirty-six Poetic Immortals* made. These copies were produced in monastic scriptoria or by the painters of the imperial Tosa School that held high positions in the Bureau of Painting (*Edokoro azukari*). The Tosa School[33] painters encompassed the native *Yamatoe-e* style in the Muromachi period and carried it onto a sophisticated professional level in the skilled painting of Tosa Mitsunobu (土佐光信, 1434?–1525) (Figs. 15, 23). Starting from the 15th century the Tosa School competed for influence with the Kanō School[34], both reaching full bloom in the 17th century. Though the Kanō School derived its style and themes from Chinese painting, the Tosa and Kanō Schools were quite close in expression during the Momoyama period, which is our main point of interest. Their color schemes (using brilliant natural color pigments and gold) were almost identical and the main difference was in scale and concept (Figs. 17,18). The Kanō painters focused on large details and decorative type of paintings on large screens and walls of noble palaces and monasteries, while the Tosa paintings were based on miniature and narrative scroll paintings. Kanō inspiration was derived from the Chinese *Kanga* (or *Kara-e*) and Tosa from the Japanese *Yamato-e* painting. In the 16th century, Kanō Motonobu (狩野 元信, 1476–1559) painted both black-and-white ink landscapes and colourful narrative scrolls (such as *Shuten Dōji emaki*) derived from the native *Yamato-e* style, that were often copied in later centuries (Fig. 17). As late as 1640, shogun Iemitsu had a scroll of the *Sanjūrokkasen* drawn by Iwasa Matabei (岩佐又兵衛, 1578–1650),[35] a nobleman, who was a disciple of Tosa Mitsunori and a direct predecessor of the first painters of the popular Ukiyo-e Schools, as he painted the bustling daily life in Kyōto and provinces already in the Keichō era around the year 1600. A 7.5 m long *emakimono* scroll from the Museum of Fine Arts in Boston[36] attributed to Iwasa Matabei shows the complete set of the *Thirty-six Poetic Immortals* painted in colors as seated *kasen-e* portraits against blank background.

Besides the illustrated scroll format and the paper sheet format, the poets were also portrayed one by one on wooden boards as large-scale paintings. Such poets' portraits would be placed as votive pictures (*emma* 絵 馬) in a Buddhist monastery (*tera*) or a Shintō shrine (*miya*) under the protruding wooden eaves or in the *ranma* space above the sliding doors inside of a temple hall. This type of *kasen-e* is to be found, for instance, in the Jōzan-ji temple,[37] which was founded by the poet and calligrapher Ichikawa Jōzan (1583–1672) in 1641. Jōzan named the "Hall of Poetic Hermits" (Shisen-dō, 詩仙堂) after the classic Chinese poets' portraits he had hung in his study. Another famous set of Japanese *Thirty-six Poetic Immortals* is displayed in the open in the shrine of the God of Poetry (Kitano Tenmangū 北野天満宮) in the North-West part of Kyōto. A beautifully decorated, large and complete set called *Framed Thirty-six Poetry Immortals* (*Sanjūrokkasen gaku* 三十六歌仙額), which dates from the middle of the 17th century (ca 1648), was painted in glittering colors and gold on wooden boards (*hengaku*) by three painters of the Kanō School: Tan'yū, Yūsen and Naonobu[38], and has been preserved in the Konpira Sanctuary in Shikoku (Fig. 33).

But let us turn now to a predecessor of all these later fireworks of artistic fantasy, the Prague set of six *kasen-e* from around the year 1570, which is published here for the first time. It offers six sheets out of the thirty-six ancient portraits drawn in a truly traditional *Yamato-e* style. Due to the fragmentary character of the set, there is no notice of the original provenance, nor the painter's mark (*kakihan* 書き判), nor a seal or signature, leaving the remarkable set of naive figures open to further scrutiny. The first striking feature is the size: the Prague *kasen-e* are much larger than the usual format of *kasen-e* fragments cut out from a scroll. Each single sheet of this set has the measurements of 51.8 x 36.8 cm, indicating that the paper was not used horizontally (as in hand-scrolls), but rather vertically (as on folding-screen panels). While the average size of fragments of illustrations from a traditional horizontal scroll *emaki* has a vertical measurement of 20 to 37 cm, the vertical size of Prague *kasen-e* is almost double the typical scroll height. The painter of these large-sized poets figures used the *gampi*[39] paper of a format called "paper which fits into a space" (*ma-niai-gami*), perhaps so as to be pasted on individual panels of a folding screen (*byōbu*) or on sliding doors (*fusuma*). The *gampi* paper and the style of calligraphic writing recall the medieval manuscripts labelled as *Nara-ehon* that were produced from the 15th to the late 17th centuries. The usage of ink and natural pigments as well as the occasional traces of liquid gold, date the work to the second half of the 16th century. The casual calligraphic style resembles the often-imitated handwriting of Fujiwara no Teika, the greatest arbiter of Japanese poetry from the early 13th century.

What becomes evident upon closer inspection is the fact that the portraits and some details on the robes have been retouched during an unskilled restoration process, perhaps ordered by a 19th century owner of the set (thick paper with commercial accounts in Japanese is used for backing of the original paper). The unsigned, anonymous painter and calligrapher who created the seated poets (but perhaps only copied them from an unknown source) was a mere artisan without much skill. He did not belong to an academic school (like the Tosa or the Kanō School), or to a monastery scriptorium (like the professional painters from temples in Nara who created the *Nara-ehon* of the Muromachi period). Rather, he belonged to the guild of town painters (*machi-eshi*) who worked for a newly established painting shop (*eya*) or a fan shop (*ōgiya*) that catered to the newly-rising townspeople clientele in Kyōto, Naniwa, Sakai or other large cities at the close of the hundred years of civil wars in the late 16th century.

Contrary to the very simplified figure-pictures in the fans, there is an evident attempt on the part of the poets' painter to add portrait features to individual poets, to create real life-like portraits (*nise-e* 似せ絵). Yet, the painter was not very skilled, which is quite clear when we compare these naïve portraits with the masterful portraits drawn by the professional painters of the Kanō for the Kompira shrine in Shikoku in 1648 (Fig. 33).[40] Regardless of the clumsy brushwork, the portraits of the seated poets of long ago are vivid, expressive and almost magical in their naïveté, individualization, and the ancient patina of four hundred years. Even though these charming *kasen-e* portraits represent only six of the complete set of the *Thirty-six Poetry Immortals*, they are among the oldest examples of poetic illustrations in Czech collections and can be considered as complementary artifacts to the more extensive example of 16th-century Japanese poetry illustration – the Prague version of *Ōgi no sōshi*. From the artistic point of view, the old pictures of *ōgi-e* and *kasen-e* from Prague collections that we present in this volume do not belong to the showcase of great Japanese art. They rather represent a mediocre daily-life pictorial production of ancient Japanese folk. However, such paintings have been seldom preserved elsewhere and this exactly is the point of their rarity and exceptionality. Without doubt, these ancient portraits retain a strange beauty of an original and authentic artistic expression. Because of the rare quality of the antique *kasen-e*, we reproduce them in a large scale together with the translation of the poems (Figs. 37–42).

The ancient tradition of painting the thirty-six poets in scrolls or on wooden boards or large paper sheets to be displayed in the *ranma* space above the sliding doors changed with the Edo period (1615–1868) into issuing a set of *Sanjūrokkasen* to be pasted on screens or to be viewed in books. In 1628 (Kan'ei 5), the Buddhist monk, tea ceremony master and calligrapher Shōkadō Shōjō (松花堂昭乗, 1584–1639)[41] created a small accordion album with thirty six poet-portraits and calligraphy of their poems written on decorated papers. It was acquired for the large private collection of Japanese illustrated books of ca. 2200 volumes assembled by Gerhard Pulverer, which is housed at the Smithsonian Institution in Washington since 2007. Shōjō was one of the "Three Brushes" of the Kan'ei era (1624–1643). His calligraphy, called "the Shōkadō-style", became popular for the next 200 years throughout the Edo period and his highly idiosyncratic handwriting of syllabic script was admired as an ideal for writing poetry. At about the same time, Tosa Mitsunori (土佐光則, 1583–1638) created an album of the *Thirty-six Poetic Immortals* glittering with gold and colors and joined by calligraphies of Konoe Nobuhiro (近衛 信尋, 1599–1649), another famous calligrapher of the time. This splendid piece of art, originally from the William Anderson Collection, is kept in a later copy by The British Museum (Fig. 18). In 1893, Ferdinand D'Este on his return from Japan donated to the Museum für Völkerkunde in Vienna a complete 17th century *kasen-e* folder of the One Hundred Poets (*Hyakunin isshu*) with their poems calligraphed on stiff *shikishi* paper decorated with abstract gold designs. A similar 17th century album with poems and minutely painted seated figures of the *Six Poetic Immortals* (*Rokkasen*) by an anonymous Tosa School follower was purchased in Japan by Joe Hloucha and preserved in the National Gallery, Prague (Fig. 35).

Fig. 36. Anonymous painter of the 19th century: **The poetess Ise watching the Dragon's Gate Waterfall** (*Ryūmon no taki*) in Yamato, ink and colors on paper, 72 x 38 cm dated Bunsei 6 (1823).
(Photo credit: National Gallery, Prague, Vm 3599)
The motif is linked with the poetess's visit to the Ryūmonji temple where she composed the poem (translated by J. Mostow):

たちぬはぬ
絹きし人も
なきものを
なに山姫の
ぬのさらすらん

tachi-nuhanu
kinu kishi hito mo
naki mono wo
nani yama-hime no
nuno sarasuran

The ones who wore the robes
that were neither cut nor sewn
are gone—
why then does the mountain goddess
continue to bleach her cloth for them?

Fig. 37. **Lady Nakatsukasa** 中務 (912?–991?) Nakatsukasa was the grand-daughter of Emperor Uda and the daughter of the prolific poet, Lady Ise. She is one of only five women numbered among the Thirty-six Poetic Immortals. She married another of the famous thirty-six poets, Minamoto no Saneakira. Many of her poems are included in the second Japanese imperial poetry anthology *Gosenshū*, issued in 951. Her poem from this anthology, no. 846, is on the theme of Love:

秋風の
吹くにつけても
とはぬかな
荻の葉ならば
音はしてまし

akikaze no
fuku ni tsukete mo
tohanu kana
wogi no ha naraba
oto ha shitemashi

He does not come
even though the autumn wind
begins to blow
and the leaves of reeds
whisper in vivid response.

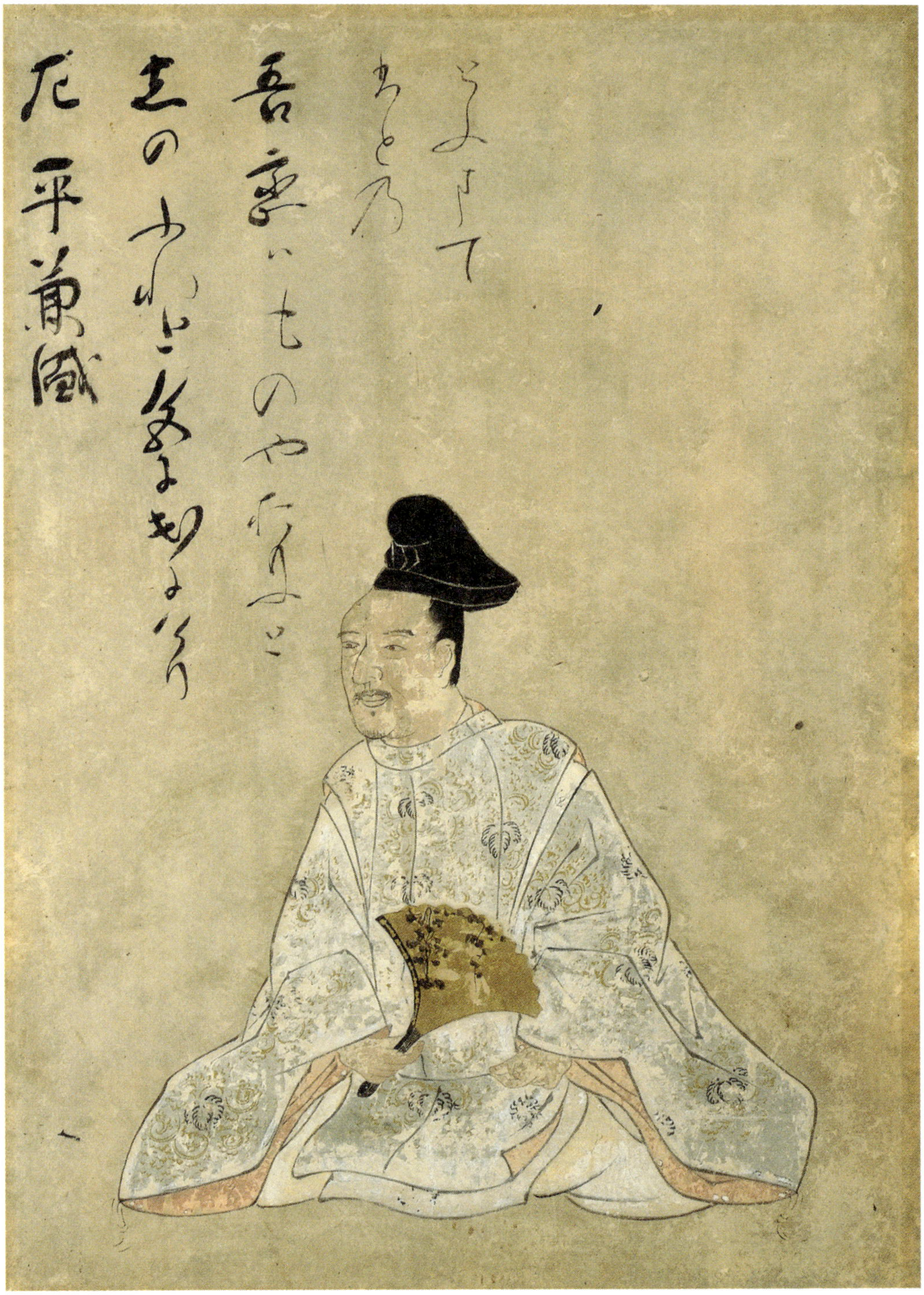

Fig. 38. **Taira no Kanemori** 平 兼盛 (?–991) Kanemori was a member of the Taira clan of warriors and a noted poet. Kanemori's poems are included in several official poetry anthologies from the Heian period. His personal collection, known as the *Kanemori-shū* (兼盛 集), remains. His daughter Akazome no Emon was a distinguished *waka* poet, though she is usually recognized as the daughter of her adoptive father, Akazome no Tokimochi. The inscribed poem from the *ShinKokinshū* collection (no. 622) is also included as no. 40 in the collection of One Hundred Poets (*Hyakunin isshu*) (translated by J. Mostow):

忍ぶれど
色にいでにけり
わが恋は
物や思ふと
人のとふまで

shinoburedo
iro ni idenikeri
wa ga kohi ha
mono ya omofu to
hito no tofu made

Even though I hide it,
it shows all over my face,
such is my longing,
so that people ask me
"What are you thinking about?"

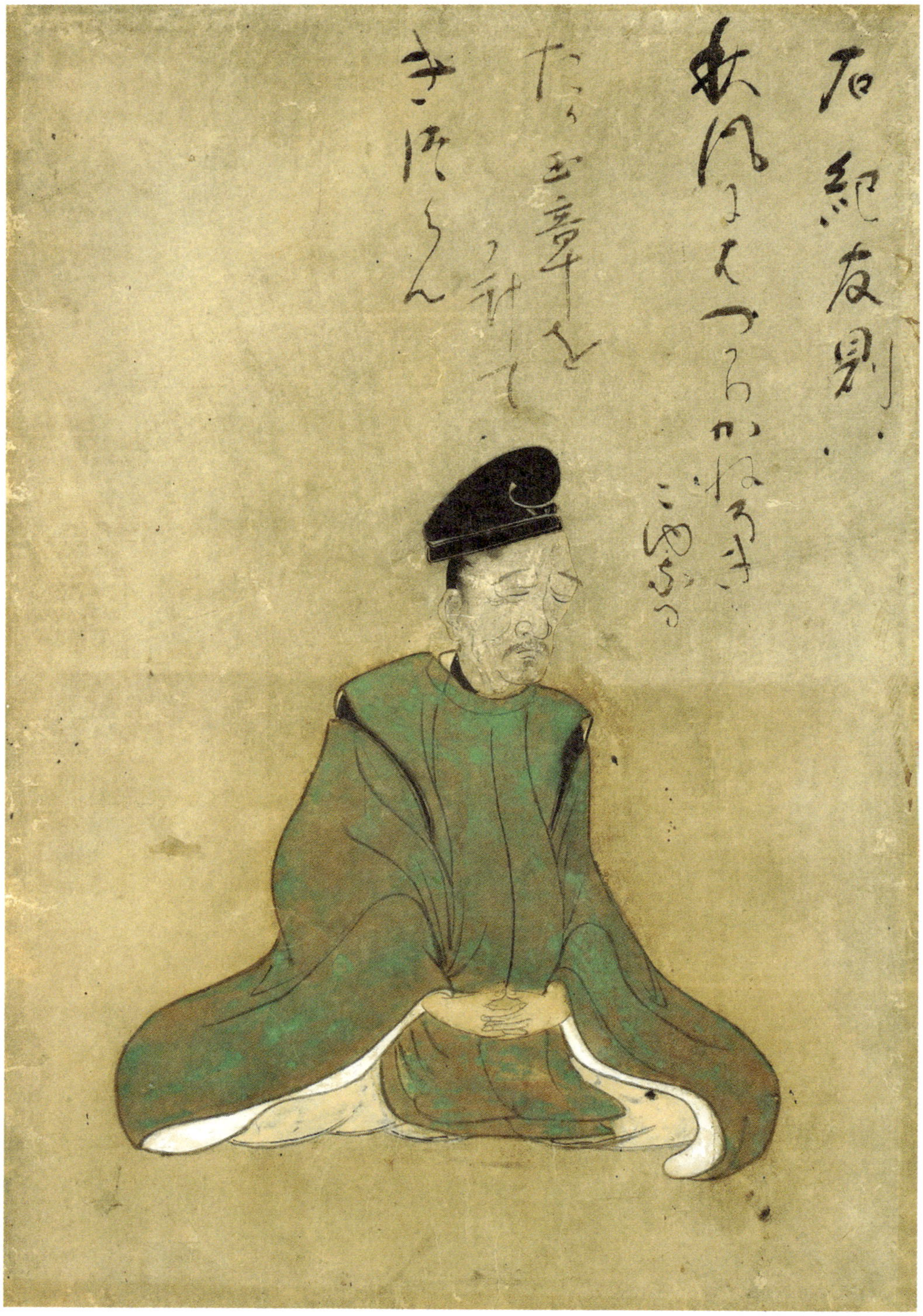

Fig. 39. **Ki no Tomonori** 紀 友則 (c. 850–c. 904) Tomonori was an early compiler of the *Kokinshū*, though he certainly did not see it to completion as the anthology includes a eulogy for him composed by Ki no Tsurayuki, his uncle and colleague in the compilation effort. Ki no Tomonori is the author of several poems in the *Kokinshū* and in later official collections. A collection of his poems from various sources appears as the *Tomonori shū*. The quoted poem is no. 207, an autumn poem from the *Kokinshū*. As Tomonori contests for the Right party, the poem is inscribed from right to left:

秋風に
はつかりかねそ
きこゆらむ
たか玉つを
かけてきつらむ

akikaze ni
hatsukari ga ne zo
kikoyunaru
ta ga tamadzusa wo
kakete kitsuramu

In the autumn wind
I hear the crying
of the wild geese,
hoping they can finally
bring your letter from the skies.

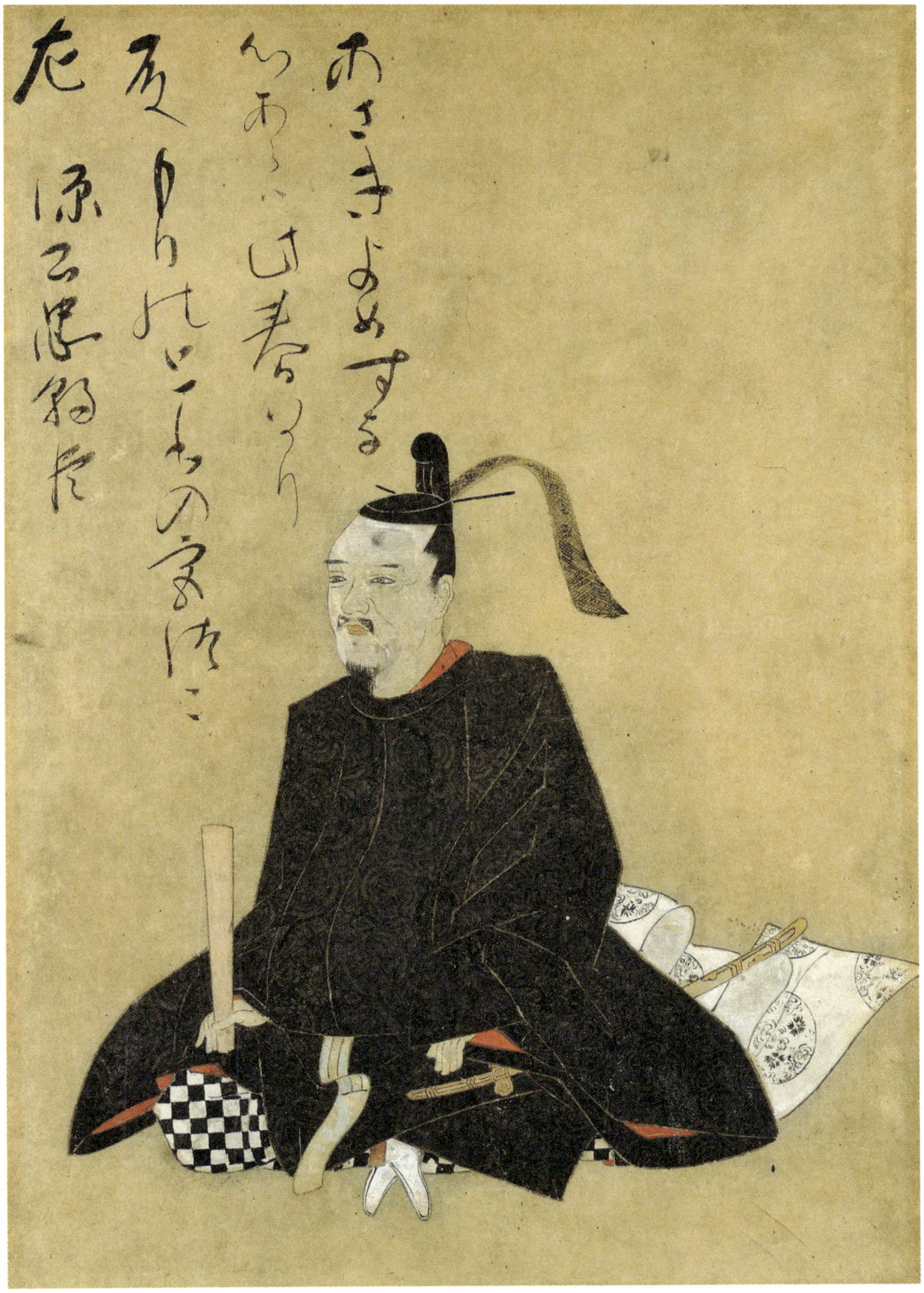

Fig. 40. **Minamoto no Kintada** 源公忠 (889–948) One of the Thirty-six Poetic Immortals from the warrior clan of the Minamoto with the court title Ason. The included poem on the topic of blossoming sakura in Spring is from *GoShūishū*, no. 1055. It uses a motif of a servant boy sweeping the leaves from the garden, which had been typical in Chinese art and poetry ever since the Tang period. Left (SA) poem written from left to right:

友もりの
とものみやつこ
心あらは
この春ハかり
あさきよめすな

tonomori no
tomo no miyatsuko
kokoro araba
kono haru bakari
asagi yomesu na

If you have a heart,
my lad, do not sweep away
the fallen leaves
in our garden
until the spring is over.

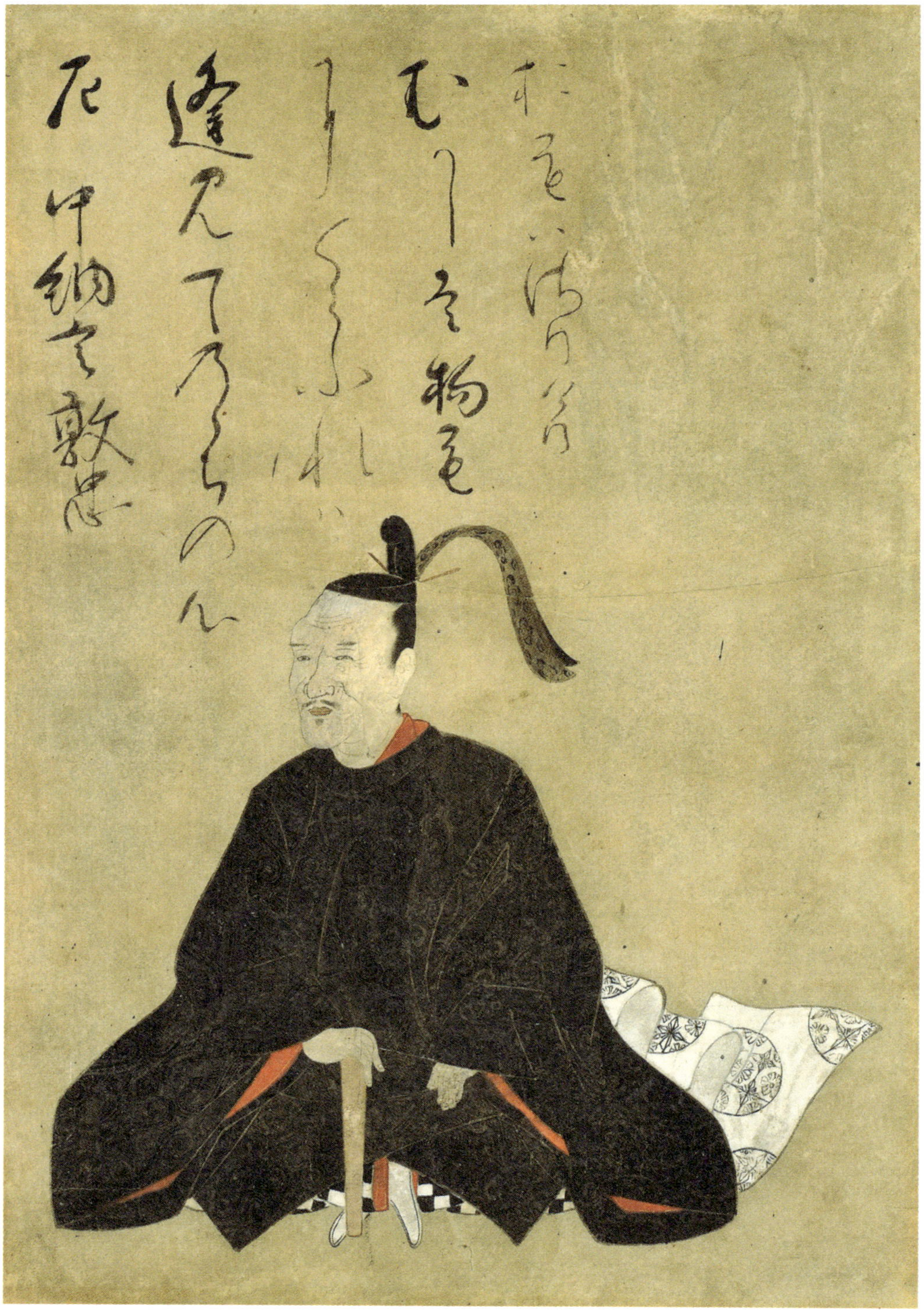

Fig. 41. **Fujiwara no Atsutada** 藤原 敦忠 (906–943) Atsutada is also known as the Hon'in Chūnagon 本院中納言, the Biwa Chūnagon 琵琶中納言 or Gon Chūnagon Atsutada 権中納言敦忠. Many of his poems written in correspondence with court women remain, and some are included in official poetry anthologies such as *Gosen waka shū*. He is a noted member of the Thirty-six Poetic Immortals and one of his poems, quoted further, is included in the famous anthology *Hyakunin isshu* (no. 43) (translated by J. Mostow). Atsutada's poem is written from left to right:

逢みての
のちの心に
くらふれは
むかしは物も
おもはさりけり

ahimite no
nochi no kokoro ni
kurabureba
mukashi ha mono mo
omohazarikeri

When compared to
the feelings in my heart
after we'd met and loved,
I realize that in the past
I had no cares at all.

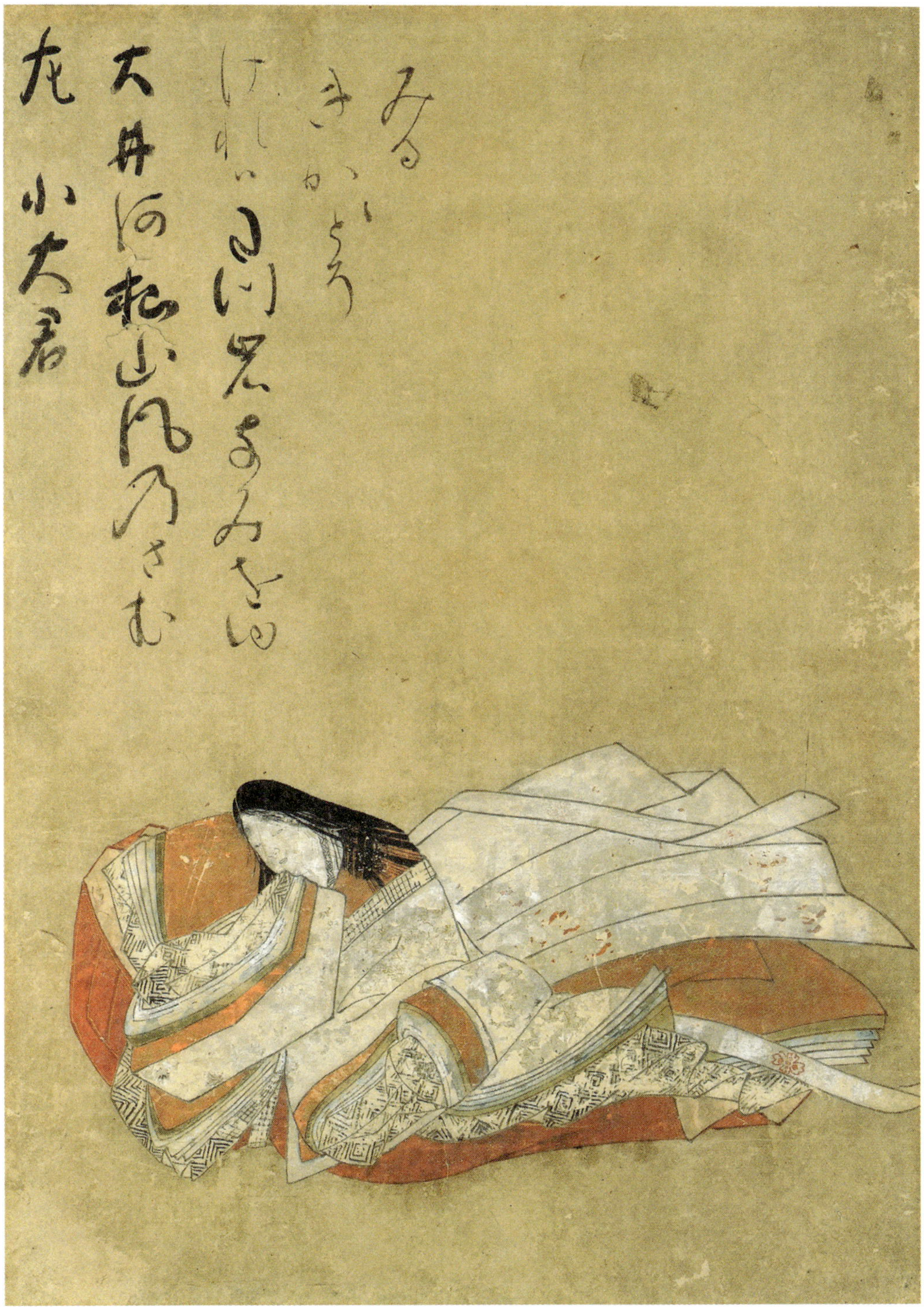

Fig. 42. **Kodai no Kimi** 小大君 (active in the 9th cent.) Also known as Ko Ōkimi, she was one of only five women numbered among the Thirty-six Poetic Immortals. Many of her poems are in Japanese imperial poetry anthologies including the *Shūi waka shū*. There are poems overlapping between her personal poetry collection *Kodai no Kimi shū* (小大君集) and Ono no Komachi's personal collection. Her poem is a Spring poem, no. 2 from *Goshūishū*. This poem is inscribed from left to right, being a poem composed by the Left party.

大井河
杣山風の
さむけれハ
たつ岩なみを
ゆきかとそみる

ohoigawa
somayama kaze no
samukereba
tatsu ihanami wo
yuki ka to zo miru

The cold wind
whirls down the Soma
mountain slopes
to the Ōi river in the snow.
I give up all my hopes.

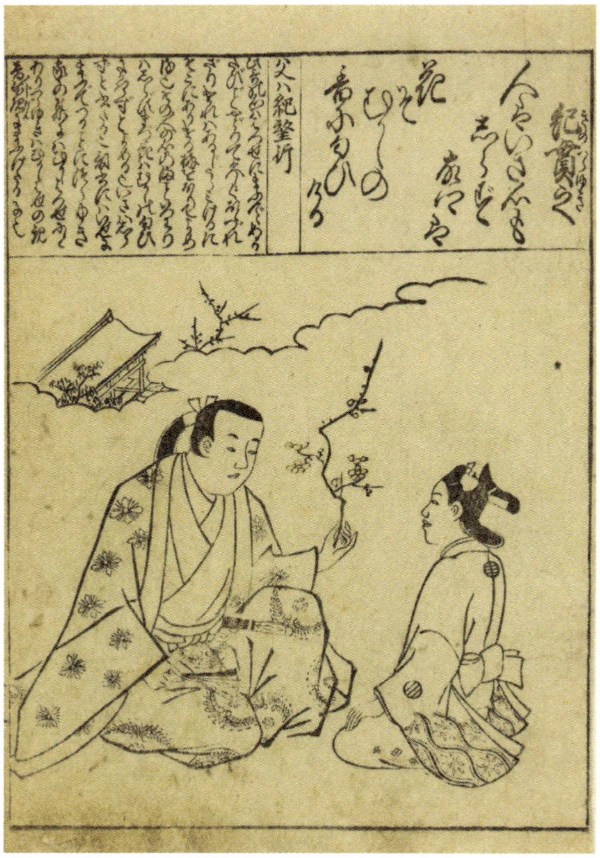

Fig. 43. **Hishikawa Moronobu** (1618–1694): The compiler of the *Kokinshū*, Ki no Tsurayuki with a young attendant and his reflective poem from *Hyakunin isshu* (no. 35). A page from Elegant Full-Figure Portraits of the One Hundred Poets (*Fūryū sugata-e Hyakunin isshu*) picture book, black and white woodcut, published by Kinoshita Jinemon, 1695.
(Photo credit: National Gallery, Prague, Vm 262)
The well-known lyrics compare the ever-changing heart of men and the never-changing scent of cherry blossoms.

人はいさ
心もしらす
故郷は
花ぞむかしの
香に匂ひける

hito ha isa
kokoro mo shirazu
furusato ha / no
hana zo mukashi no
ka ni nihohikeru

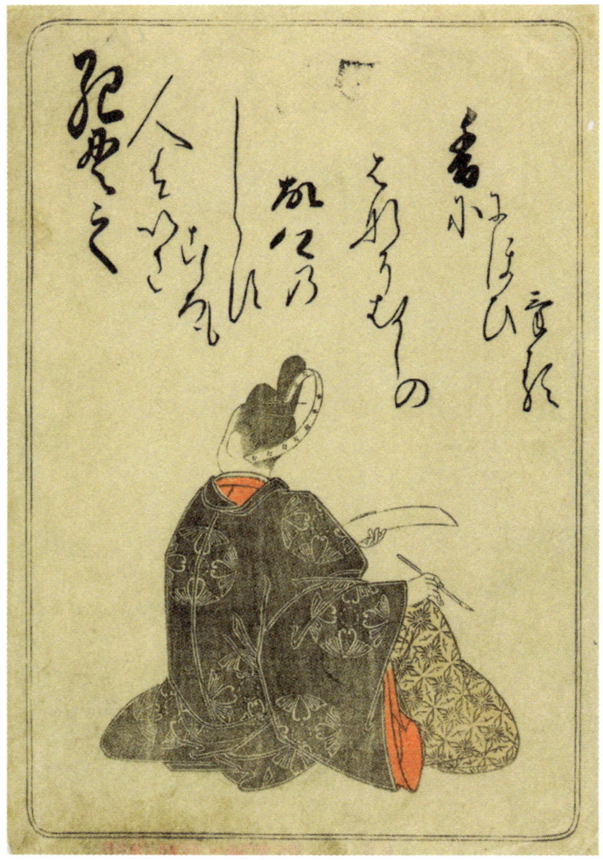

Fig. 44. **Katsukawa Shunshō** (1726–1793): Poet Ki no Tsurayuki, from the album The Hundred Poets Brocaded in the Eastern Weave (*Nishiki hyakunin isshu Azuma ori*, 錦百人一首あつま織), calligraphy in Shoren-in style by Sayama Chikayuki, published by Kariganeya Ginosuke and Seikichi, Edo, colour woodcut *nishiki-e*, 28 x 18.2 cm, 1775.
(Photo credit: National Gallery, Prague, Vm 1038)
Poem 35 from Hyakunin isshu *is the same as in Fig. 43 (translated by J. Mostow). It reads from left to right:*

With people, well,
you can never know their hearts;
but in my old village
the flowers brightly bloom with
the scent of the days of old.

Starting from the 17th century, painted books evolved into woodblock printed books. Many early printed books contain *kasen-e* figures thanks to the popularity of the *Sanjūrokkasen.* The *Hyakunin isshu,* a chronological collection of one hundred poems by one hundred poets active between the 7th and the 13th centuries, which was compiled by Fujiwara Teika in 1236, became highly popular from the 17th century on. The assembly of thirty-six or one hundred seated poets was often published in woodcut printed pictorial albums to be enjoyed in privacy, and later even on small cards for playing social games (*uta-garuta*). But it definitely was *Ise monogatari* that appeared most frequently among early printed poetic books. The earliest *Ise Stories* edition with black and white pictures by an anonymous painter was calligraphed for print in the style of the most accomplished artist among the "Three Brushes", Hon'ami Kōetsu (本阿弥光悦, 1558–1637), as early as the Keichō era (1595–1615).[42] *Kōetsu-bon* became the term for early books calligraphed by Kōetsu, such as the *Sanjūrokkasen* edition dated from ca. 1610. It was the same Kōetsu who calligraphed poetry on hand-painted scrolls or sheets of paper pre-decorated with abstracted natural

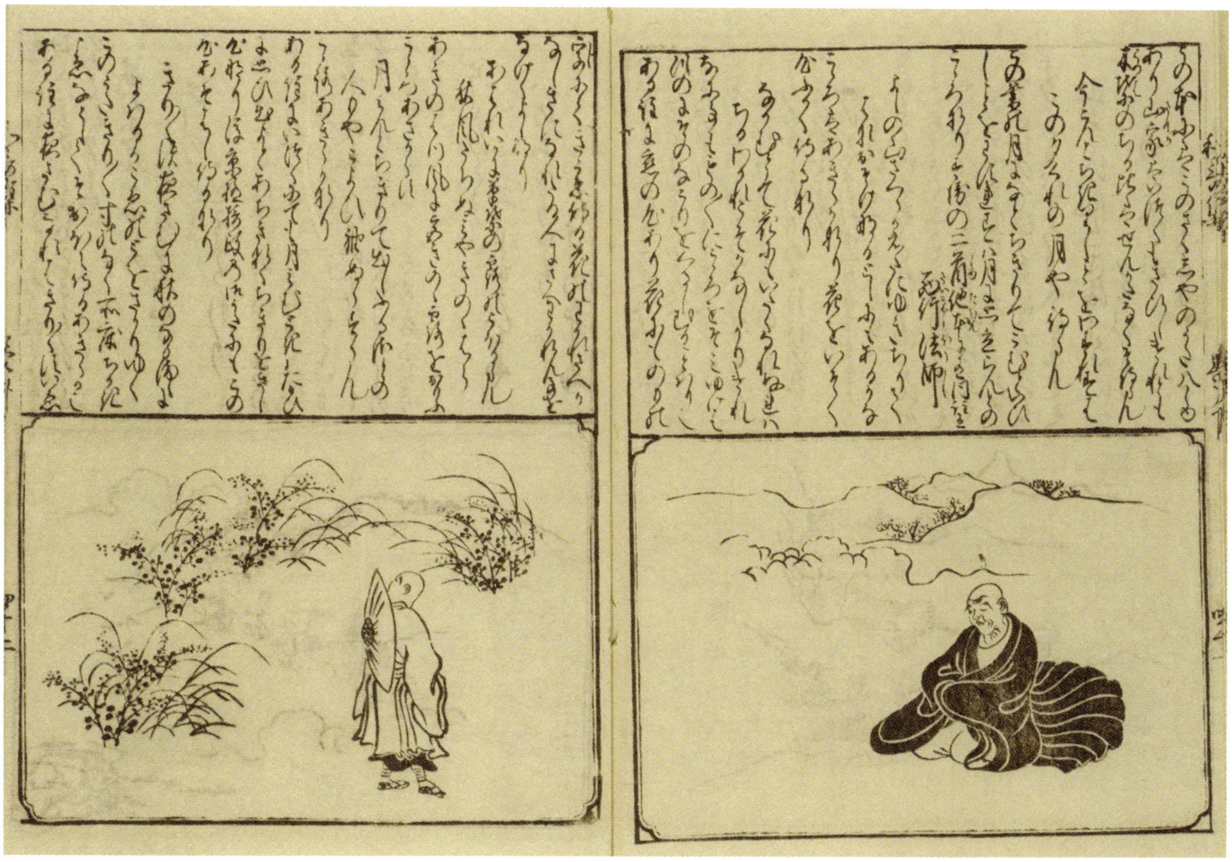

Fig. 45. **Hishikawa Moronobu** (1618–1694): **Double-page with poems by Monk Saigyō** from the 3rd part of the illustrated book Private Selection of Poems with Commentaries (*Jisan kachū* 自讃歌註), 3 parts in one volume, 88 pp, black and white woodcut, 27.2 x 18.5 cm, published by Suwaraya Mohei, Edo, ca. 1685.
(Photo credit: National Gallery, Prague, Vm 262)
This anthology of 170 poems by 17 poets from the age of the ShinKokinshū *was compiled by the* renga *master Sōgi hōshi (1421–1502) in 1485 and was still very popular in the Jōkyō era (1684–1688) when Moronobu illustrated it with pictures of seated poetes* kasen-e *and* Yamato-e *like scenes depicting the contents of the* waka *poetry.* Hyakunin isshu *became more popular than this collection of verse later in the Edo period. On the reproduced double-page (41 ura, 42 omote), we can see two illustrations but the commentary in the upper part (kashira) offers five poems by the wandering monk and excellent poet of nature, Monk Saigyō.*
On the left-hand side we see him walking among grass plain of Miyagi no hara near Sendai and composing a poem (ShinKokinshū, *300*):

あはれいかに
草葉の露の
こぼるらむ
秋風立ちぬ
宮城野の原

aware ika ni
kusaba no tsuyu no
koboruramu
akikaze tachinu
Miyagino hara

How sad to observe
the dew drops torn away
from the leaves of grass
in the raging winds of Fall
on Miyagino Plain.

The seated figure of Saigyō on the right is set against the backdrop of Yoshino hills near the ancient capital of Nara. The poem is from ShinKokinshū *(Spring, 79)*:

吉野山
さくらが枝に
雪ちりて
花おそげなる
年にもあるかな

yoshino yama
sakura ga eda ni
yuki chirite
hana osoge naru
toshi ni mo aru kana

This year I feel
the blossoms will bloom late
In the Yoshino Hills
White snow scatters still
on the barren cherries twigs.

The preceeding poem to the right is a variation on a Kokinshū poem by Monk Sosei by Fujiwara no Hideyoshi (1184–1240) from the ShinKokinshū (Love, 1203):

今こむと
ちぎりしことを
わすれずは
このゆふくれの
月や待らむ

ima kon to
chigirishi koto wo
wasurezu ha
kono yufukure no
tsuki ya matsuran

I swore to you
to come by and see you soon.
That is why you might
keep waiting for the moon
all along this endless twilight.

Fig. 46. **Nishikawa Sukenobu** (1671–1750): **"Castaway shells"** (*Utsusekai*) – a double-page no. 18 of A Picture Book of Poems about Sea Shells (*Ehon kaikasen*), 1st of 3 volumes, black and white woodcut, 19.4 x 26 cm, published by Hishiya Jihei in Kyōto, 1749. (Photo credit: National Gallery, Prague, Vm 1307_19)
The Book of Shells *presents a series of various shells joined by beauty figures, metaphoric poems and commentaries. The poem on the "castaway shell" (utsusekai) uses a word-play on the "world of sorrows" (ku no sekai), the verb "beat, crash" (utsu), and the noun "reality" (utsusu). The poem above the standing beauty reads:*

波のうつ
み島の浦の
うつせ貝
むなしきからに
われやなるらん

nami no utsu
Mishima no ura no
utsusekai
munashiki kara ni
ware ya naruran

Am I as empty
as a castaway shell
cast by waves
on the shore of Mishima
struck by the crashing waves?

motifs in silver and gold by the painter Tawaraya Sōtatsu (俵屋宗達, ca. 1570–ca. 1643), as mentioned above (Fig. 8). This edition's illustrations, showing the triangular figures of poets seated on tatami mats with embroidered edges (*agedatami kasen-e*), were cut into the woodblocks after paintings of Tosa Mitsushige (土佐光茂, ca. 1496–1559)[43] who perpetuated the mediaeval practice of depicting *kasen-e*. The eighteen poets for the Left side begin the book, followed by the eighteen Right Party contestants – which is quite unusual as most of the preceding scrolls and following books show the competing poets in firmly set couples of Left and Right parties. What is important is the large size of this volume (32.8 x 25.8 cm) which is quite similar to the Prague version of *Ōgi no sōshi.* Monochrome ink editions called *Saga-bon* were among the artistic movable-type-printed books made in Saga in during the first four decades of the 17th century. These printed books set the high standards for the future of printing from solid woodcut blocks, which developed into a remarkable and wide spread industry during the following three hundred years. Thanks to the lively book culture and the 250 year-long spell of complete peace during the Edo period, the Japanese were able to achieve a high degree of spiritual cultivation. Even then, of course, the lyrical

Fig. 47. **Nishikawa Sukenobu** (1671–1750): **The poetess Izumi Shikibu** (active in the early 10th century), double-page 5B, 6A from the Illustrated Album of Reeds (*Ehon nezamegusa*), 3 volumes, black and white woodcut (later edition with with stencil coloring, *kappazuri*), 21.6 x 15.7 cm, published by Kikuya Kihei, Kyōto, 1744. (second printing of ca. 1760). (Photo credit: National Gallery, Prague, Vm 3828_06)
Izumi is depicted in her study with books bound in the Edo-period fashion. She is looking pensively into the autumn garden with a rock. This scenery is usually used for the author Murasaki Shikibu, who created her Genji monogatari *at Ishiyamadera, famous for its rocks. The poem is one of full 100 poems of this court lady preserved in the imperial anthologies.*

山寺の
入相の鐘の
声ごとに
今日も暮れぬと
聞くぞ悲しき

yamadera no
iriai no kane no
koegoto ni
kefu no kurenu to
kiku zo kanashiki

How sad to hear
the evening bells tolling
from the mountain temple
and to know that lonely night
is coming near with every sound.

poetic tradition formed a formidable stream within the development of the culture of the "floating world" (*ukiyo*) and its images – Ukiyo-e.

The Thirty-six Poetic Immortals were among the illustrated books (*ehon, sashiehon*) designed by the first Ukiyo-e master Hishikawa Moronobu (菱川 師宣, 1618–1694)[44] (Figs. 43, 45), who firmly established the stylistic features of popular painting and the graphic art of Ukiyo-e which started blossoming around the Genroku Era (1688–1704). This era marked the climax of cultural revival in the western cultural center of Kansai around Kyōto and Ōsaka. Ōsaka artist and scholar Tachibana Morikuni (橘守国, 1679–1748), the author of the early 18th century encyclopedia of "Chinese" knowledge (*Morokoshi kinmō zui*), painted and annotated a two-volume classical *kasen-e* album under the title *Ehon nezashi takara* in 1745. Western Ukiyo-e culture was exemplified by the illustrator Nishikawa Sukenobu (西川助信, 1671–1750), who successfully imitated the classical Tosa School idiom of *Yamato-e* painting and copied the intricate "scattered" *chirashigaki* calligraphy in woodblock printed books with poems, such as the poetry books of sea shells, weeds, pines, etc., all illustrated with charming plump figures of contemporary beauties (Figs. 46, 47).

Fig. 48. **Katsukawa Shunshō** (1726–1792): A girl under a willow tree by a brook, the syllable "ka" from the 48-sheets series Ise Stories in Fashionable Brocade Pictures (*Fūryū nishiki-e Ise monogatari*), signed: Katuskawa Shunshō-ga, color woodcut, aiban 22.2 x 15.2 cm, ca. 1770–73.
(Photo credit: The British Museum, 1942,0124,0.10.6)
Illustration to Episode 50 of The Ise Stories with the widely-known anonymous poem "yuku midzu ni" (Kokinshū, 522) included in the Prague Ōgi no sōshi as no. 31:

yuku midzu ni	The greater folly
kazu kaku yori mo	lies not in writing figures
hakanaki ha	on a flowing stream,
omohanu hito wo	but in loving loyally
omofu narikeri	one who has no love for you.

Fig. 49. **Suzuki Harunobu** (1724–1770): The famed beauty Ono no Komachi with a fan, color woodcut, 27.3 x 20 cm, ca. 1765–70.
(Photo credit: The British Museum, 1906,1220,0.62)
This print is a full-colour plagiarism of the elegant figure of Ono no Komachi from the black and white book Ehon Tokiwagusa *by Nishikawa Sukenobu (1671–1750). The 9th century poetess is dressed in the twelve-layered robe* (jūni hitoe), *and holds a massive fan* (hiōgi) *of the Heian period, decorated with sakura flowers, which associate with Komachi's most famous poem* (Hyakunin isshu, *no. 9, translated by J. Mostow):*

hana no iro ha	The colour of the flowers
utsurinikeri na	has faded indeed
itadzura ni	in vain
waga mi yo ni furu	have I passed through the world
nagame seshi ma ni	while gazing at the falling rains.

Fig. 50. **Hosoda Eishi** ((1756–1829): The Poetess Saigū Nyōgo (Princess Kishi) with a fan and a modern lady with a child from the series Thirty-six Poetic Immortals in Modern Disguise (*Yatsushi Sanjūrokkasen*), color woodcut nishiki-e, chūban, 23.7 x 18.2 cm, 1799.
(Photo credit: West-Bohemian Museum, Pilsen, 0 94)
Eishi set the classical poetess seated behind a screen in justaposition to a contemporary gentle lady in modern hairdress, joined by a servant child. The quoted poem (Shūishū 451) on tuning the koto *zither by the wind is translated for Figs. 10, 22, 31 and is also included as no. 2 in the Prague version of Ōgi no sōshi. The concept of each of the five illustrations of the same poem is quite different.*

koto no ne ni	The wind through the pines
mine no matsukaze	on the peak closely resembles
kayofurashi	the sound of the zither--
idzure no o yori	from which, slope or string,
shirabe-someken	does it begin to play?

Fig. 51. **Katsushika Hokusai** (1760–1849): The poetess Ono no Komachi behind a screen from a *Rokkasen* series, color woodcut, signature Katsushika Hokusai-ga in the lower left corner, signature of the calligrapher Tōnan-sho next to the poem calligraphed in the Kōetsu style, color woodcut, 38 x 25.4 cm, ca. 1810.
(Photo credit: The British Museum, 1860,0414,0.321)
The long-lived master of Japanese Ukiyo-e *painting and prints created this print with the famous poem by Ono no Komachi as a display of his mastery of the few swift simplified outlines* (ryakuga) *that form the girl's garment. The poem about the changing heart of men* (Kokinshū *797) is quoted also in Fig. 32 (here with a change in the last verse:* hana ni zo ari*).*

iro mihede	The only flower
utsurofu mono ha	which keeps on changing color,
yo no naka no	which whithers here
hito no kokoro no	and blossoms elsewhere then,
hana zo arikeru	lives in the hearts of men.

When the center of illustrated book production shifted from Kansai to Edo (called also the Eastern Provices, Azuma) during the first half of the 18th century, many Edo artists, who called themselves *Yamato-eshi* (i.e., Okumura Masanobu, Kaigetsudō School artists), tried hard to learn the noble style of the imperial capital. In Edo, a new type of ethereal beauties was introduced by Suzuki Harunobu (鈴木春信, ca. 1626–1770) together with multicolored "brocade" prints (*nishiki-e* 錦絵) around 1765 (Fig. 49). His slender modern girls from teahouses were often posing as poets of the past in paraphrases called *mitate* (見立). Harunobu's follower Isoda Koryūsai (1735–1790) playfully re-worked the *Thirty-six Poetic Immortals* into beautiful courtesans from the "northern quarters" (*Hokurō yatsushi Sanjūrokkasen*, 1770–72). The two or three decades around the year 1800 mark the "golden age of Ukiyo-e". By the close of the 18th century, since the woodcut technique had made remarkable progress, large editions of colored books were sold on the market, and the revival of poetry reached its peak of popularity in gorgeously executed books, such as in the album of *Sanjūrokkasen* dating from the year 1794 and painted by the actor-print master Katsukawa Shunshō (勝川 春章, 1726–1793) with a gentle color scheme and dynamic lines (Figs. 34, 48). In 1799, the noble poets of the past were confronted with present day beauties in *Thirty-six Poetic Immortals in Modern Disguise* (*Yatsushi Sanjūrokkasen* 窶し三十六歌仙) by the "aristocrat" among plebeian illustrators, Hosoda Eishi (細田栄之, 1756–1829) (Fig. 50). Eishi, who was of samurai stock, soon turned to producing classical *kasen-e* albums like *Thirty-six Female Poetic Immortals* (*Onna Sanjūrokkase*n, 1801). Several excellent artists who specialized in portraying beauties and actors (*bijin-e, yakusha-e*) created images, which became the still unsurpassed symbols of Japanese beauty. Kitagawa Utamaro (喜多川 歌麿, c. 1753–1806) portrayed famed courtesans from the "green houses" (*seirō*) as noble ladies in close details of the *ōkubi-e* (large heads) on silver or yellow background (Fig. 66). In the series *Six Poetic Immortals in Five Seductive Moods* (*Goirozome rokkasen*) he painted the poetess Ono no Komachi as being seduced by the sex-repulsive courtier Ōtomo no Kuronushi – a vivid lascivious scene on a plain silver background. The founder of the mighty Utagawa School, Toyokuni I (歌川豐國, 1769–1825) specialized in actor prints, yet he painted also the *Thirty-six Poets* in a realistic vein and with psychological insight (Fig. 54).

Literati painters (*bunjin* 文人), too, loved to playfully invent thirty-six poetic immortals among contemporary folk and illustrate them with free brush outlines of the seated poets. An example of the literati style may be found in the *kasen-e* by the noted haiku poet and *bunjin-ga* painter Yosa Buson (与謝 蕪村, 1716–1784). Buson painted thirty-six *haiku* poets from the lineage of Matsuo Bashō as *kasen-e* in his highly abbreviated style joined by his remarkable calligraphy and its woodcut edition was printed posthumously as *The Thirty-Six Poetic Immortals of Haikai* (*Haikai sanjūrokkasen*, 1799). The title was re-cut and rearranged for a new edition entitled *Buson Sanjūrokkasen*, published in Edo in 1828. From the late 18th century, allegorical usage of the *Sanjūrokkasen* became fashionable with the popularity of "witty verse" (*kyōka* 狂歌). The famous writer Santō Kyōden (山東 京伝), who was also a painter under the name of Kitao Masanobu (北尾 政寅, 1761–1816), painted humorous portraits of his contemporaries disguised as famous poets with comic poems in his book *Library of Witty Verse in the Eastern Style* (*Azumaburi kyōka bunko* 吾妻曲狂歌文庫, 1786) (Fig. 53). An extremely simplified rendering called "abbreviated pictures" (*ryakuga* 略画) became popular with Masanobu's pupil Kitao Masayoshi (北 尾 政美 alias Kuwagata Keisai 鍬形蕙斎, 1764–1824), who reached an extreme of pictorial condensation. Masayoshi's style became familiar through the 15-volume album of Hokusai *manga*. Besides this popular manual of painting motifs, Katsushika Hokusai (葛飾北斎, 1760–1849) created several *ryakuga* albums full of playful tiny figures of contemporary commoners, and he even painted a *Rokkasen* series with *kasen-e* silhouettes drawn in several simplified outlines (Fig. 51). Hokusai illustrated *The Thirty-six Poetic Immortals of Haikai* (*Haikai Sanjūrokkasen*), which was published by an Edo association of *haikai* poets Reiki-ren and the publisher Bizen in Bunsei 10 (1827).[45] The number of 36 *kasen* may have inspired the famous painter to his epoch-breaking landscape series *The Thirty-six Views of Fuji* (*Fugaku Sanjū rokkei*, 1829–31) where Fuji Mountain is featured in basic outlines and colour-scheme as a simplifed visual equivalent of the concise *haiku* form.

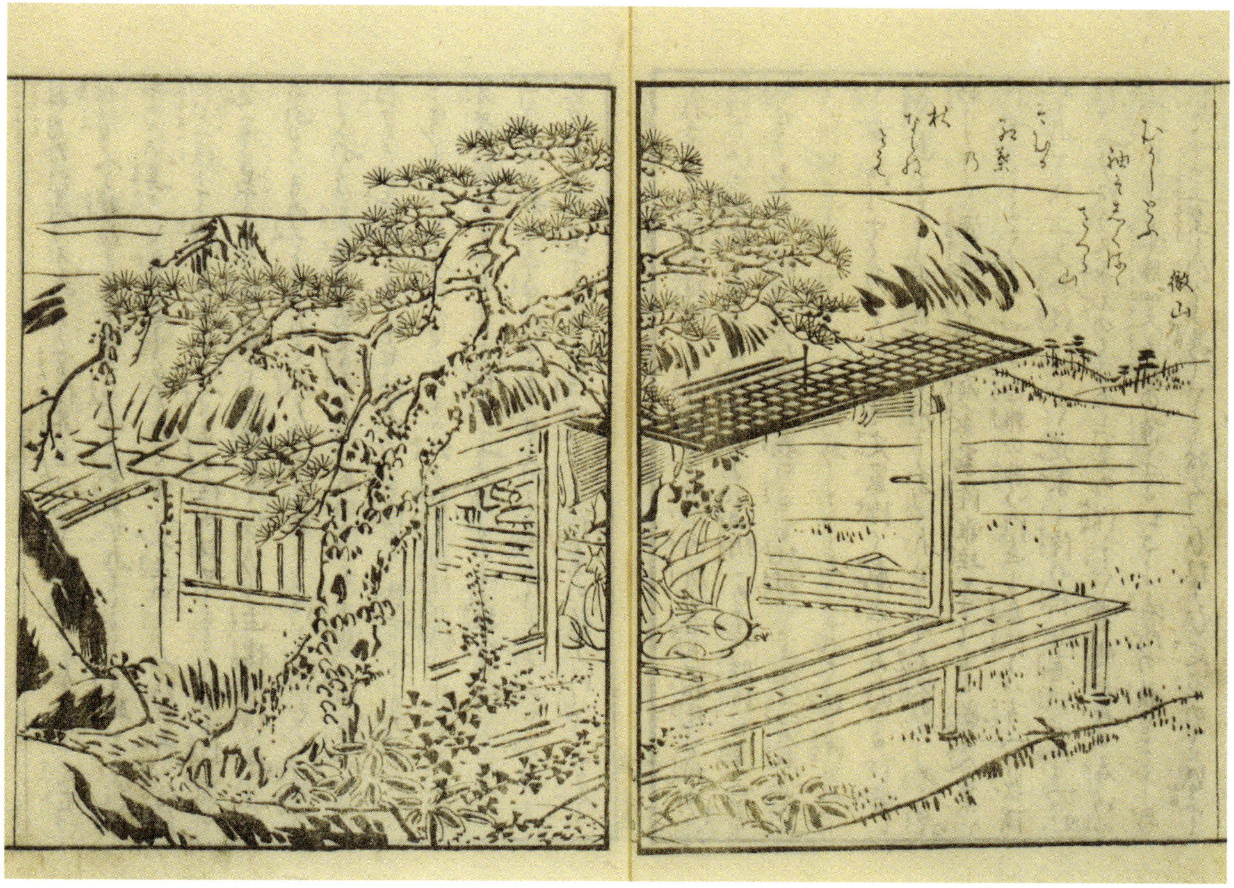

Fig. 52. **Ōishi Matora** (1794-1833): The poet Teika in his hut at Ogura Mountain, black and white woodcut on paper, double-page illustration form the 9th volume of One Hundred Poets with Tales for One Night Each (*Hyakunin isshu hitoyo gatari*), 9 volumes in blue slip cover (*chitsu*), published by Tsurugaya Kyūbei, Ōsaka, 25.7 x 18.5 cm, 1833.
(Photo credit: National Gallery, Prague, Vm 3806a-i)
This large compendium offers beautiful calligraphies of the one hundred poems of Hyakunin isshu (One Hundred Poems by One Hundred Poets), collected by Fujiwara no Teika at the Ogura Mountain in Kyōto around the year 1236. Ōishi Matora was a prolific illustrator from Ōsaka who was capable of combining the classical illustrations in the Tosa School vein with free-hand ink painting in literati style, such as on the illustration above showing humorous picture the compiler Teika himself, following poem no. 97 of the Hyakunin isshu.

The pupils and adherents of the Utagawa School represented the mainstream among Ukiyo-e broadsheet and book illustration designers throughout the 19th century. The cheap *kusazōshi* editions of *Sanjūrokkasen*, and *Hyakunin isshu* became extremely popular. During the first half of the 19th century, the ever-expanding market was flooded with cheaply produced books presenting the *Thirty-six Poetic Immortals* as women, warriors, artisans, Yoshiwara beauties, actors, etc., often joined with humorous *kyōka* poems (Fig. 53, 56). The classical *waka* collection of the *One Hundred Poets* (*Hyakunin isshu*) came to the fore, illustrated with *kasen-e* pictures. In 1818, the famous Ōsaka actor Nakamura Utaemon III, known also as Shikan by his *haimyō* (or *haiku* name), came to Edo and Akatsuki Kanenari (暁鐘成, 1793–1860) depicted him in one hundred different Kabuki roles joined with witty poems with very intricate associations to the contents of the contemporary Kabuki stage (Fig. 56). Kanenari also illustrated the *Ogura hyakushu ruidai banashi*, a three-volume book of anecdotes linked to the themes of poems in the *Hyakunin isshu*. In 1833, Ōsaka *bunjin-ga* painter Ōishi Matora (大石 真虎, 1794–1833) illustrated a nine volume black-and-white edition of *One Hundred Poets with Tales for One Night Each* (*Hyakunin isshu hitoyo gatari*) by Ozaki Masayoshi with double-page illustrations in the classical Yamato-e-Tosa vein, yet he combined historical explications with anecdotes illustrated in the free-wheeling literati style (Fig. 52). In 1836, Keisai Eisen (渓斎 英泉, 1790–1848), who specialized in beauty paintings (*bijin-e*), illustrated in

Fig. 53. **Kitao Masanobu** (1761–1816): The *kyōka* poet Hamabe no Kurohito with an *orihon* of poems and his own comic poem. A sheet from The Library of Witty Poems in the Eastern Style (*Azumaburi kyōka bunko* 吾妻曲狂歌文庫.), color woodcut *nishiki-e*, published by Tsutaya Jūzaburō (Kōshōdō), 25.9 x 17.5 cm, 1786.
(Photo credit: National Gallery, Prague, Vm 4282)
This collection of humorous kyōka poems follows the line established by Masanobu's teacher Kitao Shigemasa in his kyōkabon A Sack Full of Old and New Mad Poems about the One Hundred Poets (Hyakunin isshu Kokin kyōka fukuro), which was also published by Tsutaya Jūzaburō in Tenmei era. The poet's name, "Black man from the shore", is a funny variation on the famous classical poet Yamabe no Akahito ("Red man from the mountains") and his poem is as follows:

kuitaranu	The dumpling-shaped moon –
uwasa mo kikazu	a single one for China
Kara Yamato	and our Yamato –
tatta hitotsu no	does not listen to complaints
mochi no tsuki kana	that we have nothing to eat.

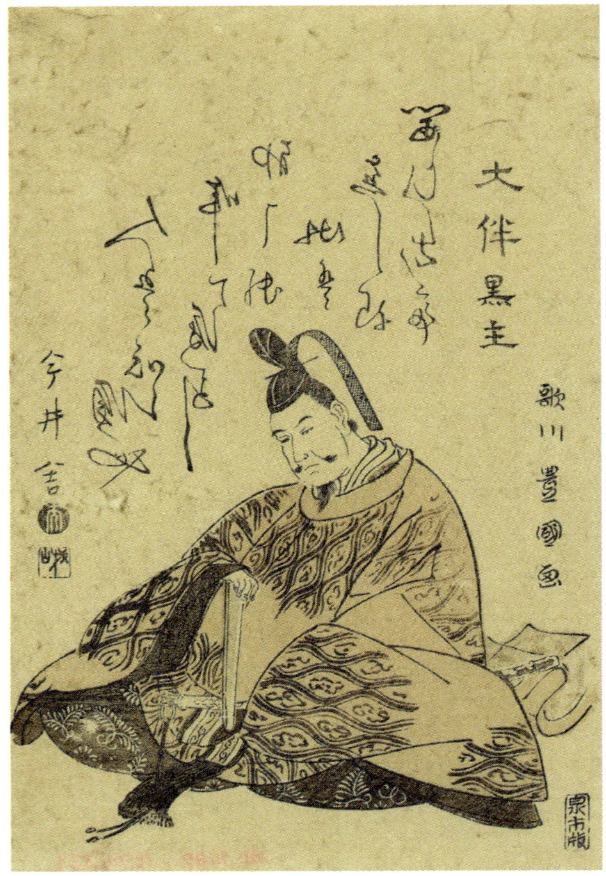

Fig. 54. **Utagawa Toyokuni** (1769–1825): Realistic *kasen-e* portrait of Ōtomo no Kuronushi (9th century) from a a set of Six Poetic Immortals (*Rokkasen*), woodcut printed from 2 color blocks, chūban size 23.6 x 16.2 cm, signature: Utagawa Toyokuni-ga, the mirror-turned calligraphy (*kagami moji*) signed Imai-sha, two personal seals of the calligrapher (*rakkan*) Hage, Ga ("Bald Mountain"), publisher's mark: Sen-Ichi-han (Izumiya Ichibei), 1787 (Year of the Sheep).
(Photo credit: National Gallery, Prague, Vm 1038).
Toyokuni was a master of actor prints and this kasen-e picture was obviously produced at the beginning of his career. The realistic facial expression of the pensive poet is achieved with simple graphic means. The intricate calligraphy, written intentionally to be read in mirror, conveys the desparate feelings of the author of a famous Kokinshū *love poem (KKS 735):*

omohidete	Since I am in love
koishiki toki ha	I go out in sad reveries.
hatsukari no	Wild geese high above
nakite wataru to	are flying by and shedding tears –
hito shirurame ya	Is she aware of all this?

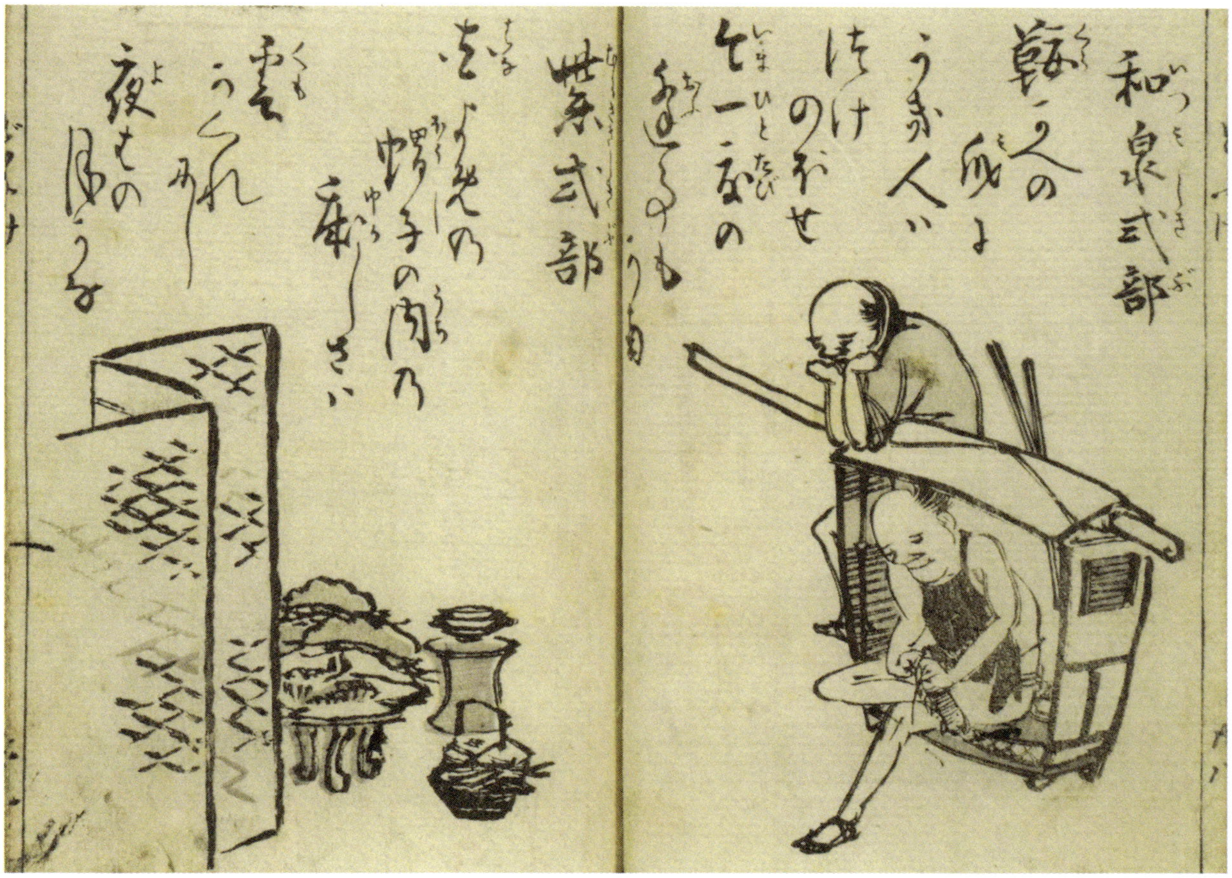

Fig. 55. **Takenouchi Bizan** (1780–1854). A double-page with variations of poems by Izumi Shikibu and Murasaki Shikibu from Comic Poem Variations of the One Hundred Poets (*Kyōka Hyakunin Isshu*) with a subtitle "Throwing stones into the dark night" (*Yamiyo wo tsubute*), black and white woodcut, 112 pp, 17.3 x 11.7 cm, published by Takenouchi Magobei, Edo, 1833. (Photo credit: National Gallery, Prague, Vm 1298)

On the left page there is a kyōka *on the* Hyakunin isshu *poem (no. 57) by Murasaki Shikibu (973–1025?) (also SKKS 1499), which reads (translated by J. Mostow):*

meguri aite
mishi ya soretomo
wakanu ma ni
kumo-gakurenishi
yoha no tsuki-kana

As I was wondering
whether or not I had seen it
by chance,
it became cloud-hidden
- the face of the midnight moon!

The kyōka humorous version quotes two lines of the original classical poem in the manner of a honkadori *variation:*

hanayome no
bōshi no uchi no
yukashisa ha
kumo-gakurenishi
yoha no tsuki kana

The beauty of the bride
in her lovely wedding hat
disappeared in no time –
it became cloud-hidden
as the face of the midnight moon!

On the right page there is a kyōka *on the* Hyakunin isshu *poem (no. 56) by Izumi Shikibu (976?–1030) (also* Goshūishū*), which reads (translated by J. Mostow):*

arazaramu
kono yo no hoka no
omohide ni
ima hito-tabi no
afu goto mogana

Among my memories
of this world, from whence
I will soon be gone,
oh, how I wish there was
one more meeting now with you!

The parody on the poem illustrated in the right-hand page reads:

kurakahe no
mi ni ukihito ha
tsukenobose
ima hito-tabi no
afu koto mogana

Pilgrim on the road
seat your body to the saddle
of my palanquin!
Oh, how I wish there was
one more meeting now with you!

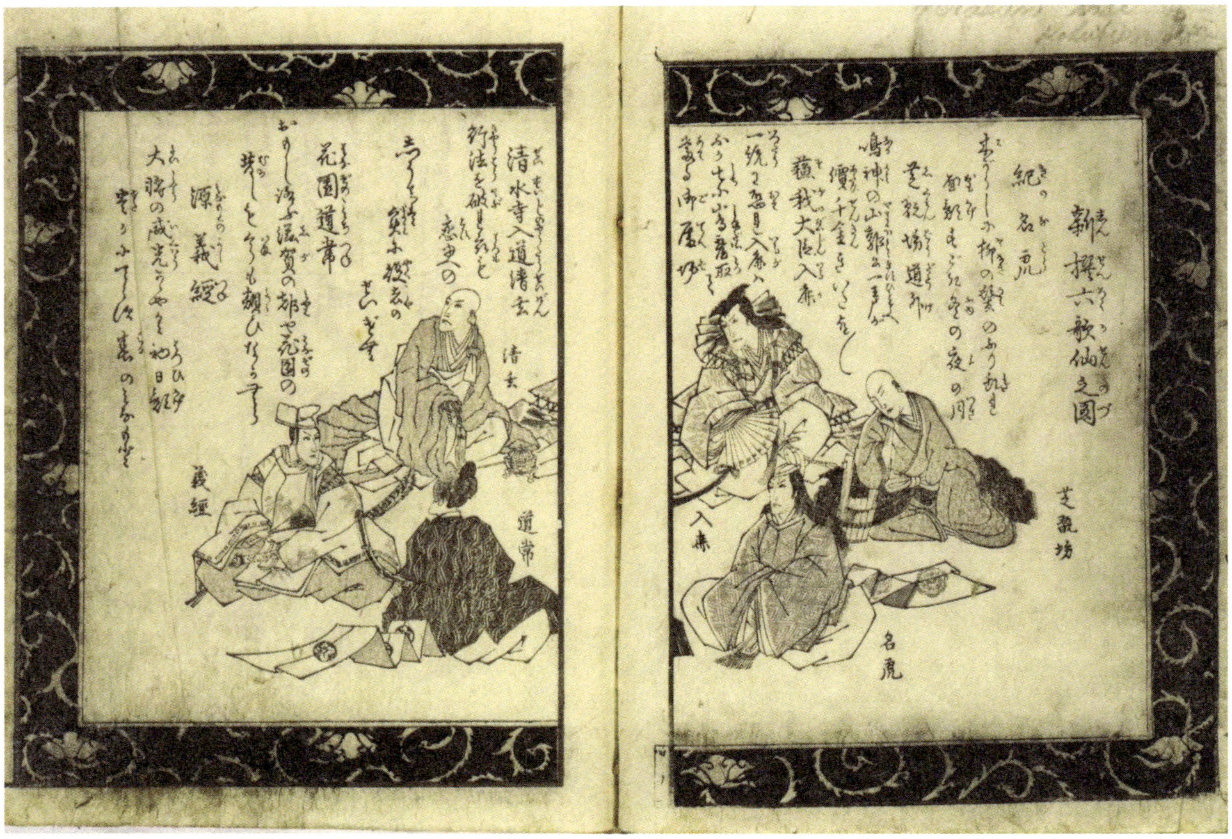

Fig. 56. **Akatsuki Kanenari** (1793–1860): Ōsaka actor Nakamura Utaemon III, also known as Shikan (1778–1838) posing as the Six Poetic Immortals in six different roles, a double-page from the *kyōka* comic verse album Shikan's Precious Library of the One Hundred Poets (*Shikan Hyakunin isshu tamabunko*), I vol. complete in 109 pp, black and white woodcut, 25.7 x 18.7 cm, published by Kawachiya Tasuke and Shioya Chōbei in Ōsaka and Tsuruya Kiemon and Kinsuke in Edo, 1819.
(Photo credit: National Gallery, Prague, Vm 3868)

On the double-page entitled New Selection of Rokkasen (Shinsen Rokkasen no zu) *there are six* kasen-e *pictures of Shikan in the* Kabuki *roles of (from right to left): Ki no Natora, Shikanbō Dōge, Soga Daijin Iruka, Seisuiji Nyūdō Seigen, Hanazono Michitsune and Minamoto Yoshitsune. The adjoining* kyōka *poems are highly allusive humorous pieces targeted at afficionado* Kabuki *lovers with many hints about recent* Kabuki *production. Utaemon III, who held the name of Nakamura Shikan I from the* 2nd *lunar month of 1818 to the* 9th *lunar month of 1819 when he was performing in Edo, was a great star in many male and female roles as well as quick change dance performances. Kanenari promptly illustrated his abilities in one hundred roles alluding to the* Hyakunin isshu. *The first poem, to give an example, where Shikan is posing as the ghost of Ki no Natora, evokes the freezing atmosphere of a ghost story on the* Kabuki *stage.*

kogarashi ni	The willows' hair
yanagi no kami no	is disheveled and torn
furimidare	by raging winds
omokage sugoki	How cruelly the moon stares
fuyu no yo no tsuki	in the cold air of the wintry night.

Another witty poem on Nakamura Shikan in the role of Hanazono Michitsune plays with the surname of the actor, which means "the inner village" and the special, secluded position of the vast and beautiful villa of Emperor Hanazono (today's Myōshinji Temple) within the capital of Kyōto (in Shiga province):

omoshirofu	Hanazono Palace
Shiga no miyako ya	in the capital of Kyōto
Hanazono no	- both in the past and now -
mukashi mo ima mo	has had a very special position
tokuhi Nakamura	as the inner village - Nakamura.

Fig. 57. **Utagawa Kunisada** (1786–1865): Three famous actors as the blossoms of Japan (*Waka no sannin*) – introductory illustration of the first volume of The Thirty-six Poetic Immortals among Actors (*Yakusha sanjū rokkasen*), vol. 1, 15 pp, black and white woodcut with an additional grey block, luxurious print with blind printing effects on thick *hōsho-gami* paper, published by Nishimuraya Yohachi, Edo, 25.5 x 18.5 cm, 1835. (Volumes 2 and 3 were never published).
(Photo credit: National Gallery, Prague, Vm 4010)
The title of this illustration Waka no sannin (和花の三人) *uses a homonym phrase* (kenyōgen), *playing with the "Three Young Blossoms" and the "Three Gods of Poetry".* Waka no sanjin (和歌三神) *are three ancient gods protecting poetry, adored since the Heian period: Deity of Sumiyoshi Shrine (Sumiyoshi Myōjin,* 住吉明神), *Deity of Tamatsushima Shrine (Tamatsushima Myōjin* 玉津島明神), *and the* Manyōshū *poet Kakinomoto no Hitomaro* (柿本人麻呂). *The three famous actors therefore stand in dignified poses, acting in a paraphrase (mitate) on the Gods of Poetry, as well as in the roles labelled next to the attached poems. From right to left, they are:*

1) ***Matsumoto Kōshirō** V (1765–1838) in the role of the lord of robbers Ishikawa Goemon from the play* Sanmon Gosan no Kiri. *The kyōka describes "the high-nosed"* (hanadaka) *Kōshirō as an actor who has been unsurpassed in the past and present:*

Kōshirō to	Among all actors
oshieraretemo	of the past and present time
dekigataki	Kōshirō
yakusha no naka no	is hard to imitate
kokon maremono.	so rare is his art.

2) ***Ichikawa Ebizō** V (known as Danjūrō VII till 1836, 1791–1859) in the role of Genkurō Yoshitsune from the historical play* Yoshitsune senbonzakura. *His kyōka reads:*

oyadama no	The gentle Yoshitsune
taishō nareya	the grassroot person
wasa ogi no	the Minamoto clan
Minamoto ni shite	played by the general of actors
gei no Yoshitsune.	the rounded-eye Danjūrō.

3) *Female roles actor* (onnagata) ***Iwai Tojaku** (until 1832 Hanshirō V, 1776–1847) as Mikazuki Osen in the drama* Shitennō Yagura no Ishizue *with the poem:*

kumoi yori	The slender moon
arawarenikeri	appears on mountains edge
hiōgi	on the third night
yama no ha ni ōu	as a cedarwood fan
mikazuki no mayu.	descending from the realm of the clouds.

Fig. 58. **Utagawa Kuniyoshi** (1797–1861): The poetess Suō no Naishi (1037?–1109), sheet no. 67 from the series One Hundred Poems by One Hundred Poets (*Hyakunin isshu no uchi*), color woodcut *nishiki-e*, published by Ebisu, 1842. (Photo credit: Municipal Museum, Olomouc, G 9499)
Kuniyoshi ventured into illustrating the most popular set of classical waka *poems of the Edo period, the* Hyakunin isshu, *in a time when censorship restrictions of the late Tempō era limited his favorite warrior themes. Kuniyoshi offers a variation on classical* Yamato-e *designs as carried over to the Edo period by the Tosa and Sumiyoshi Schools, using the brilliant technique of brocade pictures* (nishiki-e). *He depicts two seated court ladies in their typical attire, one seen from behind with a wide fan hiding her face, and a courtier peeping into the private parlor under the bamboo blinds and offering his arm as a pillow. (Translation by J. Mostow):*

haru no yo no	With your arm as my pillow
yume bakari naru	for no more than a brief
temakura ni	spring night's dream,
kainaku tatan	how I would regret my name
na koso oshikere.	coming, pointlessly, to 'arm.

Fig. 59. **Utagawa Kuniyoshi** (1797–1861): Nakura Station by the Plain of Musashi, sheet no. 40 from the series Sixty-nine Stations along the Kisokaidō Road (*Kisokaidō rokujūkyū tsugi no uchi*), Subtitle: Narihira and the Nijō Empress. Color woodcut nishiki-e, ōban 36 x 25 cm, published by Kazusaya Iwazō, 1852–53.
(Photo credit: William Pearl, kuniyoshiproject.com)
This impressive print illustrates Episode 12 from The Ise Stories (Ise monogatari), *where Narihira hides with his beloved empress, with whom he eloped from the palace, in the high grass of Musashi Plain. In the background, the palace guards, who are trying to trace the couple, are getting ready to burn down the grass. This motif has been illustrated hundreds of times, yet Kuniyoshi's pictorial concept is quite original. The poem from the* Kokinshū *(no. 17), included also in Prague* Ōgi no sōshi *as no. 13, reads: (Translation by J. Mostow)*

musashino ha	Do not burn today
kefu ha na yaki so	the grass on Musashi Plain.
waka-kusa no	Gentle as dew
tsuma mo komoreri	my love hides in here
ware mo komoreri.	and I am with her.

Fig. 60. **Utagawa Kunisada** (1786–1865): The Kabuki actor Sawamura Tanosuke III (1845–1878) as the ferryman Tombei's brave daughter Ofuna from the play *Shinrei Yaguchi no watashi*, from the series Mirror of Handwriting of Famous People of Today (*Imayō meika – Jihitsu kagami*), color woodcut, ōban, published by Maru-toku-han (Bakura-chō, Edo), carved by Yokogawa Hori-Take (Chōchiku), combined censorship and dating seal: *Aratame*, Year of Monkey, 10 month, 1860. The same series data apply for nos. 60–62. (Photo credit: National Gallery, Prague, Vm 4248, h, e, f.)
Sawamura Tanosuke III, the most talented actor of female roles (onnagata) *of the early Meiji period, is depicted here at the age of a mere 15 years. A few years later, however, this actor got gangrene and his legs were cut off by the American surgeon Hepburn- the creator of the transcription system of Japanese into the Latin letters (Hepburn script). The young plain country girl Ofuna, daughter of an evil ferryman, falls in love at first sight with the famous warrior Nitta Yoshimine. She saves his life by sacrificing herself. The play reaches a climax in the scene of the drum beating with a scabbard after Ofuna has been fatally stabbed. This scene is suggested by the drum hanging in the right hand upper corner. The poem written by the young actor speaks of Ofuna's unrequitted love:*

aikyō no
hiraki hajime ya
ume no hana

The tender blossoms
of the plum tree just opened
for the first love.

Fig. 61. **Utagawa Kunisada** (1786–1865): The Kabuki actor Ichikawa Danjūrō IX (1838–1903) in the role of Kamakura Gongorō Kagemasa in the play *Shibaraku* – the typical role of *aragoto* or "robust style of acting" among the Eighteen Famous Plays (*Jūhachiban*) of the Ichikawa actor family.
The crest of the actors bearing the name Danjūrō was the peony. Here the young son of Ichikawa Ebizō V (or Danjurō VII) still has the name of Kawarasaki Gonjūrō and the poetic name Shisen (Violet Fan), but soon he will become Danjurō IX, and acquire the poetic name (haimyō) Sanjō. Both poetic names are signed under the haiku poem written in the actor's own handwriting, which speaks about the fate of the Ichikawa actors who have the responsibility to continue the great family tradition:

watakushi no
tegara de ha nashi
fuyu botan

It is not due to my own
talents that I may act
as the winter peony.

Winter here refers to the fact that his father, the great actor Ebizō V, died a year ago, leaving him an orphan with the burden of the family tradition. In 1832, Danjūrō VII passed the great traditional name of Danjūrō to his handsome talented son Danjurō VIII. Since the young Danjūrō committed suicide in 1854, the name became ritually unclean, yet Gonjūrō had the courage to bring the name to a new spell of glamor by becoming Danjurō IX, the greatest actor of the Meiji period.

Fig. 62. **Utagawa Kunisada** (1786–1865): Ichikawa Ichizō III (acting under that name 1830–1865) in the role of Soga Jūrō Sukenari, the older of the two Soga brothers in the Soga vendetta (*Soga no taimen*) plays.
Jūrō is a typical soft and refined role of the "gentle style of playing", called wagoto ("Japanese type"). The thin, white, melancholic, soft-spoken and feminine wagoto hero is the opposite of the strong, red, loud and ruffian male roles called "the rough style" (aragoto) (see Fig. 61). Jūrō's poem speaking of the marsh "iso" hints at his lover, the dancer Ōiso, whom he married just for one short night before he would lose his life in the vendetta night-fight with his father's murderer Kudō Suketsune in his hunting camp under Mount Fuji. Thanks to the spectacular setting, the famous vendetta play was given as a New Year Kabuki performance.

Nami araki	How alluring is
hi ha ka mo kashi	the scent of plum on the marsh
iso no ume	beaten by wild waves.

Fans with actors' bust portraits, as shown in this series, were actually carried by Kabuki *theatre fans when the Tempō era restrictions faded away in 1860s before the start of the Meiji period (1868).*

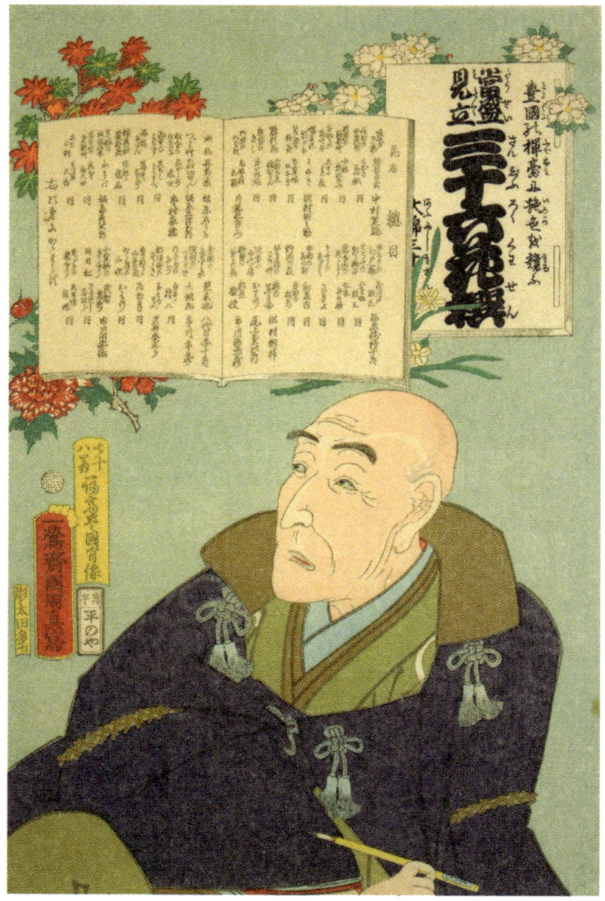

Fig. 63. **Toyohara Kunichika** (1835–1900): Portrait of the Ukiyo-e master Utagawa Kunisada (1786–1865) at 78 years of age. The title sheet of the *mitate* series the Selection of Thirty-six Flowers among Contemporary Kabuki Actors (*Tōsei mitate – Sanjū rokkasen*, 當盛見立 三十六花撰), color woodcut, *ōban*, published by Hiranoya, Edo, carved by Ota Tashichi, dating and censorship seal *aratame*, 1863.
(Photo credit: British Museum, no. 2005,0630,0.1)
A large bust portrait (nigao ōkubi-e) *of the great master of actor prints (see Figs.60-62) is set against a list of 36 actors and their* Kabuki *roles in the* mitate *series* The Selection of Thirty-six Flowers among Contemporary Kabuki Actors, *which employs a homonymous word play on* The Thirty-six Poetic Immortals. *Kunisada, alias Toyokuni III (1786-1865), was the most prolific master of* Kabuki *prints in the late Edo period, as his oeuvre of Ukiyo-e designs is estimated to surplus 30,000 sheets. He is portrayed here at the age of 78, when he survived his rivals, the Ukiyo-e masters Hokusai, Hiroshige, and Kuniyoshi. Kunisada's pupil Kunichika, the most appreciated* Kabuki *stage painter of the future Meiji period, duly acclaims his master's superiority by saying that the actor portraits of his series "are competing with the glamorous Toyokuni brush-style".* (Toyokuni no fudenami ni iroka wo kisou).

the classical Tosa style a large encyclopaedia of practical knowledge for women (*Nichiyō zatsuroku fujin shubunko*), which comprised fully illustrated collections of poems of *Hyakunin isshu, Sanjūrokkasen, Ōmi hakkei* (*Eight Views of the Ōmi Province* with poems), methods of wrapping up gifts, arranging flowers, playing *go* and *koto*, bringing up children, welcoming guests, etc. but also a full text of the educational classics *Onna imagawa* of the "Rules for Women" type of textbooks (*onna chōhōki*). The title of this large (178 pp.) volume for everyday use was *Shūgyoku Hyakunin isshu Ogura shiori* (*The Superior Jewel Compendium of One Hundred Poems by One Hundred Poets from Ogura*).[46] The popularity of this book is evident from an almost immediate second edition, as it was re-published again by Suharaya Mohei in 1850. Five other publishers joined to share the immense financial costs involved in cutting woodblocks for such a large compilation. But uniting forces among publishers and distributors for large and luxurious color editions of Ukiyo-e books and broadsheets was quite a normal practice, namely in the years following the crisis of Tempo Era in the years 1834–38 and the censorship measures of the Tokugawa regime which restricted the Ukiyo-e market, theatres and publishers after 1842 for over a decade.

The most remarkable development in *kasen-e* pictures occurred in the large-size colour woodcuts (*ōban nishiki-e*) produced by the Utagawa School of Ukiyo-e. Modern variations and paraphrases called *mitate* (見立) became extremely popular and the numbers 36, 53, 69 or even 100 became set numbers for series of colored *nishiki-e* prints. Utagawa Kuniyoshi (歌川国芳, 1797–1861) would draw charming variations on *waka* poems in his technically excellent *Hyakunin isshu* series (Fig. 58) or in his landscape series depicting the Kisokaidō road (Fig. 59). By the mid-19th century, most *mitate* prints centered on Kabuki actors. There are series of prints by the Utagawa School masters, and especially by Utagawa Kunisada (歌川国貞, 1786–1865), offering large busts of Kabuki actors figuring as one of the *Thirty-six Poetic Immortals* and referring to the old poems. In the series *The Mirror of Calligraphy of the Famous Personalities of Today* (*Imayō meika jihitsu kagami*) Kunisada combines fans with *haiku* poems written in the famous Kabuki actors' own hands with portrait busts in roles that inspire poetic puzzles (Figs. 60–62). Kunisada's pupil Toyohara Kunichika (豊原 国周, 1835–1900) portrayed his master on the introductory sheet of his series *The Selection of Thirty-six Flowers among Contemporary* Kabuki *Actors* (*Tōsei mitate Sanjū rokkasen,* 1863), where he plays on homonyms *kasen* 歌仙 "poetic immortal" and *kasen* 花撰 "selected flowers" (Fig. 63). Many other fanciful variations on the *Sanjūrokkasen* series and picture books on poetry were published well into the modern Meiji period (1868–1912).

The selection of graphic sheets combining the poet's figure in ancient attire with poetry shows the late Edo-period developments of these pictorial puzzles that had started in the witty games with fans at the Heian court and continued through the *ōgi no sōshi* of the 16th and 17th centuries. We can see that classical poetry was freely appropriated by each new generation and adapted to contemporary tastes. New layers of connotations were laid on the traditional culture, both literary and artistic, especially during the long epoch of peace in the Edo period. At the end of this long cultural tradition, the principle of the puzzle employed in the paraphrase *mitate*, which evokes all imaginable allusions and connotations from Japanese history, literature, art, and drama, reached the complexity, fragility, and intricacy of a spider's web. This, exactly, is the great advantage of the long and continuous cultural tradition of Japan.

During the first public research done by Americans after the opening of Japan to the "higher civilization" of the West in 1868 an astonishing fact came to light, that 40 % of the male and 18% of the female population of the Japanese were able to read fluently.[47] That means that Japan at that time was a highly literate country of the contemporary world. This high ratio of literacy may have led to the incredibly quick tempo of adoption by the island country of Western standards in all spheres of social life. A parliamentary system built on hitherto unknown democratic principles, jurisdiction, industry, agriculture, navy, army, transportation, science, medicine, journalism and media, music, fine arts, literature, drama, photography and very soon also film – all these innovations were absorbed by the Japanese in two generations. This admirable capacity of Japanese culture started deep in the past with composing fragile poems…

(Endnotes)

1 Brush (*fude*), ink stick (*sumi*), paper (*kami*), together with the ink rubbing stone (*suzuri*) are called The Four Treasures of the Scholar's Study (*bunbō shihō* 文房四宝 or *bunbō shikō* 文房四候).

2 The set of twenty sheets of *Ehon wakashū* (Prague version of *Ōgi no sōshi*, NG Vm 725) was published for the first time in the catalogue of the *sato-gaeri-ten* type of exhibition entitled *Message of Beauty from Prague (Praha no bi no tayori)* at the Kyōto National Museum in 2002. Prior to this date *Ehon wakashū* was published by Helena Honcoopová in an overall description in the following catalogues of the National Gallery, Prague: *Masterpieces from the National Gallery, Prague*, 1997, *Books cut into the wood*, 1997, A *Descriptive Catalogue of Japanese Illustrated Books in the National Gallery, Prague*, 1998.The set of six poets portraits (*kasen-e*, Prague private collection) is introduced here for the first time.

3 The six out of 36 *kasen-e* were acquired through purchase from a U.S. antique market by a private collector from Prague quite recently, in 2012. Their provenance is unknown.

4 This dating has been suggested as the most probable date of the set's origin by Prof. Hiroyuki Kanō during a personal consultation in November 2012. The set might have been painted just at the close of the century of the Warring State Period (*Sengoku jidai*) – at about the time Oda Nobunaga entered Kyōto to install centralized power and re-consolidated the war-haunted and destroyed city, even though he himself caused great damage by uprooting the Enryakuji Temple complex on Mt. Hiei in 1571.

5 *Ganpishi* 雁皮紙, formerly known as *hishi* 斐紙, is paper made from the fiber of the *ganpi* plant (Lat. Diplomorpha sikokiana honda or Wikstroemia sikokiana). Along with *choshi* 楮紙 (mulberry paper) and *mashi* 麻 紙 (hemp paper), *ganpishi* is one of three traditional handmade papers dating back to ancient times. In the Heian period fine *ganpishi*, known as *usuyō* 薄様, was used by court ladies for writing letters and poems in *kana* かな script, and as wrapping paper. (http://www.aisf.or.jp/~jaanus/deta/g/ganpishi.htm. 8.5.2013)

6 An alternative term for the "bird's-eye view" is "view from above" (*fukan zuhō* 俯 瞰 図法). It, however, has nothing to do with the Renaissance type of perspective, which is called *enkinhō* 遠近法 in Japanese and was occasionally used much later, from the 16th century in the so called "perspective pictures" (uki-e), inspired by the imported Western copperplates.

7 The practice of depicting court ladies from behind was much later adapted by Ukiyo-e painters for pictures of seated or standing courtesans. It has evolved into the so-called *mikaeri bijin* – a standing beauty looking back over her shoulder at a client (viewer). Both the seated court ladies of *Yamato-e* and the turning beauties of *Ukiyo-e* became icons typical for Japanese art.

8 The curving outline of *Yamato-e* is called "the iron-wire drawing line" (*tessenbyō* 鉄線描) in the terms of the variety of eighteen calligraphic lines in use in figural ink painting (*jinbutsu jūhachibyō* 人物十八 描). This term was coined much later during the Ming dynasty in China (1368–1644).

9 The most famous painting guild in Nara was the Shōnami-za 勝南院座 connected to the Ichijōin Hall 一乗院 of Kōfukuji temple.

10 This *Nara-ehon*, called alternatively *Kachō Fūgetsu* 花鳥風月, has been published in the Keiō University *Nara-ehon* database under the numbers KL 003 and BL 008. (see Bibliography, the Keiō University *Nara-ehon* database). In 2014, Joshua Mostow published in his *Courtly Visions* (see Mostow 2014) a detailed commentary on *Kachō Fūgetsu* (pp. 167,175) and included a complete translation of this tale by R. Keller Kimbrough as Appendix B of the same title (pp. 311–323).

11 The wide bat-fans became popular from the Kamakura period. The bat *kōmori* 蝙蝠 is a symbol of good luck, as the Sino-Japanese reading for 蝠 *fuku-bat* is identical with *fuku-luck*.

12 Similarly to these two games, pairs of painted clam shells were also used as courtly amusements (*kai-awase, kai-ōi* 貝覆い). Another popular game was the floating of sake cups on a stream in a garden – contestants had to compose a poem before the cup reached them, or drink its contents as a penalty. (http://www.aisf.or.jp/~jaanus/deta/o/ougi.htm, 12. 12. 2012)

13 *Hokkyō*, "the bridge of Law", is the highest of the three ranks in Buddhist clergy hierarchy (*hōin, hōgen, hokkyō*). (The same terms were used as ranks for medicine doctors and painters. Similar to Latin term "laureatus").

14 In 1615, Hon'ami Kōetsu founded an extraordinary art colony in Takagamine in the north-west suburbs of Kyōto, where many lacquer pieces, pottery marvels, paintings and calligraphies of innovative artistic quality were produced. He (with Shōkadō Shōjō and Konoe Nobutada) was counted among the "Three Brushes of the Kan'ei Era" (*Kan'ei no sanpitsu* 寛永の三筆), that is, the three best calligraphers of the time. These three calligraphic styles were often imitated on various poetry scrolls and publications during the Edo period.

15 Sōtatsu used simplified and highly abstracted natural motifs in combination with the *tarashikomi* technique (wet and blurring ink and paint) and layers of golden and silver leaf and dust decoration to create an idiosyncratic style of a painting, which led to the establishment of the decorative painting tradition of the Rimpa School in the 18th and 19th centuries.

16 Suzuki Jun, catalogue of the exhibition *Kasen-e of the Edo Period (1600–1868): The Transformation and Originality of the Courtly Beauty in Ehon (Illustrated Books)* at the National Institute of Japanese Literature (Kokubungaku Kenkyū Shiryōkan), 2009, no. 72.

17 Makoto Yasuhara in her study (see Bibliography) lists all the extant versions of *Ōgi no sōshi* and their names, for example, the Mingeikan copy containing 102 poems, the Nezu collection copy with 100 poems, and the Suntory version with only 30 poems.

18 The Prague *Ōgi no sōshi* was definitely made as a book, as all the twenty sheets are numbered in the right lower corner of each sheet. Yet its size might have been several millimeters larger, as some of the page numbers have been cut in half, probably during a later remounting and backing of the paper, which had carelessly been scribbled upon in ink on the reverse side.

19 Suzuki Jun, catalogue of *Kasen-e of the Edo period*, no. 1. (see the note 16).

20 The "Keichō to Genna era" dating was at first suggested in correspondence with the present day best Japanese *Nara-ehon* specialist, Prof. Ishikawa Tōru, before he came to Prague to scrutinize the book *in situ*. He came twice in 2014. When he saw the actual condition of the Prague *Ōgi no sōshi*, he inclined to the earlier, late 16th century date of origin. This corresponds with the already mentioned view (see note 4) of the important connoisseur of art, Professor Kanō Hiroyuki of Dōshisha University, who dated the Prague *Ōgi* volume to around 1590.

21 The term "genius" is sometimes used as the translation of the term *kasen*. In Chinese mythology, there was a group of Eight Immortals (Chinese *pinyin Baxian*, Jap. *Hassen*) designating a group of eight shaman-like eccentrics who lived quite freely beyond social structures and could perform miracles. In the theory of linked *renga* poetry, the same word denoted the usual length of a linked poem of the humorous *haikai no renga* type, which consisted of thirty-six stanzas. *Kasen* in this way became a synonym for the numeral thirty-six.

22 The Six Poetic Immortals from the 9th century (*Rokkasen*) include the following: Poetess Ono no Komachi, and poets Ariwara no Narihira, Sōjō Henjō, Kisen Hōshi, Bunya no Yasuhide and Ōtomo Kuronushi. All of them, excluding the last one, are also incorporated into the famous collection of *One Hundred Poems by One Hundred Poets* (Hyakunin isshu) compiled by Fujiwara no Teika in 1236. However, only the first three had been incorporated into the *Thirty-six Poetic Immortals (Sanjūrokkasen)* selection by Fujiwara no Kintō in the early 11th century.

23 Fujiwara no Kintō (藤原公任, 966–1041), also known as the Shijō Dainagon 四条大納言, was the most accomplished poetic arbiter and man of learning of the 11th century. He was the son and heir of the Great Minister (*dajō daijin*) Tadayori, and made an exceptional career at the imperial court, especially after the "almighty" Fujiwara no Michinaga came to power. He was the author of his own private poetry collection, compiler of imperial collections *Shūishū* 拾遺抄 and *Kingyokushū* 金玉集, and he also compiled the collection of highlights of both Chinese and Japanese poetry for public recitation, *Wakan rōeishū* 和漢朗詠集. He wrote the first Japanese poetics, still greatly inspired by Chinese theories, such as *Waka kuhon* 和歌九品, *Shinsen zuinō* 新撰髄脳, *Karongi* 歌論議, *Shijō Dainagon Uta-makura* 四条大納言歌枕, etc. In around 1009–10, he compiled the *Sanjūrokkasen*, called *Sanjū rokunin-sen* 三十六人撰 in his time. (http://www.asahi-net.or.jp/~sg2h-ymst/yamatouta/sennin/kintou.html, 8. 5. 2013)

24 The term *Sanjūrokkasen* is alternatively translated as "The *Thirty-six Geniuses of Japanese Poetry*", "*The Thirty-six Immortals of Poetry*", "*The Thirty-six Immortal Poets*", or, most often, "*The Thirty-six Poetic Immortals*".

25 Prince Tomohira (aka Guhei Shinnnō 具平親 王, 964–1009), known also as Chigusa-dono (千種殿) or GoChūshoō (後中書王 The Latter Learned Prince), was the seventh son of the Emperor Murakami and excelled in many fields of arts and learning (Chinese, calligraphy, yin-yan cosmogony *on'yōdō*, music etc.), but first of all, he composed poetry and had deep interest in its theory, competing with the supreme arbiter of poetry, Fujiwara no Kintō. His personal poetry collection has been lost, so that only 42 of his poems remain in the imperial anthologies, but thanks to him, such anthologies like *Wakan rōeishū* and *Sanjūrokkasen* were assembled upon his order by Fujiwara no Kintō. (http://www.asahi-net.or.jp/~sg2h-ymst/yamatouta/sennin/tomohira.html, 12. 9. 2013)

26 The first four poets (Hitomaro, Tsurayuki, Mitsune, Lady Ise) and the two last poets (Taira no Kanemori, Lady Nakatsukasa) are represented by ten poems in the original selection by Kintō, which was at first called *Sanjū rokunin-sen (Selection of 36 People)*.

27 Fujiwara no Norikane (1107–1165) 藤原範兼 created his own selection of *Gorokurokusen*, that is *Sanjūrokkasen*, before Shunzei, but it never gained wide popularity and is known today under the title *Thirty-six Poetic Immortals of the Middle Ages* (*Chūko sanjū rokkasen* 中古三十六歌仙).

28 The circumstances and rules of poetry contests from the time of their utmost popularity during the reign of ex-emperor Go-Toba at the turn of the 12th century are described in detail in Huey's *The Making of Shinkokinshū* (see the Bibliography).

29 The oldest *uta-awase* record dates from the year 913. A very extensive poetry contest of 600 rounds, the *Roppyakuban uta-awase*, was judged by Fujiwara no Shunzei (Toshinari) in 1192. Under the patronage of the ex-emperor GoToba a poetry contest of one thousand five hundred rounds (*Sengohyakuban uta-awase*) reached a record in number of recited poems. (See: Švarcová, 2005, p. 248).

30 The *Thirty-six Poetic Immortals* (*Sanjūrokkasen*) are listed below in pairs representing the Left (*SA*) and the Right (*U*) party. (R marks 3 poets from the *Rokkasen* set; there are 5 women poets marked as poetesses; * marks 6 poets from the Prague fragment).

1. Kakinomoto no Hitomaro SA
2. Ki no Tsurayuki U
3. Ōshikōchi no Mitsune SA
4. Ise U poetess
5. Otomo no Yakamochi SA
6. Yamabe no Akahito U
7. Ariwara no Narihira SA R
8. Sōjō Henjō U R
9. Sosei Hōshi SA
10. Ki no Tomonori* U
11. Sarumaru no Taifu SA
12. Ono no Komachi U R poetess

13. Fujiwara no Kanesuke SA
14. Fujiwara no Asatada U
15. Fujiwara no Atsutada* SA
16. Fujiwara no Takamitsu U
17. Minamoto no Kintada* SA
18. Mibu no Tadamine U
19. Princess Kishi, Saigū no Nyōgo SA, poetess
20. Ōnakatomi no Yoritomo U
21. Minamoto no Muneyuki SA
22. Minamoto no Shigeyuki U
23. Fujiwara no Toshiyuki SA
24. Minamoto no Saneakira U
25. Fujiwara no Kiyotada SA
26. Minamoto no Shitagō U
27. Fujiwara no Okikaze SA
28. Kiyohara no Motosuke U
29. Sakanoue no Korenori SA
30. Fujiwara no Motozane U
31. Sanjōin Nyokurōdo Sakon (Kodai no Kimi)* SA, poetess
32. Fujiwara no Nakafumi U
33. Onakatomi no Yoshinobu SA
34. Mibu no Tadami U
35. Taira no Kanemori * SA
36. Nakatsukasa * U, poetess

31 Sugawara no Michizane (菅原道真, 845–903), aka Kan Shōjō (菅丞相) or Kanke (菅家), was an important statesman, poet and calligrapher of the late 9th century under whose influence the tributary relationship of Japan to Tang dynasty China was abolished (894). After his protector, Emperor Uda, died, his enemies caused Kanke to be sent into exile in Dazaifu on the island of Kyūshū where he passed away from sorrow. Already during the 10th century he was deified as Tenman Tenjin 天満天神 – the Shintō *kami* of learning and poetry. Many shrines were founded in his name, the oldest being Kitano Tenman-gū in northern Kyōto. His attributes are an ox (the animal he used to ride into exile) and the five-petal blossom of the plum which embellishes his robe as a family crest (*kamon*). Although he was a master of Chinese poetry, a famous *waka* poem depicts a miracle (described also in his legends) of his favorite plum, which had flown from his garden in to join him in exile: "My plum blossoms! / Do not forget your scent / in the early spring / when the eastern wind blows / even though you have lost your master." (東風吹かば/にほひをこせよ/ 梅花 / 主なしとて/ 春を忘るな. *Kochi fukaba / nihohi okoseyo / ume no hana / aruji nashi tote / haru wo wasuru na*).

32 The two scrolls of the *Satake-bon Sanjūrokkasen* were dismantled into sheets with the individual poets in 1919. These fragments are found in various collections nowadays; Kodai no Kimi is kept by the Tōkyō National Museum.

33 The Tosa School (土佐派 Tosa-ha) was a painting academy connected with the imperial court and the Bureau of Painting (*edokoro*) where its members worked as official painters (*edokoro azukari* 絵所領), starting with Tosa Mitsunobu (1434?–1525?). The painters specialized in illustrating courtly subjects and classical narratives (such as *Genji-e*), poetry (*uta-e*) and later also bird and flowers (*kachō-ga*) using the *Yamato-e* style. Their work excelled in fine line work, carefully and minutely drawn details, brilliant colors and a rich application of gold. Later in the 16th century, a side branch of the Tosa School was established in Edo by Sumiyoshi Jokei (住吉如慶, 1561–1633), called the Sumiyoshi School (住吉派). Both reached their apex during the latter half of the 17th century, creating, for example, large *Rakuchū rakugai zu* and continued in their rather stereotyped academic activities until the late Meiji period when they underwent a reincarnation as *Nihonga* 日本画, the stream of traditionalist "Japanese painting".

34 The Kanō School (狩野派 Kanō-ha) was the most influential Japanese painting academy from the late 15th until the 20th century. Its founding masters became famous by creating the golden and green murals for the magnificent palaces of the Momoyama period in Kyōto, but with the Edo period they started serving as the exclusive artists (*goyō eshi*) of the shōgunate in Edo and split into many branches with hundreds of adherents.

35 Iwasa Matabei's mysterious life was detected from the period's documents by Sandy Kita in his biography *The Last Tosa: Iwasa Katsumochi Matabei, Bridge to Ukiyo-e* (412 pp), University of Hawaii Press, Honolulu, 1999.

36 The *Thirty-six Poetic Immortals* scroll by Iwasa Matabei in Boston Museum of Fine Arts measures 27.2 x 751.1 cm and can be visited on the Museum's web-site under inventory no. 11.7734. The famous American collector William Sturgis Bigelow donated it to the Museum of Fine Arts in Boston around 1900. (http://www.mfa.org)

37 Jōzanji is located in Kyōto's North-East part of Sakyō-ku, Ichijōji.

38 Kanō Naonobu (狩野尚信, 1607–1650), or Shōsei, was born in Kyōto as the son of Kanō Takanobu, and was the younger brother of Kanō Tan'yū (狩野 探幽, 1602–1674). As early as 1623 he was appointed *goyō eshi* (court painter) at the shogun's court, and in 1626 he worked together with his brother on the decoration of Nijō Castle, the seat of the Tokugawa shoguns in Kyōto. He was very successful as a painter: in 1630 he was summoned to Edo and given an estate, where he founded the Kobikichō branch of the Kanō School. His brother and he are seen as the greatest Kanō artists of the early Edo period. The set of large *Sanjūrokkasen* portraits painted on wooden boards in Konpira Sanctuary in Shikoku was co-produced by Kanō Tan'yū, Naonobu and Yūsen.

39 In the Kamakura and Muromachi periods two types of *ganpishi* developed: *torinoko-gami* 鳥の子紙 and *ma-niai-gami* 間似合紙. *Torinoko*, or "chick paper" took its name from its pale yellowish color, said to resemble baby chicks. *Ma-niai-gami* ("paper which fits into a space") takes its name from its size, which matches half the size of the average *fusuma* sliding door space. When used for a *fusuma* door or a *byōbu* folding screen, powdered stone was added to the paper to reduce its elasticity and give it fire resistance.

40 The court poetess active in the 9th century Kodai no Kimi, 小大の君, or Kimi no Ōkimi きみの大君, or Sanjōin Nyokurōdo Sakon, should not be mixed up with Nukata no Ōkimi (known also as Nukata no Himemiko 額田 姫王) of the 7th century, the consort of Tenmu Tennō and the poetess of the *Man'yōshū* collection. Ōkimi was a title for queen.

41 Shōkadō Shōjō was the abbot of the Shintō-Shingon Buddhist sanctuary of Iwashimizu Hachimangū.

42 This album has been recently exhibited at the National Institute of Japanese Literature as part of their exhibition *Kasen-e of the Edo period (1600–1868)* as cat. no. 6 with a commentary by Suzuki Jun. (see note 16).

43 Tosa Mitsushige, also known as Mitsumochi, was the son of Mitsunobu and is best known for illustrating the *Dōjōji engi emaki* depicting Princess Kiyohime's transformation into a serpent-dragon – a legend that was turned into the Noh, Jōruri and Kabuki drama theme "Musume Dōjōji".

44 Hishikawa Moronobu was born as the son of a countryside fabric dyer in Chiba. He moved to Edo around 1665 and he died there after 30 prolific years of painting and designing illustrated books during the period of the greatest upheaval of cultural activities at the close of the 17th century, in the Genroku Era (1688–1704).

45 *The Thirty-six Poetic Immortals of Haikai* (*Haikai sanjūrokkasen*) is a book compiled by Hisensai Shō and published in Edo with Hokusai's illustrations in 1827. This *chūbon*-sized book signed Tōto Katsushika Iitsu-ga is stored in the Boston Museum of Fine Arts under the accession number 1997.819.

46 The complete set of *Hyakunin isshu* with Eisei's illustrations from this edition was reproduced in the Czech translation of the *One Hundred Poets* by Helena Honcoopová and published in the National Gallery, Prague as *Sto básní* in 1997.

47 Peter Kornicki, *The Book in Japan: A Cultural History from the Beginnings to the Nineteeth Century*, Brill, Leiden, 1998 (498 pp.), edition University of Hawaii Press, Honolulu, 2011 (p. 411).

Fig. 64. **Hidaka Tetsuō** (1791–1872): Bamboo, fan-painting (*senmenga*), ink on paper, 14.8 x 47 cm, inscription: "Painted by Tetsuō on an Autumn day, Ansei 2" (*kinoto u shūjitsu, Tetsuō*), 1855.
(Photo credit: The British Museum, 1973,0226,0.91, purchased from Jack Hillier, 1973)
Fans with ink painting often offered the popular topic of the Three Friends of Winter, that is the Bamboo, Pine and Plum, that symbolized the ideal qualities of an educated man, so called "literati" (bunjin). *Hidaka Tetsuō* (日高 鉄翁, *aka Tetsuō Somon* 鉄翁 祖門) *from Nagasaki belonged to Literati* (bunjin-ga) *or Nanga School and specialized in bamboo and orchid paintings.*

JOE HLOUCHA: COLLECTOR OF THE PRAGUE BOOK OF FANS

Helena Honcoopová

The greatest Czech collector of Japanese art was undoubtedly the prolific travel-book and *Japonérie* writer Joe Hloucha (1881–1957) whose huge legacy of almost nine thousand Japanese artifacts is kept by the Náprstek Museum in Prague (founded 1862). Over two thousand graphic sheets and books have been acquired by the Collection of Oriental Art of the National Gallery, Prague (established 1952). Though many collectors interested in Japanese art brought as many as an estimated 50,000 Japanese art and crafts objects to the Czech lands over five centuries (starting from the first Jesuit missions in the late 16th century), none of them can compare to Joe Hloucha.

The son of a brewer from the small central Bohemian village of Podkováň, Josef moved to Prague (to the famous St. Thomas Brewery rented by his father) in 1895 – one year after the large Czecho-Slavonic Exhibition in Prague, which aroused vivid interest in ethnographic studies and far-away countries. The exhibition, which attracted over two million visitors, had been organized by the founder of the first Czech Industrial Museum, Vojtěch Náprstek (1826–1894) who was the pivotal figure in the modernization of Czech society and inspired many of his contemporaries to "open the window to the world" and to take interest in non-European cultures. A number of 19th and 20th century travelers, scholars, entrepreneurs, writers and artists contributed their collections of ethnographic, art and crafts objects to Náprstek's museum. One of Náprstek's friends was the first Czech globetrotter Josef Kořenský (1847–1938), a teacher and paleontologist who visited Japan during his two round-the-world journeys in 1893–1894 and 1900–1901 and wrote two books about Japan.[1]

Josef Hloucha happened to be his nephew; he started reading books about Japan and collecting Japanese things at an early age, as he greatly admired his uncle. Young Josef studied in the library of the Náprstek Museum, which became the center of progressive intellectual life in Prague during the three closing decades of the 19th century. The young collector Josef did not meet the founder of the museum in person, as Náprstek died in 1894, but he helped his widow Josefa to organize the Náprstek Museum collections from all over the world and studied all available books on Japan.

Josef and his older brother Karel decided to become writers. While Karel was writing a novel on the recently concluded Russo-Japanese War, Joe (which became Josef's artistic name) published his first *Japonérie* novel *Sakura in a Gale* (*Sakura ve vichřici*) in 1905. It almost instantly became a best-seller, and was later reprinted eleven times. The readers of the sentimental novel set in Tōkyō and describing an unhappy love-affair between a young art collector and a Japanese girl named Sakura, admired especially the true-to-life description of the Japanese environment, customs and art.

In fact, the novel was written before Hloucha, aged 25, accomplished his first dream-trip to Japan on his round-the-world journey in 1906. He spent four months in Ōsaka and Tōkyō and purchased many works of art, studying diligently all he could get to know about things Japanese. He had a compatriot advisor in Karel Jan Hora (1881–1974)[2], the manager of a Chicago-based gas company in Ōsaka, who could speak fluent Japanese and helped him to find fine and cheap graphic sheets and illustrated books in the Kansai region – a fact which accounts for the remarkable collection of Ōsaka prints, more than one

Fig. 65. Joe Hloucha with a *jinrikisha* during his first journey to Japan in 1906. The picture is signed and annotated in the bottom right corner "Travelling in the Japanese manner".
(Photo credit: Arcimboldo gallery, Prague)

thousand sheets in number, in the Czech Republic. Most of the precious collection of almost a thousand Ukiyo-e albums and illustrated books (*ehon*) kept by the National Gallery, Prague now, were collected in that year.[3] Even though we can find no evidence of where and when the Prague *Ōgi no sōshi* was purchased in the detailed diary-like books that Hloucha kept for the whole of his life, the rare manuscript was most probably acquired during his Kyōto sojourn in 1906.[4]

After coming back to Prague, Hloucha annotated, enlarged and exhibited his collections and continued to write books on Japanese themes.[5] Before and after the First World War Hloucha published thirteen titles, some illustrated by lithographs of Japanese graphic art from his collections and even bound in the Japanese manner by sewing folded sheets together in a soft cover. His stories, public lectures and studies on Japanese history, architecture and manners were often illustrated by his own photographs, as he took many of his own pictures on glass plates and assembled over 500 photographs. Books by and on Hloucha were embellished by illustrators showing the manly Hloucha during his travels. His writings on Japan started with *Japonérie* fiction in the Pierre Loti (1850–1923) vein, but in the 1920s, as his knowledge of things Japanese grew, he wrote serious sociological and literary studies comparable to the writings of Lord A. B. Mitford (1837–1916) or Lafcadio Hearn (1850–1904).

Hloucha continued his art collecting, purchasing many Japanese, Chinese and also European and Czech Gothic art items at European auctions. He also continued to promote Japanese culture in many magazines and public lectures. With his brother Karel he made his living as a successful entrepreneur. In 1908 he started running a Japanese tea-house, the Yokohama, built according to his own design by the architect Jan Kotěra, first at a large Chamber of Commerce Exhibition site and then in the newly constructed Lucerna Palace in central Prague (1909–1915). Another Japanese-style restaurant, bar and dancing lounge run by the Hloucha brothers was the Alhambra in the very heart of Prague (1915–1924). In 1924, Hloucha built Villa Sakura in a Japanese style in Roztoky near Prague; its garden was decorated with *yaezakura* and *momiji* trees, Chinese lions (*karajishi*), stone lanterns (*tōrō*), and a lake with golden carp *koi* spanned by a vaulted *taiko* bridge. On a plot adjacent to Hloucha's villa, the large Japanese-style Sakura Hotel was built by the architect Illich in 1929. It became a famous excursion spot for the Prague bourgeoisie, offering Japanese *sakura* viewing, kimono-dressed waitresses and jazz music to dance to.[6] Thanks to Hloucha, Roztoky became the "Little Japan by Prague" – alleys of *sakura* still bloom there each spring.

In 1926, however, Hloucha sold his Villa Sakura and started his second journey *autour-du-monde*, stopping in Japan for five months. This second journey was even more fruitful than the first one as far as art collecting was concerned, even though the collector was greatly distressed by the damage caused by the Great Earthquake of 1923. He devoted much care to collecting Buddhist sculpture, altarpieces, statuary, lacquer-ware and porcelain this time, as he had more money. Moreover, he was assisted by the newly established Embassy of Czechoslovakia (becoming friends with the ambassador Josef Švagrovský[7]), which was founded as a result of the new European division after World War One in 1918.

In November 1929, Hloucha was able to organize his First Exhibition of Non-European Arts and Crafts on the precincts of the huge Prague Trade Fair Palace. He exhibited the results of thirty years of collecting in an astonishing volume and quality. There were art objects from Persia, Africa (Congo, Cameroon, Liberia, Togo, Nigeria), Oceania (the Marquees Islands, the Solomon Islands, New Guinea), Burma, Siam, Tibet, Hong-Kong, China, and – above all – Japan. And Hloucha offered a collection of 1175 pieces to the state for a small amount of money (a million and a half of Czech crowns). He wished the state to build a new modern museum of non-European art for the huge collection. His biographer of the time, Šmejkal, wrote the following: "In the interest of the state and of the nation, the government is obliged to save this precious treasure for the state and make it the foundation of a future Ethnographical Museum, which should replace the old-fashioned Náprstek Museum. Will the state buy similar treasures from abroad in the future for a great deal of money?"[8] There was a lot of support for this new museum project in the press, a ministerial committee was established to prepare the new museum, but the typical Czech bureaucracy worked slowly and the overall economic crisis intervened to stop the plan.[9]

The Second World War started by bringing disaster and depression. Hloucha deposited a part of his collection in ministerial storehouses, and sold the best artifacts of his collection to the Arts and Crafts Museum in Prague where an exhibition of Japanese crafts was held in 1943. He kept on studying and collecting Czech Gothic and Baroque art. During the Second World War, Hloucha started writing a book on Ukiyo-e based on his own huge collections of over six thousand prints. Yet his knowledge of Japanese was limited and he relied on English, German and French books and on the expertise of a more experienced Czech connoisseur of Ukiyo-e, the Benedectine friar and poet Sigismund Bouška (1867–1942), who studied Ukiyo-e from 1907, made his first exhibition in 1911 and annotated Ukiyo-e collections both for the Náprstek Museum and for Hloucha. Bouška died during the war, while writing his own version of Ukiyo-e history.[10] Both Bouška's and Hloucha's wartime manuscripts on Ukiyo-e have been lost. Hloucha's only monograph on Japanese art, entitled *Hokusai – The Man Mad about Painting*, was printed in Czech (by Orbis) in 1949 and in English (by Artia) in 1954. Starting from the latter part of 1950s, however, many of Hloucha's woodcuts appeared in a series of five books on Japanese prints that were written by the founder of the Collection of Oriental Art of the National Gallery, Prague, Lubor Hájek (1921–2000).[11]

Hloucha did not travel to Japan for a third time. He became too old to venture on a long trip. For the three free years after the Second World War, Hloucha could observe the unusual bloom of Czech Oriental studies, being an honorary member of various cultural committees and enjoying peace, respect and welfare. Then in 1948, the Communists launched a coup d'état, and Hloucha had to observe the gradual cultural and social decline of his nation helplessly. In 1955, he was forced by the pro-Soviet regime to pass his Japanese collections to the state in exchange for a small pension. His treasures of non-European art, 8,792 pieces in total, mostly from Japan (6756) and China (614), were transported to the Náprstek Museum during the next year, while he was helping with the documentation. The Japanese collection included over 3,554 prints, 530 photographs, 85 netsuke, 77 *tsuba*, 380 ceramics, fine lacquer-ware and many paintings and Buddhist altarpieces and statues. As well there were ethnographical objects like toys and fans, bamboo baskets and furniture. Hloucha died suddenly after the process. He died aged 76, penniless, childless, with no posterity. None of his dreams regarding the future of his collection came true. Still, he died nobly, for he managed to collect for his native country, as a single private person, what other countries spent generations collecting.

(Endnotes)

1 Kořenský's first travelogue was recently published in an English translation by Miriam Jelínková. Josef L. Kořenský, *In Japan (1893–94)* (Prague: Karolinum, 2013).

2 Winkelhöferová, Vlasta: "The First Czech Specialist in Japanese Studies and a Capable Businessman, Karel Jan Hora" (První český japanolog a zdatný obchodník Karel Jan Hora). In: *Krajané ve starém Orientu (Our Natives in the Old Orient)*, edit. Obuchová, Ľubica, published by Czech Oriental Society, Praha, 2008, pp. 100–115.

3 The complete library of Hloucha's Japanese books was inherited by the Oriental Institute of the Czech Academy of Sciences after his death in 1957, yet the National Gallery, Prague was able to gain all the woodcut illustrated Japanese books amounting to almost a thousand volumes in 1975. They were catalogued and published in a descriptive catalogue in English in 1998 (see the Bibliography: Honcoopová, Koike, Rezner, 1998).

4 The Hloucha collection of *ehon* was more or less completed in 1906, as evidenced by a 1910 list of 750 books hand-written in green ink and stored in the Hloucha archive in the Náprstek Museum. Yet in 1949, Hloucha enlarged this part of the collection by purchasing 60 books from the legacy of the graphic artist Emil Orlik, who stayed in Japan in 1900 for one year so as to learn woodcut technique. See: Kraemerová, 2007, note 73, p. 41.

5 Hloucha's early writings published before WWI (such as *My Madame Chrysanthéme, Letters by an Unknown, Flood, Pavilion of Horrors)* are typical *Japonérie* writings. His later books from the 1920s, however, *(Little Japanese, The Town of a Thousand Temples, Fairy Tales of Japanese Children, The Selllers of Smiles, Among Gods and Demons*, etc.) are competent studies of Japanese ethnography, history and culture.

6 In 1939, the Sakura Hotel turned into a war field hospital and later it was greatly ruined during the forty years of the communist regime. It serves as a hospital still today.

7 Josef Švagrovský served as the Ambassador at the Czechoslovak Embassy in Tōkyō from 1923 to 1928.

8 J. V. Šmejkal: *Milenec Nipponu – Tři lásky Joe Hlouchy (The Lover of Nippon – The Three Loves of Joe Hloucha),* Prague, 1931, p. 98.

9 Hloucha offered his collection in a large auction held in Berlin one year later, on December 3rd and 4th, 1930. Even though Hloucha sold a part of his collections (namely the African art) in the Berlin auction, most of it, fortunately, returned home to Prague.

10 A major part of Bouška's collection of Japanese prints, focused on the early period Ukiyo-e, has been acquired by the Náprstek Museum. A small part is archived in the Memorial of Czech Literature at Strahov Monastery in Prague.

11 The five titles on Ukiyo-e history written quite early after the atrocities of WW2 by the young Asian art specialist from the National Gallery, Lubor Hájek, were published only in foreign languages and they were never printed in Czech. Hájek's titles cover early period Ukiyo-e, the age of Harunobu, the age of Utamaro, Ōsaka prints, and a review of Japanese graphic art (all issued by the Publishing House Artia, Prague, 1956–1973). It is typical of a small nation like the Czech one (10 million inhabitants), that there does not exist any book in the native language on the history of Japanese Ukiyo-e, even though three Czech scholars, Bouška, Hloucha and Hájek, wrote books on the topic.

Fig. 66. **Kitagawa Utamaro** (1753–1806): **A Maiden that Seldom Meets Love** from the series The Love Book from an Anthology of Poems (*Kasen koi no bu – Mare ni au koi*, 歌仙恋の部稀二逢恋), color woodcut, ōban size 38.5 x 25.2 cm, published by Tsutaya Jūzaburō, ca 1793–94. (Photo credit: The British Museum, 1906,1220,0.331, purchased from Arthur Morrison, 1906)
One of the five sheets in the poetic (kasen) *series of "large busts" of beauties* (bijin ōkubi-e) *portraits a young maiden from a rich merchant family (safely-guarded, well-dressed and with a perfect coiffure), who secretly gestures to a long-unseen lover. As a modern variation* (mitate) *on classical love poetry, the naïve girl poses for a poetess who waits for her lover in vain. Utamaro's girl portraits are still unsurpassed as epitomes of Japanese female beauty. Also the incredible technical skills of Edo carvers and printers of color woodblocks displayed on this print are worth of notice, as they had been brought to perfection in the Golden Age of* Ukiyo-e, *which blossomed during two or three decades around the year 1800.*

APPENDICES

APPENDIX A
SELECTED BIBLIOGRAPHY

* Brazell, Karen (edit.): *Twelve Plays of the Noh and Kyōgen Theaters,* Ithaca: Cornell University, East Asia Papers, no. 50.

* Brower, Robert H.: *Conversations with Shōtetsu,* Center for Japanese Studies, The University of Michigan, 1992.

Brower, Robert H. and Earl Miner: *Japanese Court Poetry*, Stanford University Press, 1961.

* Brower, Robert H. and Earl Miner: (transl.): *Fujiwara no Teika's Superior Poems of Our Time*, Stanford University Press, 1967.

* Carpenter, John T.: *Reading surimono*, Leiden – Boston: Hotei publishing, 2008.

* Chibbett, David: *The History of Japanese Printing and Book Illustration.* Tōkyō: Kodansha International, 1977.

* Clark, Timothy: *Ukiyo-e Paintings in the British Museum,* British Museum Press, 1992.

* Coudenhove, Gerolf: *Vollmond und Zikadenklänge, Japanische Verse und Farben,* C. Bertelsmann Verlag, 1955.

* Cranston, Edwin A (edit.): *A Waka Anthology,* Volume Two: Grasses of Remembrance, Stanford University Press, 1993.

* Fiala, Karel (transl.): *Příběh prince Genjiho* (Genji monogatari by Murasaki Shikibu), translated into Czech in 4 volumes, Praha - Litomyšl: Paseka, 2002–2006.

* Forrer, Matthi (edit.): *Essays on Japanese Art presented to Jack Hillier*, London: Roberts G Sawers, 1998.

* Hillier, Jack & Lawrence Smith: *Japanese Prints – 300 years of albums and books,* British Museum, 1983.

* Hillier, Jack: *The Art of the Japanese Book.* 2 vols. London: Philip Wilson for Sotheby's, 1987.

* Honcoopová, Helena: *Knihy řezané do dřeva (Books Cut into the Wood)*, catalogue of Japanese illustrated books, National Gallery, Prague, 1997.

* Honcoopová, Helena, Koike Masatane, Alam Rezner: *Japanese Illustrated Books and Manuscripts from the National Gallery, Prague,* A Descriptive Catalogue, National Gallery, Prague, 1998.

* Honcoopová, Helena: *Kunisada, Mistr pozdního japonského dřevořezu, (Kunisada, Master of the Late Japanese Woodcut)* National Gallery, Prague, 2005.

* Huey, Robert N. *The Making of Shinkokinshū.* Cambridge, MA: Harvard University Asia Center, 2002.

* Huey, Robert (trans): "Sakuragawa: Cherry River", *Monumenta Nipponica*, vol. 38, no. 3 (Aut.1983).

* Ishikawa, Tōru: *Naraehon to Naraemaki no uchū* (*The Cosmos of Nara-ehon and Nara-emaki*), Tōkyō: Shibunkaku Shuppan, 2010.

* Ishikawa, Tōru: *Nyūmon Nara-ehon emaki* (*Introduction to Picture Books and Scrolls from Nara*), Tōkyō: Shibunkaku Shuppan, 2009.

* Katō, Shūichi: *Form, Style, Tradition: Reflections on Japanese Art and Society*, Berkeley: University of California Press, 1971.

* Katō, Shūichi: *A History of Japanese Literature – The First Thousand Years*, Macmillan Press 1979.

* Keyes, Roger: *The Male Journey in Japanese Prints*, University of California Press 1989.

* Keyes, Roger: *Surimono*, Kodansha, 1984.

* Kornicki, Peter: *The Book in Japan: A Cultural History from the Beginnings to the Nineteenth Century.* Leiden: Brill, 1998.

* Kraemerová, Alice and Jan Šejbl: *Japonsko, má láska – Český cestovatel a sběratel Joe Hloucha* (*Japan, my love. The Czech traveller and collector Joe Hloucha*), Praha: Národní muzeum, 2007.

* Mason, Penelope: *History of Japanese Art*, New York: Harry N Abrams Inc, 1993.

* Meech, Julia and Jane Oliver (eds.): *Designed for Pleasure: The World of Edo Japan in Prints and Paintings,* 1680–1860 University of Washington Press, 2008.

* Miner, Earl: *An Introduction to Japanese Court Poetry.* Stanford: Stanford University Press, 1968.

* Miner, Earl: *Japanese Linked Poetry, An account with translations of haikai and renga poetry,* Princeton University Press, 1979.

* Miner, Earl, Hiroko Odagiri, and Robert E. Morrell, eds., *The Princeton Companion to Classical Japanese Literature,* Princeton University Press, 1985.

* Mostow, Joshua: *Pictures of the Heart: The Hyakunin Isshu in Word and Image.* University of Hawai'i Press, 1996.

* Mostow, Joshua S.: „A New "Classical" Theme: The One Hundred Poets from elite to Popular Art in the Early Edo Period" in Elisabeth Lillehoj (ed.): *Critical Perspectives on Classicism in Japanese Painting, 1600–1700*, Honolulu: University of Hawai'i Press, 2004.

* Mostow, Joshua: *At the House of Gathered Leaves: Shorter Biographical and Autobiographical Narratives from Japanese Court Literature.* University of Hawai'i Press, 2004.

* Mostow, Joshua and Henk J. Herwig: *The Hundred Poets Compared: A Print Series by Kuniyoshi, Hiroshige, and Kunisada,* Leiden – Boston: Hotei Publishing, 2007.

* Mostow, Joshua and Royall Tyler: *The Ise Stories: Ise monogatari,* University of Hawai'i Press, 2010.

* Mostow, Joshua S.: Courtly Visions. *The Ise Stories and the Politics of cultural Appropriation*, Leiden – Boston: Brill, 2014.

*Munsterberg, Hugo: *The Japanese Print A Historical Guide*, John Weatherhill, 1988.

* Murase, Miyeko: "Fan Paintings Attributed to Sōtatsu: Their Themes and Prototypes." *Ars Orientalis* 9 (1973), pp. 51-77.

* Murase, Miyeko: *Bridge of Dreams, Mary Griggs Burke Collection of Japanese Art,* New York: The Metropolitan Museum of Art, 2000.

* Ōta, Shōko (ed.): *Edo no shuppan bunka kara hajimatta imēji kakumei (The Visual Revolution Initiated by Edo Publishing Culture)*, Kanazawa geijutsugaku kenkyūkai, Kanazawa, 2007.

* Pekarik, Andrew J.: *The Thirty-six Immortal Women Poets A poetry album with illustrations by Chobunsai Eishi*, Barrie & Jenkins, 1991.

* Sakomura, Tomoko: *Pictured Words and Codified Seasons: Visualizations of Waka Poetry in Late Sixteenth- and Early Seventeenth-Century Japan* (unpublished Ph.D. dissertation), Columbia University, 2007.

* Shirane, Haruo (ed.): *Early Modern Japanese Literature: An Anthology, 1600–1900.* Columbia University Press, 2002.

* Shively, Donald H.: "Popular culture", *The Cambridge History of Japan,* vol. 4, Cambridge, 1991.

* Suzuki, Jun: *Kasen'e of the Edo period* (1600–1868) – *The Transformation and Originality of the Courtly Beauty in Ehon (Illustrated Books)*, Tōkyō: National Institute of Japanese Literature, 2009.

* Suzuki, Daisetz T.: *Zen and Japanese Culture*, Princeton University Press, 1970.

* Švarcová, Zdenka: *Japonská literatura 712–1868*, Praha: Karolinum, 2005.

* Tokuda, Kazuo and Yasuhara, Makoto: *Gakushūin joshi daigaku toshokan shinshutsu Ōgi no sōshi no shōkai (Introduction to the newly published Book of Fans from the Gakushūin)*, Gakushūin University Papers no 15, 1994.

* Tsuji, Eiko: *Zaigai Nihon jūyō emaki shūsei* (A selection of important Japanese picture scrolls in foreign collections), 2 vols., Tōkyō: Kasama shoin, 2011.

* Tyler, Royall (transl.): *Japanese Noh Dramas.* London: Penguin Books, 1992.

* Tyler, Royall (2010): see Mostow, Joshua and Royall Tyler: *The Ise Stories.*

* Ueda, Makoto (transl.): *The Old Pine Tree and Other Noh Plays.* Lincoln: University of Nebraska Press, 1962.

* Watson, William (ed.): *The Great Japan Exhibition Art of the Edo Period 1600–1868*, London: Royal Academy/ Weidenfeld & Nicolson, 1981.

* Watson, Burton: *Kanshi: The Poetry of Ishikawa Jozan and Other Edo-Period Poets*, North Point Press, 1990.

* Yasuhara, Makoto: *Ōgi no sōshi no kenkyū – asobi no geibun (A Study of the Books of Fans – A Playful Poetic Genre)*, Tōkyō: Pelikan-sha, 2003.

Databases

ASAHI NET, Yoyo no utabito,
(comprehensive repertory of *waka* with biographies of poets)
http://www.asahi-net.or.jp/~sg2h-ymst/yamatouta/sennin.html

ART RESEARCH CENTRE =ARC, Ritsumeikan University,
Kyōto, (*kuzushiji,* Ukiyo-e, Kyoto maps and many other db)
http://www.dh-jac.net/db/arcnishikie-e/searchp.htm

HATHI TRUST DIGITAL LIBRARY, Michigan University,
(selected titles of illustrated books)
http://babel.hathitrust.org/cgi

HŌSEI UNIVERSITY, Tōkyō
(resource materials concerning Noh drama, librettos etc.)
http://aterui.i.hosei.ac.jp/oguchi/nogaku/index.htm

JAANUS =Japanese Architecture and Art Net Users System
(English on-line Dictionary compiled by Dr. Mary N. Parent)
http://www.aisf.or.jp/~jaanus/

KEIŌ UNIVERSITY, Tōkyō, database of Nara-ehon
(international db of Nara-emaki compiled by Ishikawa Tōru)
http://dbs.humi.keio.ac.jp/naraehon/index-e.html

KOKUBUNGAKU KENKYŪ SHIRYŌKAN = NIJL = National Institute of Japanese Literature, Tōkyō
http://www.nijl.ac.jp/

NATIONAL DIET LIBRARY = NDL, Tōkyō
(92 000 items of old books dating to 1868, English interface)
http://dl.ndl.go.jp

NICHIBUNKEN, Jap. Culture Research Institute, Kyōto
(database of Japanese waka poetry with indices, etc.)
http://www.nichibun.ac.jp/graphicversion/dbase/database.html

PRINCETON UNIVERSITY LIBRARY
http://library.princeton.edu/databases/subject/japanese-studies

TOKYO METROPOLITAN LIBRARY=METRO
(1 800,000 prints, old and rare books, maps, magazines etc.)
https://catalog.library.metro.tokyo.jp/

WASEDA UNIVERSITY, KOTENSEKI, Tōkyō
(database of classical Japanese literature incl. manuscripts)
www.wul.waseda.ac.jp/kotenseki/search.php

WASEDA UNIVERSITY, ENPAKU, Tōkyō
(database of 57,500 theatrical prints, no English interface)
www.enpaku.waseda.ac.jp/db/enpakunishik/search.php

APPENDIX B
LIST OF ILLUSTRATIONS

APPENDIX C
CHART OF IMPERIAL ANTHOLOGIES (*chokusenshū* 勅撰集)

NO. 順番	ANTHOLOGY 勅撰集	EMPEROR 下命者	DATE 成立年	COMPILERS AND POETS 撰者	MAIN POETS REPRESENTED 最多入集歌人	NO. OF POEMS 総歌数
1	Kokin shū 古今集 KKS	醍醐天皇 Daigo	905	Ki no Tsurayuki, 紀貫之•Ki no Tomonori 紀友則•Mibu no Tadamine 壬生忠岑	Ki no Tsurayuki 紀貫之 (872–945)	1111首
2	Gosen shū 後撰集 GSS	村上天皇 Murakami	951	Kiyohara Motosuke 清原元輔•Ōnakatomi Yoshinobu 大中臣能宣•Minamoto no Shitagō 源順•Sakanoue no Mochiki 坂上望城	Ki no Tsurayuki 紀貫之	1425首
3	Shūi shū 拾遺集 SIS	花山院 Kazan-in	c. 1007	Emperor Kazan-in 花山院 (967–1008)	Ki no Tsurayuki 紀貫之	1351首
4	Goshūi shū 後拾遺集 GSIS	白河天皇 Shirakawa	1086	Fujiwara Michitoshi 藤原通俊 (1047–1099)	Izumi Shikibu 和泉式部 (976–1030)	1218首
5	Kinyō shū 金葉集 KYS	白河院 Shirakawa-in	c. 1125	Minamoto no Shunrai 源俊頼 (1055–1129)	Minamoto no Shunrai 源俊頼	665首
6	Shika shū 詞花集 SKS	崇徳院 Sutoku-in	1144–51	Fujiwara no Akisuke 藤原顕輔 (1090–1155)	Sone no Yoshitada 曾禰好忠 Izumi Shikibu	415首
7	Senzai shū 千載集 SZS	後白河院 GoShirakawa-in	1188	Fujiwara no Toshinari (Shunzei) 藤原俊成 (1114–1204)	源俊頼 Minamoto no Shunrai	1288首
8	Shinkokin shū 新古今集 SKKS	後鳥羽院 GoToba-in	1205	Fujiwara no Ariie 藤原有家•Fujiwara no Teika 藤原定家•Fujiwara no Ietaka 藤原家隆•Fujiwara no Masatsune 藤原雅経•Jakuren Hōshi 寂蓮	Saigyō, Jien, Jakuren, Shunzei, Shikishi, GoToba-in, Kunaikyō	1978首
9	Shinchokusen shū 新勅撰集 SCSS	後堀河天皇 GoHorikawa	1235	Fujiwara no Sadaie (Teika) 藤原定家 (1162–1242)	Fujiwara no Ietaka 藤原家隆 (1158–1237)	1374首
10	Shokugosen shū 続後撰集 SHGSS	後嵯峨院 GoSaga-in	1251	Fujiwara no Tameie 藤原為家 (1198–1275)	Fujiwara no Teika 藤原定家 (1162–1242)	1377首
11	Shokukokin shū 続古今集 SHKKS	後嵯峨院 GoSaga-in	1265	Fujiwara/Kinugasa no Ieyoshi 藤原家良 (1192–1264)•Fujiwara no Tameie 藤原為家•Fujiwara no Motoie 藤原基家 (1203–1280)	Munetaka Shinnō 宗尊親王 (1242–1274)	1915首
12	Shokushūi shū 続拾遺 SHSIS	亀山院 Kameyama-in	1278	Fujiwara no Tameuji 藤原為氏 (1226–1286)	Fujiwara no Ietaka 藤原為家 (1158–1237)	1459首
13	Shingosen shū 新後撰 SHGSS	後宇多院 GoUda-in	1303	Fujiwara/Nijō Tameyo 二条為世 (1282–1338)	Fujiwara no Teika 藤原定家 (1162–1242)	1607首
14	Gyokuyō shū 玉葉 GYS	伏見院 Fushimi-in	1312	Fujiwara/Kyōgoku Tamekane 京極為兼 (1254–1332)	Fushimi-in 伏見院 (1265–1317)	2800首
15	Shokusenzai shū 続千載集 SHSZS	後宇多院 GoUda-in	1320	Fujiwara/Nijō Tameyo 二条為世 (1282–1338)	GoUda-in 後宇多院 (1267–1324)	2143首
16	Shokugoshūi shū 続後拾遺集	後醍醐天皇 GoDaigo	1326	Nijō Tamefuji 二条為藤 (1275–1324)•Nijō Tamesada 二条為定 (1293–1360)	Fujiwara no Tameuji 藤原為氏 (1221–1285)	1353首
17	Fūga shū 風雅集 FGS	花園院 Hanazono-in	1344–46	Kōgon no in 光厳院 (1313–1364)	Fushimi-in 伏見院 (1265–1317)	2211首
18	Shinsenzai shū 新千載集 SSZS	後光厳天皇 GoKōgon	1359	Fujiwara/Nijō Tamesada 二条為定 (1293–1360)	Nijō Tameyo 二条為世 (1250–1338)	2365首
19	Shinshūi shū 新拾遺集 SSIS	後光厳天皇 GoKōgon	1364	Nijō Tameakira 二条為明 (1295–1364)	Nijō Tametō 二条為藤 (1341–1381)	1920首
20	Shingoshūi shū 新後拾遺集 SGSIS	後円融天皇 GoEn´yū	1384	Nijō Tametō 二条為遠•(1341–1381)•Nijō Tameshige 二条為重 (1325–1385)	Nijō Yoshimoto 二条良基 (1320–1388)	1554首
21	Shinshokukokin shū 新続古今集 SSHKKS	後花園天皇 GoHanazono	1439	Asukai Masayo 飛鳥井雅世 (1390–1452)	Asukai Masayori 飛鳥井雅縁 (1358–1428)	2144首

Total number of *waka* poems in 21 Imperial Anthologies 33 277

APPENDIX D
LIST OF FIRST LINES
A: POEMS INCLUDED IN THE FACSIMILE

POEM NO.	FIRST LINE	JAPANESE	ENGLISH
	AFUMI NARU		See ŌMI NARU
	AFUSAKA NO		See ŌSAKA NO
92	AKATSUKI NO	あかつきの	I do not learn / from our unhappy partings
24	AKI NO YO NO	あきのよの	The light, here and there / of the crescent moon
115	AKIBANA NO	あきばなの	In the autumn is it / indeed most moving
10	ARAKANE NO	あらかねの	Coming from the earth / of hard iron
76	AU TOKI WA	あふときは	Although i think / I have exhausted all I had to say
88	BASHŌ HA NI	はせをはに	The banana-leaves / sometimes the wind
112	E NI KAKU MO	えにかくも	Even painted as a picture / they scatter
49	FUDE MO YOSHI	ふてもよし	The brush is good / the ink-good Sumiyoshi
33	FUJI NO NE WA	ふちのねは	The height of / Mt. Fuji's peak
62	FURU YUKI NI	ふるゆきに	In the falling snow / the bamboo in the garden
61	FURUSATO NO	ふるさとの	Ah, the flowers of the attending ash
98	FUTATSU ARU	ふたつある	The names of the plant /are two:/longing-and forgetting
44	GOKURAKUNO	こくらくの	Inside paradise, as well / since I take a seat, indeed
82	HAMA CHIDORI	はまちとり	O beach-plovers! / although your traces may return
22	HANA MO USHI	はなもうし	The cherry blossoms are frail / and the gales are cruel
51	HANA NARABA	はなならは	If they were flowers / how many times on my sleeves
9	HANA SAKABA	花さかは	They said that / if the cherries bloom, they would send word
72	HARUKA NARU	はるかなる	Ah, to be alone / among the rocks
8	HITO NO KONO	人のこの	Thinking that they say / that a person's child
91	HONOBONO TO	ほのぼのと	Faintly, faintly / through the morning mist
106	HONOKA NI MO	ほのかにも	Had I not at least / tied a knot around
50	IKADASHI YO	いかたしの	Hey, Raftsman! / Wait! There is something I would ask you
38	ISOGAZUBA	いそかすは	If he had not hurried / they would not have got so wet
54	KAGIRI AREBA	かきりあれは	Since there is a limit / I have come to see the moon
66	KARAKOROMO	からころも	Robe from Cathay / long and comfortably worn
107	KARASAKI NO	からさきの	The pine of Karasaki / has become twain
20	KARI-KURASHI	かりきらし	Having spent the day hunting / at Katano
18	KASASAGI NO	かささきの	When I see the whiteness / of the frost that lies
64	KAWAZU NAKU	かはすなく	Do their reflections / appear in the Kaminabi River
99	KAZE FUKEBA	かせふけは	When the wild wind blows / out upon the sea white waves
116	KIKU DANI MO	きくたにも	Ah, the distant voice of the stag / crying in the foothills

POEM NO.	FIRST LINE	JAPANESE	ENGLISH
111	KIKU YA IKA NI	きくやいかに	Do you hear it? / Even the wind in uncertain skies
113	KIMI GA YO NO	きみがよの	As an example / of how long / my lord shall live
102	KIREBA USHI	きれはうし	If I cut them, it's sad / if I do not cut them, then it will
103	KIRI NO HA NO	きりのはの	The fallen leaves of the paulownia / have also become difficult
3	KIRI NO KI NO	きりのきの	At the start / the wood of the paulownia
86	KOISHIKU WA	こひしくは	If you long for me / come, if even only for a visit
25	KOKORO TO YA	こころとや	Do the leaves themselves / decide to change color?
52	KOMA TOMETE	こまとめて	There is no shelter / for me to stop my horse
53	KONO UCHI MO	このうちも	He envies / even the one in the cage / the mountain-tit
85	KŌRI IRU	こほりいる	Entering the ice / do the mndarin ducks,, too
2	KOTO NO NE NI	ことのねに	The wind through the pines / on the peak closely resembles The same poem is also in Figs. **10, 22, 31, 50**
104	KOYA NO IKE	こやのいけ	The irises / mixed with the flags
55	KUMANO NARU	くまのなる	If only I could pass / the silent Otonashi River
73	KUMO NO IE NI	くものいへに	Even if one can snag / a wild horse/ in a spider web
45	KUSA NO NA MO	くさのなも	Even the names of grasses, / depending on where you are,
83	KUZU WA URAMI	くすはうらみ	The kuzu is bitter / and the pampas beckons
59	MATSUKAGE NI	まつかけに	Even the beribboned cock / of Osaka barrier
108	MI WO SUTETE	みをすてて	Even if they discard their lives / will they regret the flowers
12	MICHINOBE NO	みちのへの	Ah, The Spring mountain-man / with his bundle of brushwood
56	MIWATASEBA	みわたせは	When I gaze afar / the hue of the cherrey mixes
1	MIYAKO MADE	ミやこまて	the Chinese zither / of Karakoto
17	MIZU NO OMO NI	ミつのおもに	When I count / the shining moon-waves
96	MOMIJI-BA NO	もみち葉	The deep colour / of the autumn leaves
34	MOMOTOSE NI	ももとせに	Only one year shy / she is, of a full hundred
100	MONO IEBA	ものいへは	Since he spoke / my father was buried under
7	MONONOFU NO sakuragari shite	ものゝふの さくらかりして	A warrior / hunting for cherry blossoms
39	MONONOFU NO yoroi ni masaru	もののふの よろひにまさる	Even though the paper robe / has replaced the armour
47	MONONOFU NO yumihari tsuki no	もののふの ゆみはりつきの	The warrior / draws his bow by the light
13, **59**	MUSASHINO WA kefu ha na yaki zo	むさしのは けふはなやきそ	Oh no, please today / do not burn Musashi Plain!
77, **20**	MUSASHINO WA tsuki no izubeki	むさしのは つきのいすへき	There are no mountains / from which the moon can rise
5	NAGAMUREBA	なかむれは	As I look out / the leaves of bamboo are white

POEM NO.	FIRST LINE	JAPANESE	ENGLISH
109	NARUKO WO BA	なるこをは	Bird clappers in fact / by the wind of their own wings
79	NATSU NO YO NO	なつのよの	In the length of time / required to take a fan
6	NONOMIYA NO	のゝミやの	A carriage of flowers / adorned with the autumn grass
21	ŌMI NARU	あふミなる	Let them now begin / the Tsukama Festival
81	ŌIKAWA	おほひかは	I hear them sending /the raft of cedar
93	ONAJIKU WA	おなしくは	If it's all the same / I will die in the Spring
43	ONOZUKARA	をのつから	When, by chance, / they meet, do they say:
60	ŌSAKA NO	あふさかの	In the shade of the pines / scooping up pure water
58	OSOROSHI YA	おそろしや	Oh, how terrible! / It will certainly lead to our separation
15	OTO NI KIKU	をとにきく	Striking out to gaze / At Drum Falls o high repute
14	SAHOHIME NO	さほひめの	Ah, The Spring landscape / where the horsetails
114	SAKAE YUKU	さかへゆく	The prospering / houses of arrow and bow
57	SAKISOMESHI	さきそめし	When the wind blows / on the cherry blossoms
26	SAKURA CHIRU	さくらちる	The wind that blows / beneath the trees
95	SHINOBUYAMA	しのふやま	Ah, Mount Shinobu / I would gladly find a way
90	SATSUKI MATSU	さつきまつ	When I smell the scent / of the mandarine orange blossoms
69	SHINOHARA YA	しのはらや	The low bamboo field / with greens from Sano
28	SHISHI NARABA	ししならは	With boars / four times four / should make sixteen
4	SHITA MOMIJI	したもみち	The evening showers / of the mountains where the lower
30	SHIZU NO ME GA	しつのめか	The humble woman / grows used to raking up
80	SUMIYOSHI NO matsu no koma yori	すみよしの まつのこまより	As I gaze out / from between the trees of pine
118	SUMIYOSHI NO matsu ni fuji aru	すみよしの まつにふちある	Since it is an august reign / with wisteria in the pines
105	TATSUTAGAWA	たつたかわ	Tatsuta River: / the autumn leaves seem in disarray
19	TAZUNE KITE	たつねきて	Lost in contemplation / of the blooms all day
42	TOBIKIYURU	とひきゆる	The heron / flying off into the clouds
63	TOKIWA NARU	ときはなる	The evergreen / pine is famous but
67	TOKUSAKARU	とくさかる	Reaping weeds from the space between the trees
29	TORA TO MITE	とらとみて	Although / the arrow pierces the stone
71	TOSHI WO HETE	としをへて	The years pass and / as for the waters that become
119	TSUKI MIREBA	つきみれは	When I see the moon / it is first of all the capital
35	TSUKIKAGE NO	つきかけの	As the moonlight strikes / so do the oars of boats
70	TSUKI KAKUSU	つきかくす	When the branches / of the cherry blossoms grow thick
117	UGUHISU NO	うくひすの	The skinny legs / of the bush warbler

POEM NO.	FIRST LINE	JAPANESE	ENGLISH
11	USHI NO KO NI	うしの子に	Don't get stepped on / by the calf of the bull
120	UTSU NO YA NI	うつのやに	The crying / of the deer hit
32	UTSU OTO NO	うつをとの	The sound of its beating / has stopped for a while
89	UZURA NAKU	うつらなく	There is not a day / that the waves of pampas
16	WAGA KOI WA tada maruoke ni	わかこひハ たゝまるおけに	My longing / is just like a square lid
87	WAGA KOI WA Yodo no kawase ni	わかこひは よとのかはせに	My love is like / the carp swimming upstream
101	WAGA KOI WA Futami no ura no	わかこひは ふたみのうらの	My love is like / the shells lying thickly
27	WAGA YADO NO yahe yamabuki ha	わかやとの やへやまふきは	Double-petalled yamabuki / blooming near my lodging
41	WAGA YADO NO kiku no shiratsuyu	わかやとの きくのしらつゆ	The white dew of the mums / at my house
112	WE NI KAKU MO		See E NI KAKU MO
110	WARE BAKARI	われはかり	Although I think / if there was someone
94	YAMA TAMORU	やまたもる	The figure indeed / of the scarecrow who guards the field
40	YAMABITO NO	やまひとの	The mountain man: / both his umbrella and brushwood
36	YAMADERA NO haru no yube wo	やま寺の 春のゆふへを	When I come / to see the spring twilight
78	YAMADERA NO koi no kokoro wa	やまてらの こひのこころは	What kind of thing / is the feeling of love
46	YAMATA-MORU	やまたもる	Near a small hut / that guards the mountain paddies
65	YO MO AKEBA	よもあけは	Come dawn's early light / o yes, in the tank you go
84	YO NO NAKA NI	よのなかに	The short-lived beings / in this world are like
75	YOKO HASHIRU	よこはしる	The crabs that run / sideways between the reeds
23	YORITE KOSO	よりてこそ	I will come closer / and see who she is
74	YOSO NI MITE	よそにみて	They look elsewhere / and make to go home
37	YUKI FUREBA	ゆきふれは	When the snow falls / accompanied by
68	YUKI KURETE	ゆきくれて	Journeying on / were I to make the shade beneath the trees
48	YUKI NARABA	ゆきならは	If it were snow / how many times then would I
31, **48**	YUKU MIDZU NI	ゆくみつに	The greater folly / lies not in writing figures

APPENDIX D
LIST OF FIRST LINES
B: POEMS INCLUDED IN THE ESSAYS AND PICTURE CAPTIONS

FIG. NO.	FIRST LINE	JAPANESE	ENGLISH
41	AHIMITE NO nochi no kokoro ni	逢ひ見ての のちの心に	Having met e my love / Afterwards my passion was
39	AKIKAZE NI hatsukari kane zo	秋風に 初雁がねぞ	In the autumn wind / I hear the crying /of the wild geese
18, 37	AKIKAZE NO fuku ni tsukete mo	秋風の 吹くにつけても	He does not come / even though the autumn wind
34, 55	ARAZARAMU kono yo no hoka no	あらざらむ この世のほかの	Among my memories / of his world, from whence
45	AWARE IKA NI kusaba no tsuyu no	哀れいかに 草葉の露の	How sad to observe / the dewdrops blown away
49	HANA NO IRO HA utsurinikeri na	花の色は うつりにけりな	The color of the flowers / has faded indeed
55	HANAYOME NO bōshi no uchi no	花嫁の ぼうしのうちの	Beauty of the bride / in her lovely wedding hat
58	HARU NO YO NO yume bakari naru	春の夜の 夢ばかりなる	On a short spring night / Resting in your arms
43, 44	HITO HA ISA kokoro mo shirazu	人はいさ 心もしらず	No one can rely / on the changing heart of men.
32, 51	IRO MIEDE utsurou mono wa	色見えで うつろふものは	The only flower / which keeps on changing color
33	IWABASHI NO yoru no chigiri mo	岩橋の 夜の契りも	The promise to cross / the Ishibashi bridge at night
7	KAKU BAKARI hekataku miyuru	かくはかり へかたくみゆる	Though it may seem / hard and worthless to live
10	KIMI GA TAME haru no no ni idete	きみがため 春の野にいでて	Only for your sake / I walk out to spring meadows
56	KOGARASHI NI yanagi no kami no	こからしに やなきのかみの	The willow's hair / is disheveled and torn
53	KUHITARANU uwasa mo kikazu	くひたらぬ うわさもきかす	The dumpling-shaped moon / a single one for China
55	KURAKAHE NO mi ni ukibito ha	鞍かへの 身にうき人は	Pilgrim on the road / seat your body to the saddle
55	MEGURIAHITE mishi ya soretomo	めぐりあひて 見しやそれとも	We have met by chance / in the midnight moonlight
30	MIWA NO YAMA ika ni machimimu	三輪の山 いかにまち見む	No matter how long / I keep waiting for love
20	MUSASHINO HA tsuki no izubeki	武蔵野は 月のいつべき	There are no mountains / from which the moon can rise
20	MUSASHINO HA tsuki no irubeki	武蔵野は 月のいるべき	There is no hill / on Musashi Plain
8	NAGAMUREBA chiji ni mono omou	ながむれは 千々に物思ふ	I stare at the moon / dwelling in thousands of thoughts
46	NAMI NO UTSU Mishima no ura no	波のうつ 三島の浦の	Am I as empty / as the naughty shell / cast by waves
42	OHOIGAWA Somayama kaze no	大井川 杣山風の	The cold wind / whirls down the Soma

FIG. NO.	FIRST LINE	JAPANESE	ENGLISH
10	OKUYAMA NI momiji fumiwake	奥山に 紅葉踏み分け	Deep in the mountains / as I wade through the fallen leaves
54	OMOHIDETE kohishiki toki ha	思ひ出て 恋しきときは	Since I am in love / I go out in sad reveries
35, 50	OMOHITSUTSU nurebaya hito no	思ひつつ ぬればや人の	Deeply in love / I spend my days long
38	SHINOBUREDO iro ni idenikeri	忍ぶれど 一色にいでにけり	Though I would hide it, / In my face it still appears
36	TACHI-NUWANU kinu kishi hito mo	たちぬわぬ 絹きし人も	The ones who wore the robes / that were neither cut nor sewn
40	TONOMORI NO tomo no miyatsuko	おのもりの とものみやつこ	If you have a heart / my lad, do not sweep away
30	UGUHISU NO koe nakariseba	うぐひすの こゑなかりせば	If not the warbler / who would welcome with songs
47	YAMADERA NO iriai no kane no	山寺の 入相の鐘の	How sad to hear / the evening bells tolling
45	YOSHINO YAMA sakura ga eda ni	吉野山 桜が枝に	This year I feel / the blossoms will bloom late

APPENDIX E
GENERAL INDEX

X Numbers in italics indicate numbers of Poems in the Facsimile
X Bold numbers indicate Figures
X Regular numbers indicate pages

N

Ō

R

S

Helena Honcoopová
is director emeritus of the Collection of Oriental Art at the National Gallery in Prague, life-long specialist on Japanese art and author of about 15 monographs and catalogues, including a translation of the *Hyakunin isshu* into Czech.

Joshua Mostow
is Professor of Asian Studies at The University of British Columbia, Vancouver, Canada. His translations include the *Hyakunin isshu* and *Ise monogatari*, and he has written extensively on text-image relations in premodern Japanese culture.

Makoto Yasuhara
is a lecturer of Japanese literature at Rikkyō and Hōsei Universities, Tōkyō, specialist on *ōgi no sōshi* genre.

A BOOK OF FANS

ŌGI NO SŌSHI

扇の草子

Facsimile of an illustrated collection
of old Japanese poetry

With essays and commentary by
Helena Honcoopová
Joshua S. Mostow
Makoto Yasuhara

Collection of poetry translated from Japanese original script
by Joshua S. Mostow and his students, University of British Columbia
Acknowledgements translated into Japanese by Makoto Yasuhara
Proof-read by Jane Howard, Joshua Mostow
Edited by Martin Janeček
Graphic design and cover by Jiří Voves
Typeset by DTP Karolinum
Printed by Tiskárny Havlíčkův Brod, a. s.

ISBN 978-80-246-2518-8